*Dolores Mosquera & Anabel Gonzalez*

# Borderline Personality Disorder and EMDR Therapy

Dolores Mosquera & Anabel Gonzalez

Institute for the Treatment of Trauma and Personality Disorders (INTRA-TP)

Original title: *Trastorno Límite de la Personalidad y Terapia EMDR* (Spanish edition 2014: Madrid. Pleyades, SA.)

Translation: Miriam Ramos Morrison

Cover Illustration: David Crooks ( www.davidearlcrooks.net)

Illustrations: Nadia Santiago and Anabel Gonzalez

Copyright © 2014, Dolores Mosquera Barral
Web: www.intra-tp.com
E-mail: intratp@yahoo.com

ISBN: 978-84-617-1276-2

To our parents for everything

# Table of Contents

# Foreword by Andrew M. Leeds, Ph.D.

## Where there is no path

> "Fear always springs from ignorance."
> Ralph Waldo Emerson

It clear is from even the briefest of examinations of the scholarly literature that Borderline Personality Disorder (BPD) most commonly emerges from a history of chronic early neglect and trauma (Ball & Links, 2009; Battle, Shea, Johnson, et al., 2004; Horesh et al., 2008). Nevertheless many clinicians, even those who are trained in an evidence based method of treatment for posttraumatic stress disorder, such as EMDR therapy, tend to shudder at the prospect of treating patients with this condition. Why is this? I remember a conversation from 1993 with a fellow EMDR training supervisor who told me in a quiet aside that she routinely referred out any patient showing borderline features and did not accept referrals from colleagues of patients with a prior diagnosis of BPD. This was not a novice clinician, but one with years of experience in treating many types of trauma and who had advanced to a position of respect in her community. Unfortunately, over the last 20 years in my capacity as an EMDR trainer and an EMDRIA Approved Consultant, I have discovered that ambivalence and outright aversion to treating those most in need of effective treatment is not uncommon.

What is the source of this fear? Why do clinicians, who routinely agree to provide treatment to survivors of combat trauma, natural disasters and rape, turn away from those who show up with histories of broken relationships and domestic violence, with scars on their forearms or thighs, with misuse of prescription medication, or with a history of multiple suicide attempts? Are not these the individuals who most need our help?

I believe that clinicians' fears, doubts, and impulses to avoid providing care for those with BPD stem primarily from a lack of specialty education, training and opportunities for specialty consultation. Thus, these fears and aversions are understandable as being based on both an ethical stance of not working beyond the scope of one's education, training, and supervised experience as well as on an emotional component of fear due to ignorance. Not so many years ago, as it happens, I spoke again with that same EMDR training supervisor after she had completed an advanced EMDR training home study course I had prepared for working with survivors of severe early neglect and abuse. While this course was not specifically about borderline personality disorder, she told me that the course had opened her eyes to the nature of the issues with which patients with borderline symptoms struggle. She now understood the role of their insecure and disorganized attachments. She was able to recognize their neurological impairments in executive function that followed from years of early neglect and abuse. She said that she was now able to see that their specific impairments with self-regulation could be addressed with tools from EMDR therapy and that she was starting to work with patients with BPD. Her story added to my confidence that with better education and training more EMDR therapists can step forward to work with those who most need our help. This book takes an important step forward toward realizing that vision.

> "Coming together is a beginning, staying together is progress,
> and working together is success."
> Henry Ford

Since our fortuitous meeting at the 2010 EMDRIA Conference in Minneapolis, I have had the distinct privilege of collaborating with Dolores Mosquera and Anabel Gonzalez on several scholarly projects. I have had the opportunity to sit and talk with them for many hours. I have learned about the development of their thinking and how they approach the possibilities of applying EMDR therapy to cases that many clinicians might turn away from altogether, let alone consider offering EMDR therapy.

Before receiving initial training in EMDR therapy, both Dolores Mosquera and Anabel Gonzalez were working with highly challenging clinical populations. Dolores Mosquera was directing several clinics specialized in treating those with personality disorders. Anabel Gonzalez was working with those severe dissociative disorders in both hospital and outpatient settings. Both were challenged from the beginning of their work with EMDR therapy to find ways of using EMDR therapy with these most challenging of patients. Both are committed to fidelity in application of the standard EMDR procedures where that is possible. Both have also been quick to glean essential adaptations needed to fit EMDR to the needs of patients with BPD.

Having watched countless hours of video recordings of their work with these patients, I can affirm that their work reveals that they have encountered difficulties along the way. This is to be expected. But they have made a careful study of their successes and their blunders, and from their moments of confusion and uncertainty, they have strengthened both their conceptual grasp of how to understand what is happening within the clinical encounter, as well as the subtle simplicity of how to help their patients move forward into their full humanity. I say "simplicity", but that is of course misleading. The best work, when it is done elegantly, in the most challenging moment, nearly always looks simple; but underneath that simplicity lies a great deal of perception, thought, and choice. In this book they illuminate the interiority of their work and reveal the many lessons they have gained from their work with their patients.

Over these last four years, our collaborations have been diverse, sometimes writing or teaching together, sometimes sitting in each other's presentations. Our work includes a 2014 article published in the *Journal of EMDR Practice and Research*, "Application of EMDR therapy for borderline personality disorder" (Mosquera, Leeds & Gonzalez, 2014). In their previous book, *EMDR and Dissociation: The Progressive Approach*, they emphasized the need (as well as when and how) to use a range of modified EMDR procedures, and indeed in that book (with help from their co-authors) they enlarged the EMDR theoretical model on the nature of Dysfunctionally Stored Information to include information on psychological defenses and dissociative phobias.

In this book, they expand the stance which we took in Mosquera, Leeds, & Gonzalez (2014), that the application of EMDR therapy to BPD requires only minor adaptations of the standard EMDR procedures. This stance contrasts with one case report (Brown & Shapiro, 2006) in which eighteen months of cognitive behavioral and psychodynamic/insight-oriented psychotherapy was needed before EMDR therapy could be initiated. Nor do they call for prolonged weeks or months of stabilization with Resource Development and Installation before considering EMDR therapy with every patient with BPD. While extended preparation and even pharmacotherapy may be essential in certain cases, in many others they describe ways of adapting standard EMDR therapy procedures from early in treatment. When preparation and stabilization are needed, RDI is not the only choice they offer clinicians. They offer a broad array of adaptations and alternative procedures for every phase of treatment for working with individuals, couples and families where individuals need treatment for Borderline Personality Disorder. This book expands the information presented in our 2014 article to make the conceptual material and the practical application completely accessible to EMDR trained clinicians around the world.

> "Do not follow where the path may lead.
> Go, instead, where there is no path and leave a trail."
> Ralph Waldo Emerson

In recent years, the literature on specialty treatments for BPD has grown to include not only Dialectical Behavior Therapy (DBT: Linehan, 1993), but Transference Focused Psychotherapy (Yeomans, Clarkin, & Kernberg, 2002), Schema Focused Therapy, and Mentalization Based Therapy (Giesen-Bloo, et al., 2006). DBT remains the mostly widely know and most studied (Brazier, et al., 2006) of the evidence based therapies for BPD, but in spite of the notable evidence of DBT's effectiveness for some symptoms of BPD (Stoffers, 2012), its general rate of effective response may only be about 45%, while 31% of patients treated with DBT may remain unchanged, and 11% deteriorate (Kröger, 2013).

No one therapeutic approach works for all patients with a given disorder. I have long espoused the view that we are better served by trying to understand how best to match specific treatments to specific patient's needs rather than to pursue internecine struggles to prove one therapy superior in every case.

One of the unique contributions of the approach described in EMDR and Borderline Personality Disorder is the authors' recognition of the central role of structural dissociation (Mosquera, Gonzalez, & Van der Hart, 2011) in development and maintenance of the symptoms of BPD. While the degree of structural dissociation of the personality varies within a spectrum of BPD cases, an understanding of the role of structural dissociation may be central to the potential for greater success in its treatment. It is certainly necessary for an appropriate integration of EMDR into the care and treatment of those with this disorder.

While the treatment outcome literature on EMDR therapy for posttraumatic stress disorder is robust, it has yet to be formally studied in controlled research as a treatment for BPD. Such studies are now being organized in Europe. In time this research will tell us whether the results Dolores Mosquera and Anabel Gonzalez describe they are able to achieve can be replicated in well controlled studies. Until such research become available, clinicians can base their work on the strong conceptual and procedural foundation they have brought to this important area of clinical practice.

# Foreword to the Spanish Edition

*Borderline Personality Disorder and EMDR Therapy* addresses a complex disorder in a simple, direct, and scientific way. This work offers an introduction to the history of the borderline terminology, from Hippocratic times to current theories, and recommends a multidisciplinary intervention approach for the treatment of "borderline personality disorder".

The authors approach the phases of the EMDR protocol with skill and simplicity, explaining how to adapt them to the personality structure of a borderline client, and discussing, among other issues, how to work with defenses. Despite these having such a protective and adaptive function, though often with a dysfunctional foundation, clients will not be able to do without them until they learn new ways to handle their situations. Borderline clients often are unable to manage their internal world and their interpersonal relationships, given their dramatic mood changes and chaotic ways, especially if they have lacked internal models of healthy attachment.

In working with borderline personality disorder, it is crucial to become familiar with theories on trauma and neurophysiology, and to know that sometimes, early abuse, neglect, and psychological, physical, and emotional abuse can constitute risk factors for the development of the disorder. Thus, in phase 1 of EMDR, life experiences are addressed through the memories stored in the client's neural networks, along with the dysfunctional cognitive schemas that, repeated over time, have resulted in severely distorted beliefs. In phase 3 of the protocol, we must help the patient to identify these beliefs, so as to understand and develop a good map of all those life events that shaped the borderline personality structure.

Dissociation and dissociative phobias, which are the consequences of trauma, are also addressed in *Borderline Personality Disorder and EMDR Therapy*. Through the EMDR phases of preparation, stabilization, and processing, we will be able to adopt models of intervention (protocols) that allow us to integrate the emotional parts within a healthy and adaptive emotional personality structure.

I love how EMDR addresses the history of the borderline patient and how self-care and working with defenses, psychoeducation, and emotional regulation are the basis of the preparation phase. This will allow accessing and processing the most dysfunctional and maladaptive memories, so they can slowly become integrated into the client's life, through the dyadic dance that the therapist must establish from the very beginning. Confusion and lack of boundaries may increase if a safe and healthy relationship between client and therapist is not developed in the early stages and throughout the process of therapy.

Psychoeducation focuses on respecting other people, learning to be respected, developing clear operating guidelines, following their own pace, seeing failures as learning opportunities regarding themselves and their relationships with others, and becoming aware that the process requires time, respect and commitment.

As mentioned at the end of this book, we must guide our clients through the path of self-care. Just as homes need maintenance, we have to help them understand from the start that they need to work every day in maintaining improvement. So once the process of therapy is finished, they will be able to recognize the need to ask for help before they feel overwhelmed.

The last part of the book is devoted to addressing borderline personality disorder in the interpersonal context, in relation to family, couples, and therapy. If we understand the different types of attachment, the cognitive processes, and the constellation of symptoms that are presented, we can better understand the borderline client within their already problematic couple and family relationships.

Anxiety, fear, insecurity, feeling responsible or guilty for the client's therapy, blackmail, attacks, emotional contagion, and other aspects are elements to be considered in the therapeutic relationship with these clients. One of their common features is that they will often test us and it is difficult to remain completely neutral when this happens. They do this because they are constantly looking for "models" to help them place themselves safely and healthily in the world.

As the authors say, "What happens in therapy is the story of their lives," and I add that when they come to us, they also try to see if we will respect and understand them, and if we are going to help them reorganize their lives.

This book is recommended for therapists who work with clients with complex trauma, who are well familiarized with EMDR and properly use the basic protocol. This is a wonderful resource for those who want to delve into the borderline world, which can easily become chaotic, confusing, erratic, and unstable, where many things are yet to be built; and for those who want to understand the structure of these clients who do not know where they end and other people begin, whose huge anxiety is most often channeled through risky behaviors such as alcohol, sex, and substance abuse, which sometimes may even lead to death.

In a direct and clear way, this text addresses the disorder through each of the EMDR phases, adapting them to the client's personality. It is, therefore, a book for EMDR professionals or those who would like to integrate and adapt the EMDR model to their work with borderline personality.

In summary, I can say that this is an exceptional and practical piece of work, unique in that it integrates both an understanding of the client with borderline personality disorder and EMDR therapy. No doubt that this work is the result of combining many years of experience with these clients; profound knowledge of the borderline internal world, which can become dissociated, chaotic and terrible; and a personal, clear, simple, close, and compassionate style of communication, which therapists must have when treating these clients and is obviously the style that dominates this book.

For all of us, clinicians who are dedicated to helping our clients integrate their memories, reorganize their lives, and stop having their traumatic past in the present, reading and integrating the chapters of this book into our therapeutic toolbox will be very helpful.

I would like to thank Dolores Mosquera for the example of the story of The Three Little Pigs, which she introduces in the final chapter of the book, as a metaphor of what constitutes our work as therapists with such complex clients. Helping them heal truly is like a construction job, in which you have to continue doing maintenance work, and that takes time. The attitude of self-respect and self-care learned in the process of therapy should be maintained; relapses will become opportunities to seek help, if needed, through that open door that we must always offer our patients, once therapy is completed.

My gratitude and most heartfelt congratulations to Dolores and Anabel for having been and continuing to be pioneers in the research and treatment of severe and complex disorders, and especially for adapting the theories, methods, and protocols from masters like Onno van der Hart, Roger Solomon, Jim Knipe, and Andrew Leeds, among others, to Francine Shapiro's great discovery during that famous walk in the park in 1987. This has allowed speeding up the process of unblocking traumatic memories and integrating more adaptive memories, through the use of eye movements and the EMDR protocol.

I am thankful for having been invited to foreword this book, which captivated me for its clarity from the very first chapter and has helped me rearrange and reorganize my initial information.

I encourage the reader not yet familiar with EMDR to start learning this approach, which, along with reading this book, will surely be very useful for detecting, understanding, and treating patients with borderline personality disorder.

Francisca García Guerrero
President EMDR Spain Association
EMDR Europe Trainer

When you open a book for the first time and flip through its pages, curiosity about what it can offer often appears, especially if it is a reference work about a specific topic. We can consider a good book one that covers our expectations at both theoretical and practical levels, but even more if the contribution is new, different, and original.

When I opened *Borderline Personality Disorder and EMDR Therapy* for the first time, what caught my attention was that these expectations were covered in full. From the first chapter to the last, a therapeutic approach on borderline personality disorder from the EMDR perspective was brilliantly developed. Phase by phase, the authors described in detail how to work through every issue that may influence the treatment of this pathology, as well as the most common blocks or difficulties that the professional has to take into account in order to achieve great therapeutic success.

Borderline personality disorder becomes more understandable as we travel through these pages by the hand of the authors, the renowned psychologist Dolores Mosquera, one of the most internationally representative figures in this field, and the also international Anabel Gonzalez, psychiatrist and expert in dissociation. Together they help us reach a special understanding of the behavior of these clients and the responses and reactions they can show in therapy; everything that the EMDR therapist must take into account as to help patients with this condition, following a guided work map that provides sufficient knowledge to know where we need to go next.

Not long ago, the words trauma, attachment, and dissociation were barely linked to personality disorders, which is shown by the fact that most studies presented by the authors to verify this link are of recent years. Interesting contributions such as early trauma, hidden trauma, self-care, and defenses are addressed in detail and integrated flawlessly in this manual, resulting in a work program whose development covers the most important areas to consider. Each layer that must be uncovered, from beginning to end, from the most external to the most internal and vulnerabe, is described, as well as how to process and act on each one of these layers depending on what "comes along with it" and being aware of what may emerge. Ultimately, the novel therapist in this field feels cared for and supported at every stage of treatment, and the more seasoned therapists are enriched with a resourceful contribution to further their specialization.

This is one of those reference books that becomes a library must-have and to which we turn to consult any difficulty we do not know how to solve. It shows us how to treat this disorder with mastery, simplicity, and compassion; disorder that originally many professionals labeled as difficult to work with in therapy and which sometimes, as the authors say, is a challenge.

I want to formally recognize the good job that Dolores Mosquera and Anabel Gonzalez have done, by managing to show that beneath all these "shells" are "wounded children" waiting to work on trauma, attachment and dissociation through an approach such as EMDR, which provides everything we need to reprocess the inappropriately stored information and, through this, offer an effective recovery.

Natalia Seijo
Psychologist
EMDR Europe Facilitator and Consultant

# Part One
# Theoretical Foundation

# Introduction
# The Borderline Personality Disorder Challenge

## Let us start with the Name

The term borderline personality disorder originated from the psychoanalytical differentiation between two types of structures for understanding psychopathology: neurosis and psychosis. However, as it usually happens when trying to make classifications in psychology and psychiatry, cases that could not be framed into any of these two structures began to proliferate.

Homer´s, Hippocrates´ and Arateo´s descriptions of individuals with divergent characteristics of aggressive anger, melancholy, and mania, along with the work of Swiss author Theophile Bonet in 1684 (*folie manic-melancolique*), may be considered the background history of the later conceptualizations of borderline personality disorder, although the described symptoms overlap with bipolar disorder. From the very beginning, this is an indication of the diagnostic confusion that has always surrounded BPD. Furthermore, borderline pathology will develop later as a reflection of the limitations in mental illness classification systems, in order to accommodate clients who do not fit into any of the categories. The term borderline first appeared in 1884, when the English psychiatrist Hughes (borderline insanity) described a borderline state of madness, indicating that many people spend their entire life close to this line. In 1890, English author Rosse takes this definition and adds that the borderline states require the presence of severe obsessions, compulsions, phobias, hysteria, and neurasthenia. From then on, the borderline concept was described at times as belonging to the schizophrenic sphere, other times as an autonomous structure, and also as belonging to both (Paz, Palento, & Olmos 1977). Stern´s work in 1938, arguably the first significant work on the "borderline" clinical picture, reflects this ongoing controversy well.

The authors that classified the borderline disorder within the schizophrenia spectrum were Bleuler (1911), a psychiatrist who defined it as a latent schizophrenia; Claude (1926), who introduced the concept of schizomanias to frame certain pathological conditions developed on a schizoid background, secondary to emotional problems or infections; Fenichel (1942), who used the term marginal schizophrenia; Federn (1947), who called it latent schizophrenia; Hoch and Polatin (1949), who spoke of pseudoneurotic schizophrenia; and Ey (1955), who described schizoneurosis.

Other authors such as Bychowski (1957) differentiated latent schizophrenia from BPD, considering it a distinct structure. It has also been classified as an autonomous structure by Wolberg (1952), who spoke of borderline pathology as a result of a repetitive sadomasochistic cycle, Zetzel (1971), and Greenson (1954), among others.

Some authors, such as Schmideberg (1959), considered that borderline clients are not only borderline between neurosis and psychosis, but they remain at that point throughout life, stable in their instability. Other authors, such as Frosch (1959), Modell (1963), and Kernberg (1965) also defended the character of these disorders, both psychotic and neurotic.

Psychoanalyst Little (1966) perfectly defines how confusing this debate on what he calls borderline state or delusional transference can be: "The borderline state is a descriptive and imprecise term used to denote any mental illness not clearly neurotic, but not so obviously psychotic that the client has to be treated as insane."

Winnicott (1969) makes a similar point, saying that "the core of the disturbance is psychotic, but the client has enough psychoneurotic organization to always present with psychoneurotic or psychosomatic disorders when the core psychotic anxiety threatens crudely."

This complex debate also presents the problem that the concepts of neurosis and psychosis are not defined in the same way by all authors. In addition, beyond psychoanalytic theories, the concept of psychosis has also been used in a less concrete way, and does not coincide with the use of this term by psychoanalysis. For example, in some cases, psychosis is synonymous with schizophrenia, delusional symptoms, self-referentiality, or hallucinations. In other cases, it extends to what is called unique psychosis: a psychopathological spectrum ranging from schizophrenia to bipolar disorder, including frequent intermediate disorders. While psychoanalysts include autism among childhood psychosis, biological psychiatry clearly separates both conditions.

Perhaps what we can learn from borderline personality disorder is that the complexity of human beings and mental illness defies any attempt at classification. The difficulties of operationalizing the definitions of personality disorders has led, in recent years, to an emphasis on dimensional classifications, which relate to factors, as opposed to categorical ones, which simply tag. However, none of these options seem to solve the fundamental problem of borderline clients: To what are their symptomatically complex clinical pictures due? And above all, how can we effectively treat these clients?

Although international classifications ICD-10 and DSM-V generate great controversy among professionals, they are our common language. In this book, we will speak both of borderline personality disorder as it is defined in these diagnostic manuals and the criteria by which it is defined. Our main concern is not this deliberation, but understanding where these clients' problems come from and how to resolve them. For this reason, we will speak of trauma and attachment theories and the theoretical model of EMDR therapy as a framework from which to understand BPD and structure its treatment.

## The BPD Health Care Challenge

The issue posed by BPD clients is not only where to place the disorder or how to define it. Despite the extensive scientific debate on these issues, the treatment of these clients continues to challenge both therapeutic orientations and health care systems.

When therapists present clinical cases to explain their work, they often choose a diagnosis for which their clinical orientation fits more naturally. A cognitive-behavioral psychologist will likely present the case of a client with an obsessive-compulsive disorder, who will allow a better structuring of the tasks and will rigorously complete the assigned homework. A biological psychiatrist will likely choose a bipolar or schizophrenic client, in order to show how the appropriate pharmacological drug tapped into the precise receptor. In general, none of the predominant orientations tend to choose personality disorders as examples of their understanding of mental illness. If they refer to them at all, it is usually as confounding factors in the differential diagnosis or as aspects that interfere with treatment and make clients more "resistant" to conventional interventions. In those therapists who identify more rigidly with a psychotherapeutic model, the cognitive distortion produced by the fact that these cases do not fit in their model of mental illness is solved by stating that these clients do not suffer a "genuine mental illness."

Borderline clients have forced the different approaches to step out of their model's framework of beliefs. After a period in which these clients were traditionally considered untreatable, several authors have developed specific methods of intervention. Otto Kernberg (1967) breaks the general trend of not considering borderline clients as candidates for psychoanalytic treatment and describes an approach that stems from an in depth description of its peculiarities. Marsha Linehan (1993) develops a therapeutic strategy, based on the cognitive-behavioral model, which incorporates different elements such as mindfulness techniques. Many authors do not propose a "type of therapy," but instead suggest a specific approach for BPD. These proposals have as a common feature the integration of very different components and models.

BPD clients are also changing health care systems. Public systems, drowned by the pressure of cost reduction, are reducing their ratio of professionals to the point that psychotherapy services are becoming symbolic. In many health care organizations, the workload only allows a short half-hour "session" with the psychologist every month or every two months. Clients who are able to function with homework, who are well enough to recover without much help, who improve with medication, or who continue to feel bad but do not complain, adapt to a system that is logically deficient. BPD clients do not adapt without posing problems, generating frequent ER visits, repeated hospitalizations that are used as a last resort to stop unmanageable crisis, and a major health care expense spent on interventions that professionals consider unproductive. This has led many communities to propose specific programs for clients with personality disorders.

At a private level, treatment possibilities are greater, if the client can afford it. However, since most are individual sessions or are focused on a particular approach, they represent a limitation in the treatment of BPD. As we will see, borderline clients often require intervention both at a family and group level in addition to their individual treatment. Individuals with a borderline pathology teach us the importance of teamwork and coordination with other professionals. We are taught to leave the safe haven of our offices and our favorite orientations. They make us see the limitations of our health care offer.

## Personal Learning in Working with BPD

Borderline clients seem to have a knack for finding the weak spot of the therapist they are working with. These clients´ extreme and changing reactions will generate equally intense reactions in their conversational partner, which need to be constantly adjusted. Therapists can often find themselves reacting defensively, being carried away, or feeling confused and annoyed in the middle of a therapy session. If therapists have difficulty maintaining appropriate boundaries with clients, they will often end up in surreal situations with BPD individuals. If in their own history, therapists have traumatic experiences that have not been completely resolved, the sometimes extremely difficult histories of these clients may overwhelm them, and they may tend to avoid them. If therapists have trouble staying neutral, they will take the side of the client, the partner, or the family, in the frequent relational conflicts that these cases bring up. The therapeutic relationship in the treatment of borderline personality disorder is a constant challenge, which helps us to see if as therapists we are able to handle well a wide range of situations. It is like playing a complex musical score, where you can see if each instrument is well tuned. Borderline clients teach us the importance of supervision, work groups, and personal therapy. They are also helpful against therapists´ sense of omnipotence and our own narcissism. They bring us down to earth and make us more aware of our limitations. Treatment of borderline personality disorder is probably one of the best schools of psychotherapy.

# Chapter 1
# Trauma, Attachment, and Biology at the Origin of BPD

Several factors have been proposed as explanations for the origin of borderline personality disorder (BPD). Some authors have stressed the importance of genetic personality traits (Siever, Torgersen, Gunderson, Livesley, & Kendler, 2002) and their role as risk or protective factors regarding sensitivity to context (Steele & Siever, 2010). Others have linked bordelrine symptomatology to early attachment relationships (Barone, 2003; Buchheim, George, Liebl, Moser, & Benecke, 2007; Grover et al., 2007; Bakermans-Kranenburg & Van IJzendoorn, 2009; Newman, Harris & Allen, 2010). Some researchers report a high prevalence of trauma, particularly early, severe, and chronic trauma among adult borderline clients (Horesh, Ratner, Laor, & Toren, 2008; Tyrka, Wyche, Kelly, Price, & Carpenter, 2009; Ball & Links, 2009; Zanarini, 2000; Zanarini, et al., 2002). Biological factors and early traumatization, including attachment disruptions, seem to be the foundation from which the borderline pathology develops.

## Early Trauma and Borderline Personality Disorder

As described in PTSD's criterion A (APA, 1994), the classical view considers trauma from the perspective of the traumatic event and its features: a threat to the physical integrity of self and others. But in childhood, many perceived threats come from emotional signals and caregiver accessibility rather than from the level of actual physical danger or threat to survival (Schuder & Lyons-Ruth, 2004). One type of traumatization that is often overlooked is the so-called "hidden trauma," referring to the caregiver's inability to modulate affective dysregulation (Schuder & Lyons-Ruth, 2004).

Several studies have described frequent comorbidity between PTSD and BPD (Driessen et al., 2002; McLean & Gallop, 2003; Harned, Rizvi, & Linehan, 2010; Pagura et al., 2010; Pietrzak, Goldstein, Southwick, & Grant, 2011). Others find a relationship between BPD and emotional abuse (Kingdon et al., 2010) and different types of abuse (Grover, 2007; Tyrka et al., 2009). A history of trauma in childhood predicts poor prognosis in borderline clients (Gunderson et al., 2006). PTSD symptoms predict, along with dissociative symptoms, self-destructive behavior (Spitzer, Effler, & Freyberger, 2000; Sansone, Sansone, & Wiederman, 1995).

Zanarini (2000) reviewed the empirical literature that estimates childhood sexual abuse in BPD between 40 and 70%, compared with rates of sexual abuse in other Axis II disorders (between 19% and 26%). While many of these studies are retrospective, some include prospective measurements, and all show a significant relationship between sexual abuse, childhood abuse, BPD precursors, and BPD (Battle et al., 2004; Cohen, Crawford, Johnson, & Kasen, 2005; Rogosch & Chiccetti, 2005; Yen et al., 2002). Early abuse has been associated not only with BPD, but also with other mental disorders. However, results show that the relationship is stronger with BPD, even compared to other personality disorders. The severity of sexual abuse has also been linked to the severity of borderline features (Silk, Lee, Hill, & Lohr, 1995; Zanarini et al., 2002) and self-destructive behaviors (Sansone, Gaither, & Songer, 2002).

Battle et al. (2004) developed a multi-centric study that assessed the self-reported history of abuse and neglect experiences in 600 clients diagnosed with personality disorders (borderline, schizotypal, avoidant, or obsessive-compulsive) or major depressive disorder without PD. They found that rates of child abuse among individuals with PD are generally high (73% reported abuse and 82% reported neglect). BPD was associated with abuse and neglect in childhood more consistently than other PD diagnoses.

Graybar and Boutilier (2002) reviewed the empirical literature on BPD and several childhood traumas. They concluded that the referred rates of sexual abuse, physical and verbal abuse, and neglect among borderline clients ranged from 60 to 80%. Laporte and Guttman (1996) also studied various childhood experiences in women with BPD and other personality disorders. They found it easier for clients with BPD to refer a history of adoption, alcoholism, divorce, parental abandonment, having left home before age 16, verbal abuse, physical abuse, sexual abuse, and witnessing abuse than for clients with other personality disorders. In addition, a significantly higher percentage of clients with BPD reported multiple occurrences of more than one type of mistreatment or abuse, compared to clients without BPD. Paris and Zweig-Frank (1997) found that the degree of severity of abuse could differentiate between individuals with BPD and those without BPD.

Ball and Links (2009) reviewed the literature on trauma and BPD in the context of Hill′s (1965) classical criteria to demonstrate causality (strength, consistency, specificity, temporality, biological gradient, plausibility, coherence, experimental evidence, and analogy). These authors demonstrated that trauma could be considered a causal factor in the development of BPD, as part of a multifactorial etiological model.

Goodman and Yehuda (2002) reviewed a group of empirical studies and concluded that the overall rate of sexual abuse among BPD clients was 40-70%, compared with 19-26% among clients with other personality disorders. However, in recent years, many researchers have pointed out that the association between (remembered) childhood sexual abuse and BPD is not as strong as previous studies suggested. Golier et al. (2003) found high rates of early and throughout-life trauma in a sample of personality disorders. Borderline clients have significantly higher rates of physical abuse in childhood and adolescence (52.8% vs. 34.3%) and were twice as likely to develop PTSD. Yen et al. (2002) found that among different personality disorders, BPD participants reported the highest rate of traumatic exposure (particularly sexual trauma, including childhood sexual abuse), the highest rates of PTSD, and a younger age of the first early traumatic event.

Johnson, Cohen, Brown, Smailes, & Bernstein (1999) found that people with documented abuse or neglect in childhood were diagnosed four times more readily as having personality disorders in adulthood, after statistically controlling for age, parental education, and parental psychiatric disorders.

Sabo (1997) found an interaction between childhood trauma and borderline traits, also including elements of attachment as relevant factors. Fossati, Madeddu, and Maffei (1999) conducted a meta-analysis of 21 studies examining the relationship between BPD and sexual abuse in childhood. They found that the size of the effect is only moderate.

Studies of Childhood Trauma in BPD

| | |
|---|---|
| Zanarini (2000) | 40-70% of sexual abuse in childhood in BPD |
| Battle et al., 2004; Cohen et al. 2005; Rogosch et al. 2005; Yen et al., 2002 | Positive relationship in prospective studies of sexual abuse and physical abuse in childhood and BPD |
| Silk et al. 1995; Zanarini et al., 2002; Sansone et al., 2002 | Positive relationship between severity of sexual abuse, borderline symptom severity, and self-destructive behavior |
| Johnson et al. (1999) | People with documented sexual abuse or neglect are 4 times more likely to be diagnosed as a PD |
| Battle et al. (2004) | 73% sexual abuse in childhood, 82% neglect |
| Graybar & Boutilier (2002) | Physical and verbal abuse, sexual abuse and neglect 60-80% |
| Laporte & Guttman (1996) | BPD has multiple episodes and more than one type of abuse |
| Goodman & Yehuda (2002) | Childhood sexual abuse between 40-70% |
| Golier et al. (2003) | 52.8% of physical abuse in childhood or adolescence |
| Fossati et al. (1999) | Meta-analysis found evidence for moderate effect of sexual abuse in childhood |

## Studies on the Effects of Early Traumatization

We have previously seen the prevalence of traumatic events in BPD. However, we can analyze the relationship with borderline personality disorder from a different angle, for example, by analyzing the consequences of early and severe traumatization and seeing the similarity with BPD. Herbst, Jaeger, Leichsenring, & Streeck-Fischer (2009) state that a PTSD diagnosis does not adequately describe the impact of exposure to trauma on the developing child. Examining the prevalence of different types of interpersonal trauma and long-term effects of abuse and neglect in adolescents, 71% of traumatized adolescents did not meet criteria for PTSD. The most common diagnosis in the sample was BPD.

Some authors (Herman, 1992; Van der Kolk Roth, Pelcovitz, Sunday, & Spinazzola, 2005) have also remarked that symptoms of PTSD are only suitable to describe the consequences of isolated traumatic events, but do not include most of the features that are the result of early, severe, and chronic abuse and neglect. To describe this clinical presentation, a new category was proposed for the DSM-V: Disorders of Extreme Stress or DESNOS (Van der Kolk et al. 2005). Victims of chronic interpersonal traumas present characteristics that are not adequately described by PTSD criteria. Herman (1992) proposed a different concept, which she called Complex PTSD.

These authors have organized the symptoms into seven categories: Deregulation of (a) affects and impulses, (b) attention or consciousness, (c) self-perception, (d) perception of the perpetrator, (e) relationships with others, (f) somatization, and (g) systems of meaning. Many of these symptoms overlap with borderline criteria, supporting, from a different starting point, a relationship between early, relational, and chronic trauma and borderline personality disorder (Roth, Newman, Pelcovitz, Van der Kolk, & Mandel, 1997; Van der Kolk et al. 2005; Driessen et al., 2002; Gunderson & Sabo, 1993; McLean et al. 2003; Yen et al., 2002). Some authors (Classen, Pain, Field, & Woods, 2006) propose talking about disorganized post-traumatic personality disorder (PTPD-D) and organized post-traumatic personality disorder (PTPD-O). This category does not explain the process that leads from early traumatic experiences to adult psychopathology, which we will describe later in terms of structural dissociation. Although it fails to include many dissociative symptoms that are often present in these clients, this supports the idea that borderline symptoms are the consequence of trauma.

## Magnification or Minimization of the Influence of Childhood Trauma?

In previous sections, we have described empirical studies and meta-analyses related to the frequency of borderline clients reporting a history of trauma. In our discussions with colleagues who treat BPD clients, we found that they frequently question these data, arguing that borderline clients have a tendency to magnify, exaggerate, or make up childhood trauma in order to attract the therapist's attention. These comments do not seem to be confirmed by empirical research, which shows that information on trauma does not change when clients with BPD show improvement (Kremers, Van Giezen, Van der Does, Van Dyck, & Spinhoven, 2007).

On the contrary, the opposite problem needs to be taken into consideration: many traumatic experiences during childhood may not be remembered in adulthood (Chu, Matthews, Frey, & Ganzel, 1996). The probability of dissociative amnesia could be a factor that would lead clinicians and researchers to minimize the influence of traumatic factors in BPD.

Studies on the phenomenon of dissociative amnesia in relation to childhood trauma, and specifically sexual abuse, have led to controversial results. Herman and Schatzow (1987) found that a majority of women (general clients, not specifically BPD) who had sought treatment in a time-limited group for incest survivors experienced a complete or partial amnesia for sexual abuse at some point in the past. The overwhelming majority of these women were able to find some evidence that confirmed the abuse. Seventy-four percent could find convincing evidence that incest had occurred, such as a family member that confirmed it or, in one case, journals and other evidence of a deceased brother who had been the perpetrator. Another 9% found family members who stated that they were sure the abuse had occurred, even if they could not confirm it. Eleven percent made no attempt to confirm the abuse, leaving just another 6% who could not find valid evidence despite their efforts in this regard. Critics of this study have indicated that a number of the amnesic subjects were very young and perhaps had normal childhood amnesia, and that a clear and independent corroboration of the abuse was not obtained (Ofshe & Singer, 1994; Pope & Hudson, 1995).

A study by Briere and Conte (1993) showed that 54% of clients who reported memories of sexual abuse mentioned that they had suffered some amnesia for the abuse between the time of occurrence and the age of 18. Williams (1994) got in touch with adult women who had been treated for sexual abuse 17 years earlier at a city hospital and asked them to participate in a study on hospital services, in which they were asked about sexual abuse experiences, among other questions. Thirty-eight percent of these victims of abuse claimed to have not been abused. This denial can have multiple causes: amnesia, hiding, minimizing, etc. Terr (1988, 1991) describes amnesia and impaired memory in chronically traumatized children.

In therapies that explore and work with childhood experiences, such as EMDR, we often see recovery of early memories of abuse or recognition by the client that these stories were not initially told due to fear or shame. In our caseload (Mosquera et al., 2013), 36% reported having experienced some form of sexual abuse in childhood in the initial assessment, using the childhood family experiences scale. But interestingly, 22% answered this question with "I'm not sure whether it happened or not." Of the latter group, 18% answered this because they did not know it was sexual abuse (while clearly describing abusive situations) or because they felt responsible for it. In addition, 4% explained they were not sure because they had no memories, but instead had feelings and sexual difficulties similar to those of other sexual abuse victims. This makes a total of 44% of clients with BPD who report childhood abuse. The percentage of those who end up recovering those memories for which they were previously amnesic is uncertain, but it is not an uncommon situation. Since the assessment is not addressed in particular to this area, and working with EMDR is not directed toward the recovery of the memory, it is likely that the actual figures could be significantly higher. However, this should not make the therapist assume that all clients with BPD have suffered some kind of abuse. We need to keep in mind that memories can be modified due to a biased exploration by the therapist, so we must be careful not to induce memories in the client (Chu et al., 1996).

# Attachment and Borderline Personality Disorder

## The Concept of Attachment

Attachment behavior is an expression of an innate brain system that evolved to offer security to the child (Panksepp & Biven, 2012). He or she will search for the proximity of the parent, will use it as a safe haven when feeling upset to be comforted, and will internalize the relationship with the parent as an internal model of a secure base.

Siegel & Hartzell (2004) define what they call the ABC of attachment, based on three basic aspects of attachment between parents and children:

A. (Attunement) refers to being in sync, resonating with the other. The parent´s internal state is aligned with the child´s. This is usually accompanied by observable and contingent nonverbal cues.
B. (Balance). Regulation. The child´s body, emotions, and mental states are balanced and regulated through being attuned with the parent.
C. (Coherence). The sense of integration that children acquire through the relationship with their parents will make them feel internally integrated and connected to others.

When children with a secure attachment become adults, they will have the capacity for self-regulation, and they will be able to connect with others, as well as to seek and receive help. All these aspects are severely damaged in clients with BPD.

## Classification and Measurement of Attachment Subtypes

Several authors have defined different types of attachment, using different names for equivalent subtypes. The pioneer in the study of attachment was Bowlby (1969), followed by Mary Ainsworth (Ainsworth et al., 1978), who described three attachment behavior subtypes: secure, avoidant, and anxious. Disorganized attachment was described later (Main & Solomon, 1986). In the 1980s, the theory was extended to include attachment in adults.

For example, the anxious-ambivalent attachment style (Hazan & Shaver, 1987) has also been called preoccupied (Bartholomew & Horowitz, 1991) and resistant (Ainsworth, Blehar, Waters, & Wall, 1978). The disorganized attachment subtype (Main & Solomon, 1986) is not included in all classifications and is not evaluated by most psychometric instruments that assess attachment. This probably has great relevance in minimizing this factor in the development of BPD.

Hazan and Shaver (1987) developed the first questionnaire to measure attachment in adults. This questionnaire only distinguished between secure, avoidant, and anxious-ambivalent subtypes

Bartholomew & Horowitz (1991, 1998) presented a model that identified four categories: secure, dismissive, preoccupied, and fearful. The latter is a combination of the previous two. Based on these categories, they developed the Relationship Questionnaire (RC), which had four paragraphs, each describing one of the categories or attachment styles.

Two widely used questionnaires also do not include the disorganized attachment category: the Experiences in Close Relationships (ECR) questionnaire created by Brennan, Clark, and Shaver in 1998, and its revised version created by Fraley, Waller, and Brennan in 2000. These questionnaires have two scales of anxiety and avoidance, based on which the subjects were classified into one of the four categories of Bartholomew and Horowitz´s model. The secure style is characterized by low anxiety and low avoidance, the preoccupied style by high anxiety and low avoidance, the dismissive style by low anxiety and high avoidance, and the fearful one is characterized by high anxiety and high avoidance.

The most elaborate instrument for assessing attachment is the Adult Attachment Interview (AAI). It is a semi-structured interview and has been widely validated and empirically supported (Hesse, 1999). Unlike Hazan & Shaver and Bartolomew´s proposals that focus on adult romantic relationships, the AAI assesses the attachment that the person had in their family of origin.

Given that the AAI is the most developed instrument for attachment assessment, and because it the one that has the most direct connection with early attachment, the results contributed by the studies using this interview will be the ones we will take into consideration in this chapter. In them, as will be discussed, BPD has been linked with preoccupied and insecure-disorganized or unresolved attachment styles.

The following table shows the relationships between the AAI categories and the behavior of a 12-month-old child when he reunites with his mother after a brief separation in which he has been left with a stranger. This is the "strange situation" experiment, designed by Mary Ainsworth.

| Ainsworth et al., (1978); Main & Solomon (1986) **AAI** | George, Kaplan & Main (1985). **Strange Situation** |
|---|---|
| **Secure or autonomous**: Speaks in a coherent and interactive way with the interviewer about his experiences, whether favorable or unfavorable. Answers questions with enough, but not excessive, elaboration, going back to the conversational exchange with the interviewer. Provides a coherent narrative that can even include traumatic events. | **Secure**: Searches for physical contact, proximity, and interaction. If he startles with separation, he can be easily soothed by parents, returning to exploration and play. |
| **Dismissive**: Minimizes the discussion or the importance of attachment - related experiences. Responses are typically and internally inconsistent and often extremely short. Relationships with parents are usually described as highly favorable, but without evidence to support it, and when such evidence is provided, it tends to be at odds with the overall assessment. | **Insecure-avoidant**: These children avoid and ignore the parents at the meeting, staying busy with their toys, and can ignore the parents´ efforts to communicate. |

**Preoccupied**: The memories evoked by a question seem to absorb the subject's attention and guide their speech. This may involve a prolonged and bitter reminder of interactions with parents in childhood, which may lead to inappropriate discussions about current relationships. The person tends to ramble using vague language and can describe the parent both in a negative and positive way in the same sentence.

**Insecure-resistant**: Children alternate between appearing very independent and ignoring the mother and suddenly becoming very nervous and trying to find her. After reuniting, they cling and cry, but also look the other way and become resistant, and parents are unable to ease their discomfort.

**Unresolved or disorganized**: Often shows substantial lapses in reasoning or discourse. May express childish beliefs or fall into long silences or mindless chatter.

**Disorganized**: Children cry for their parents at the door and run in the opposite direction when the door opens, approaching the parent while turning their head away. Behavioral strategies appear to be collapsed. They may appear frozen or engage in stereotypical behaviors.

## Research on Attachment and BPD

Sabo (1997) reviewed the literature on childhood experiences among BPD clients and concluded that neglect by both parents and the absence of alternative attachment figures were very powerful traumatic factors in the development of BPD. They found that, in children who had at least one parent who supported and cared for them, possibly the existence of one or more supportive relationships could counteract the effects of trauma. Others have suggested the importance of biparental failure in the development of BPD (Zanarini et al., 2000a; Zweig-Frank & Paris, 1991).

Another major factor that has been associated with borderline pathology is parental attachment (Guttman & Laporte, 2002). Zweig-Frank and Paris (1991) found that individuals with BPD remembered their parents (both mothers and fathers) as less caring and overprotective than individuals without BPD, indicating that control without affection is characteristic of some parents of individuals with BPD. Parental behavior appears not only to affect the development of borderline pathology directly, but parental dysfunction may increase vulnerability to other risk factors, mediating the effect of other psychosocial factors. For example, Zanarini et al. (2000a) reported that women with BPD who remembered their mother as neglectful and their father as abusive were more likely to have been sexually abused by a person who was not one of their caregivers. They hypothesized that a negligent mother would not be able to protect her children from sexual abuse by a non-caregiver and an abusive father might make his daughter believe that being used or abused is inevitable.

Gunderson (1984, 1996) suggested that intolerance of loneliness was at the core of borderline pathology. He believed that the inability of borderlines to invoke a "soothing introjection" was a consequence of the failure of early attachment figures. He described in detail typical patterns of borderline dysfunction in terms of exaggerated overreactions of the insecure attached child, such as clinging, fear of dependency needs, terror of abandonment, and constant monitoring of the caregiver´s proximity.

Different authors have associated disorganized attachment with BPD, explaining how it relates to the lack of integrated schemes of the self (Barone, 2003; Lyons-Ruth, Yellin, Melnick, & Atwood, 2005; Liotti, 2004; Blizard, 2003; Fonagy, Gegerly, Jurist, & Target, 2002; Schore, 2001; Mosquera & Gonzalez, 2011). Many authors have explained BPD symptoms using attachment theory (Bateman & Fonagy, 2004). Implicitly or explicitly, Bowlby´s (1969, 1973, 1980) suggestion that early experiences with the caregiver serve to organize later attachment relationships has been used as a way to explain the psychopathology of BPD (Bateman & Fonagy, 2004; Fonagy & Bateman, 2007). For example, it has been suggested that the experience of interpersonal attacks, neglect, and abandonment threats present in the history of borderline clients may explain their perceptions of current relationships as attacking and negligent (Benjamin, 1993).

Crittenden (1997) has been particularly concerned with incorporating in his representation of the disorganization of adult attachment the deeply ambivalent and fearful style of intimate relationships, specific of borderline individuals. On the other hand, Lyons-Ruth and Jacobovitz (1999) focus on the disorganization of the attachment system in childhood as predisposing to later borderline pathology. An insecure disorganized pattern was identified as predisposing to behavioral problems.

Fonagy (2000) and Fonagy, Target, & Gerfely (2000) have also used the framework of attachment theory, emphasizing the role of attachment in the development of the symbolic function and the way in which insecure disorganized attachment can generate vulnerability to future confusion and challenges. Barone, Fossati and Guiducci (2011) assessed 140 subjects with BPD using the AAI and reported a "global attachment picture in which insecure organized (dismissing 51% and enmeshed 35%) and insecure disorganized categories (40%) were overrepresented. All of these, along with other theoretical approaches, predict that attachment representations (Hesse & Main, 2001) are seriously insecure in clients with BPD (Bateman & Fonagy, 2004). For Bateman and Fonagy, there is no doubt that people with BPD are insecure in their attachment. However, they think that the descriptions of insecure attachment from childhood or adulthood provide an inadequate clinical explanation for several reasons: anxious attachment is very common and patterns of anxious attachment in infancy correspond to relatively stable adult strategies (Main, Kaplan, & Cassidy, 1985). However, the hallmark of attachment disorders in borderline individuals is lack of stability (Higgitt & Fonagy, 1992).

Paris (1994) proposed an integrated theory of BPD etiology: a biopsychosocial model that attempts to explain how personality disorders in general, and BPD in particular, can develop. This model involves both the cumulative and interactive effects of many risk factors, such as the influence of protective factors: biological, psychological, or social influences, which act to prevent the development of the disorder. Paris thinks that temperament may predispose each child to certain difficulties, but that temperament characteristics in the presence of psychological risk factors, such as trauma or parental loss and failure, can be amplified. As an illustration, he explains that most shy children (temperament) develop from a normal shyness, but if the family environment is not supportive, introversion (trait) will be accentuated and, eventually, if it persists, will become pathological (disorder). Shyness can make a child establish social contacts characterized by anxiety and/or avoidance and a pattern of abnormal attachment. But if this persists, behaviors can begin to correspond with the criteria for dependent and avoidant personality disorders.

Another interesting aspect that Paris points out is that future BPD clients begin their lives with temperamental characteristics that are compatible with normalcy (for example, a child who is more inclined toward action than reflection), but with a reasonably adequate psychosocial environment, would never develop a personality disorder. They also state that parents of future borderline clients may themselves have a personality disorder; they may be insensitive to the needs of their children and fail to offer an adequate supportive environment.

Allen (2003) speaks of parental roles confusion. He describes how the parents of BPD clients apparently focused on their children to the point of obsession, but at the same time are angry at them. One way to understand the contradictory and seemingly irrational behavior in the families of borderline clients is to conceptualize them as reactions to a serious and persistent intrapsychic conflict regarding the role of the parent. This conflict is created and reinforced by the parents´ experience in their own families of origin. The ambivalence about parenthood is the core issue of this parental conflict (Luborsky & Crits-Cristoph, 1990). They feel as if they must solemnly sacrifice for their children, but at the same time feel overwhelmed by the responsibility and resentful about the sacrifice.

In conclusion, attachment difficulties cannot fully explain the complexity of BPD and are not the only factor for a person to develop BPD, even though it is one of the pieces of the puzzle (Mosquera & Gonzalez, 2009). While negative primary attachment experiences clearly have an adverse impact, positive experiences with other secure attachment figures may be one of the most effective protective social factors (Mosquera & Gonzalez, 2009). Those clients who, while having dysfunctional parents, had at some point in their childhood a healthy caretaker figure like a grandmother, an aunt, or even a teacher, will have a special resilience and strength that can allow them to move more easily through the therapeutic process. For them, there has been some kind of a "safe place."

## Genetic and Biological Factors in BPD

Understanding the role of environmental factors in the development of the personality does not deny constitutional factors. Far from entering this debate between constitutional and environmental origins of mental disorders, we understand that genetics influence character traits and that temperament interacts with environmental elements in a complex way. Some very extreme character traits (e.g., extreme impulsivity) may cause personality disorders with little contribution from the environment. But most cases are in the middle of the spectrum, where the relationship with primary caregivers and the presence of traumatic situations influences the development of a borderline personality disorder.

In order to develop a truly explanatory theory, it is important to include the role of genetic factors, which several investigations point to, providing however contradictory data. Plomin, DeFries, McClearn, and McGuffin (2001) state that genes account for 40-60% of the variability in normal personality traits. These normal personality traits can evolve into a personality disorder when the individual grows up with a dysfunctional attachment or a traumatic environment.

Relationships between attachment, genetics, and personality disorders are complex and have not been well established. We can consider that insecure attachment causes emotional dysregulation. But both insecure attachment and emotional dysregulation may be mediated by the same hereditary differences in temperament or personality traits (Goldsmith & Harman, 1994). Recently, the influence of environmental factors in the range of expression of genes in the phenotype has been stressed (Lobo & Shaw, 2008). Although this issue needs to be studied in reference to early attachment vs. genetic factors in the development of BPD, it suggests that the interaction between genetics and environment is probably even more complex than previously thought. Brussoni, Jang, Livesley, and MacBeth (2000) found that genes account for 43, 25 and 37% of the variability in fearful, preoccupied, and secure attachment. In contrast, it was found that the variability in the dismissive attachment was entirely dependent on environmental effects. Skodol et al. (2002) stated that those aspects of personality disorders that could easily have biological correlates were those involving affect regulation, patterns of impulse/action, cognitive organization, and anxiety/inhibition. For BPD, key psychobiological domains would include impulsive aggression associated with reduced serotonergic activity in the brain and affective instability associated with a high response of the cholinergic systems. Siever et al. (2002) argue that family aggregation studies suggest that the inheritability, not for BPD as a diagnosis but as the genetic basis of this disorder, may be stronger for dimensions such as impulsivity/aggression and affective instability, than for the diagnostic criteria.

Environmental and genetic factors differentiate better in studies with twins, but these studies are very complicated and expensive. Some twin studies analyzed the inheritable effects of attachment in children, without finding significant genetic effects. On the contrary, environmental factors explained 23-59% of the variance (Bakermans-Kranenburg & Van IJzendoorn, 2003; O´Connor & Croft, 2001). Other investigations such as Crawford et al. (2007) found that anxious and avoidant attachment is related to personality disorders (PD). They associate avoidant attachment and emotional dysregulation, concluding from their data that 40% of the variance in anxious attachment was inheritable, and that 63% of its association with the corresponding dimensions of PD was attributable to common genetic effects. Interestingly, dismissive or avoidant attachment was influenced by shared environment rather than genes.

The possibility that primary caregivers share genetic determinants with the child does not mean that it is a linear causation. All these elements (shared character traits and attachment styles), when traumatic events occur, can have multiplicative effects. For example, an impulsive father will probably have difficulties when having to regulate impulsive behavior in his child, often reacting in a critical or violent way to the child's behavior. The presence of a personality trait does not invalidate the role of the caregiver when handling this feature. On the contrary, the existence of a character trait is a vulnerability factor for the child, who is likely to be more affected by the caregiver's attitude.

The same dynamic occurs with emotional dysregulation. We mentioned before that emotional deregulation and insecure attachment may be at least partially mediated by heredity factors. It would be likely that children with a genetic tendency to dysregulate their emotions would evolve better with parents who can modulate them. When parents have no emotional regulation skills, because both children and parents share the same genetic traits, this will probably increase the child's emotional dysregulation. The effect of a dysregulated style in a caregiver may be more intense in children with a poor capacity for emotional regulation.

Another aspect related to biological factors is the debate on comorbidity and the confusion between Axis I diagnoses with a more clearly genetic or biological basis and BPD (Zanarini et al., 1998). Liebowitz (1979) argues that borderline personalities are not clearly separated from the old concept of borderline schizophrenia, while others insist on the separation between the two diagnoses (Gunderson & Kolb, 1979; Kernberg, 1979; Spitzer & Endicott, 1979; Masterson, 1976). Similarly, some authors have considered BPD as a variation of bipolar disorder (Akiskal, Chen, & Davis, 1985), while others question this idea. Probably, as we will discuss later, all of these hypothesis contain some truth. Some clients with BPD manifest atypical presentations of bipolar disorder, emotional dysregulation being a symptom of the underlying disorder.

Another biological factor closely related to the borderline personality disorder is substance abuse. This is common in people with BPD and it increases the complexity in handling such cases and, in some way, conditions the possible increase in the number of dropouts from treatment (Guimón, Maruottolo, Mascaró, & Boyra, 2007). Substance abuse is a substitute way of regulation in these clients, who use it to not think about their problems, to decrease a negative emotion or stimulate themselves, to avoid the reactivation of a traumatic event, or as self-punishment. Sometimes the drug serves as a form of self-medication. For example, cannabis is used for its soothing and hypnotic effect, or cocaine may have a paradoxically relaxing effect in borderline clients with comorbid ADHD, having a partially similar effect to the stimulants used as pharmacological drugs for this disorder. But both alcohol and illegal drugs generate numerous symptoms and exacerbate those already present. For example, alcohol triggers an already poorly regulated impulsivity, and cannabis sometimes generates paranoid reactions or increases obsessive thoughts.

According to Marsha Linehan (1993), there are individuals who are born with a biological tendency to react more intensely to lower levels of stress than others and take longer to recover. In these people, drugs can be used to patch up this difficulty in regulating their emotional states. In addition, in BPD there have been alterations described in the opioid systems, which some authors associate with addictive behaviors (Szerman, 2012).

The relationship between biological and traumatic factors in the development of BPD is complex, but the available data cannot be ignored. Some borderlines may have a biological basis and others a more traumatic basis, the weight of these factors being different for each client. In chapter 3, we will discuss a proposed sub-classification based on this idea.

In summary, the relationship between genetic factors, personality traits, and attachment styles is probably complex, and has not been clearly confirmed or refuted. The most likely situation is that genetic factors such as those contributing to emotional dysregulation may influence personality traits. And these traits could be modulated or exacerbated by the relationship with the primary caregiver (Schore, 2003 a, b).

# Chapter 2
# EMDR Therapy

EMDR therapy (Shapiro, 2001) is an evidence-based psychotherapy for PTSD (Bisson, J., Roberts, N.P., Andrew, M., Cooper, R. & Lewis, C., 2013; Bradley, R., Greene, J., Russ, E., Dutra, L., & Westen, D., 2005; Davidson, P.R., & Parker, K.C.H., 2001). EMDR stands for Eye Movement Desensitization and Reprocessing. In recent years, there have been studies and case reports showing positive results in many other mental disorders and somatic problems, including borderline personality disorder (Mosquera, Leeds, & Gonzalez, 2014). The empirical evidence for other diagnoses is less than for PTSD, but it offers a promising way to treat problems associated with adverse life experiences, such as those associated with BPD (Sachsse & Tumani, 1999; Leeds & Mosquera, 2012; Mosquera & Gonzalez, 2012; Connell-Jones, 2011; Woller, 2003; Brown & Shapiro, 2006; Ostacoli, 2010; Korzekwa, 2010; Lawson, 2004; Meijer, 2006).

The *adaptive information processing model* (AIP) on which EMDR is based, suggests that much psychopathology is due to dysfunctional storage or incomplete processing of adverse and traumatic life experiences. This alters the person´s capacity to integrate these experiences in an adaptive way.

The AIP model is based on the idea that the trend toward health is part of living organisms, and that the human mind has innate systems to heal psychological wounds, just as the body has them to heal physical wounds. EMDR procedures are aimed at unblocking these systems, turning on the individual´s self-healing capacity again. The therapist is a facilitator in this process.

## Traumatic Memories and Adverse Life Experiences

Adverse life experiences can generate similar effects as those of traumatic events defined by the DSM (American Psychiatric Association, 2013) for the diagnosis of post-traumatic stress disorder (PTSD) and trigger or exacerbate a wide range of emotional, mental, somatic, and behavioral problems (Ross, 2000; Mol et al., 2005). Under optimal conditions, new experiences tend to be assimilated by an information processing system that facilitates their connection to existing memory networks associated with similar experiences. By binding to these memory networks, the basis for knowledge and learning is created.

Traumatic and adverse life experiences may, however, be dysfunctionally stored in the memory, and consequently their connection to memory networks containing adaptive information will be inadequate or altered. These experiences, which are not fully processed, will be the ones that generate pathology.

Let us see these concepts with an example. A 36-year-old man with no psychiatric history began to have symptoms of anxiety several months ago and went on sick leave. For 11 years, he had worked for the same company with no particular problems, fulfilling his duties and interacting with his peers.

To work with EMDR therapy in this case, we need to know what was going on in the client's life when symptoms began. The client said that 6 months ago he got a new boss, with whom he began having problems almost from the start. According to the client, this boss treated him with contempt and never seemed satisfied with what he did. Interestingly enough, the other employees did not seem to have problems with the new manager, whom they considered a demanding but respectful person.

Why was this man not able to maintain his previous level of functioning with his new manager? From the AIP model, we search for all experiences connected with his disturbance. For example, by focusing on the feeling that was generated by the disapproving facial expression of his boss, the client connects with experiences at school with his fourth grade teacher, where he felt humiliated and embarrassed in front of the whole class. This memory would be considered unprocessed information that has become activated by a present trigger: his boss's face. This memory has the characteristics of a traumatic memory: vivid fragmented perceptual elements and a significant emotional charge (the teacher's gesture, the dented corner of the table he stared at when looking down, the heat in his face, the feeling in his stomach). With the activated disturbance associated with that school event, this man could not function as the capable and sociable employee he had always been.

But let us go a bit further and think about early attachment relationships, which are the basis from which to integrate the rest of our experiences. The client described a childhood like many others, with a loving mother and father who worked hard to raise three children. However, some moments of his family history still disturbed him when thinking about them, despite all the years that had gone by. In particular, he remembered the feeling of not being up to par when his older brother came home with his usual excellent grades and his father asked for his, always responding, "You have to work more." Each time the new boss asked him to do some additional work, the same feeling of being a disappointment he felt with his father became activated.

EMDR work with this client's anxiety problem would address the processing of specific memories connected with the feelings or beliefs about himself that become activated in the current situation. These memories would be the scene where his father said, "You have to work more" and the scene related to the fourth grade teacher, when he was humiliated in front of the entire class. Later, we would address the present triggers, as the boss' facial expression or the times when his boss asks him to do extra work. Finally, once the work with past and recent memories is finished, we would ask him to visualize facing the situation in the future, with an adaptive belief, that is, a positive belief about himself as a person.

## What Does the Processing of a Memory with EMDR Look Like?

EMDR facilitates the processing and integration of dysfunctionally stored information. For this, we collect perceptual, cognitive, emotional, and somatic elements from the memory, corresponding to different levels of information processing (Shapiro, 2001). Once this memory and all its components are activated, alternating eye movements are used to unblock this information. It is considered that these facilitate the innate information processing system in the brain. The therapist guides the process, helping the client to make sets of eye movements until all emotional, somatic and cognitive disturbance associated with that memory is resolved and a new adaptive belief about the self can be positively associated with it. In addition to eye movements, the use of alternating sounds or tactile stimulation (tapping) has been proposed for situations where the eye movements are not well tolerated. All of these can also be called bilateral stimulation.

The effect of bilateral eye movements on emotional processing of memories was empirically discovered and developed by Shapiro (1989). Later, various research studies have examined the neurophysiological effects of eye movements, finding decrease in the vividness of the images, parasympathetic activation and its subsequent relaxation effect, increased mental associations and memory recall, and overall disappearance of any emotional residue associated with the memories. These go from having the characteristics of a traumatic memory to becoming ordinary memories. It has been hypothesized that the effect of eye movements is due to an overload of the working memory, the activation of the orienting response, an increased inter-hemispheric connectivity, or the consolidation processes of emotional memories that are related with REM sleep, where similar eye movements occur spontaneously (Solomon & Shapiro, 2008).

Clinically, what we see is that clients begin the session working on an emotionally charged memory, and after a number of sets of eye movements, they report that the image becomes blurry, distant, or they find it difficult to access. They may also comment that they notice more relaxation or how their physical sensations are changing, moving, or decreasing. At other times, different memories come up in associative chains connected by the same emotion, memory components, the same belief, or different memory elements. In some cases, associations are symbolic, not corresponding to real memories. Regardless of the type of associations that arise, they will tend to become neutral or positive, and when going back to the memory, clients can connect it with other experiences, have another view about the self, and eventually can say, "It's in the past, it no longer affects me, it doesn't say anything negative about me."

Although this type of simple and effective processing is common in EMDR therapy, so is the emergence of various kinds of difficulties or blocks, which the therapist must help the client overcome. As we will see, BPD is a good example of how, while EMDR therapy is possible and extremely useful with these clients, the therapist's intervention usually must be more frequent and active.

# An Eight-Phase Protocol Addressing Past, Present, and Future Experiences

EMDR therapy proposes the use of standardized clinical protocols and procedures that always include two key elements: dual attention and visual, auditory, or tactile bilateral stimulation.

Dual attention refers to the need for the memory we are working on to be active in the nervous system while the individual maintains orientation to the present. The person must be noticing the perceptions, emotions, beliefs, and sensations associated with that memory, while also remaining aware of what is related to the current moment. The client must keep one foot in the past and one foot in the present. For the integration of that experience to be effective, what was experienced there and then must be able to connect with what I am here and now.

The standard EMDR protocol is structured in 8 phases. The first phase is aimed at understanding how the client´s current problem are linked to their traumatic and adverse life experiences. We then prepare the client to access and process specific memories, providing psycho-education about the presenting problem and how to work with EMDR, teaching self-regulation skills and working on the psychological structure whenever necessary, until the client is ready to treat traumatic memories. The processing of these memories is carried out according to the work plan developed in the first phase, addressing the present triggers and future situations later on. The client's responses to EMDR therapy are monitored carefully and the treatment plan is adjusted as needed. We will now describe these eight steps more in depth:

## Phase 1: Case Conceptualization and Treatment Plan.

In this phase, we collect the clinical history, including those experiences that continue to present some level of disturbance. In EMDR therapy we pay special attention to early experiences and attachment organization. We also specifically assess dissociative symptoms, because when they are present, our way of working must be modified. Emotional regulation skills and client resources and strengths are identified in order to detect the need to reinforce them before processing memories of traumatic experiences. In cases of complex trauma, psychological defenses, affect phobias, differentiation and fragmentation of the self, and many other elements must be taken into account in order to establish the therapeutic plan.

In this first phase, the therapist will build a therapeutic plan with the client, based on an understanding of how the current problem is related to incompletely processed experiences. Aspects that must be reinforced must also be identified, as pointed out earlier, as well as whether changes are needed in the procedures for accessing and processing traumatic memories. In this work plan, past experiences, present situations, and future aspects will be considered.

The pace of collecting information must be adjusted to each client. It should be initially less comprehensive in certain cases of complex traumatization, since a premature deep exploration can lead to decompensation. But in any case, at this stage, the therapist must have a working hypothesis and a reformulation of the problem and a treatment plan must be outlined with the client.

## Phase 2: Preparation

The EMDR framework must be explained to clients, so that they understand the model and the work method, and agree to work with it. It is also important to establish a sufficiently strong therapeutic relationship to provide clients with a sense of security from which to approach traumatic content. We also work on enhancing self-regulation skills and facilitating dual attention, both of which are required for reprocessing sessions. This preparation phase varies greatly in duration, depending on the clients' characteristics and needs.

## Phase 3: Assessment

After selecting a memory from the treatment plan, the clinician identifies the components of the memory that will be reprocessed. This memory is called the target.

Among the components of the memory, we identify a representative image of the worst part of the experience, a self-referential belief that the person has now when thinking of that moment, and the emotions and physical sensations associated with it that are still active. The clinician gathers baseline measurements in order to see the progression of the processing in phases 4, 5 and 6.

The first measurement relates to the belief. We look for both a negative belief about the self that is now active in relation to the memory and also a positive belief that the individual would like to have about the same experience. This seeks to promote a connection with the adaptive networks. Rating the positive belief assesses the extent to which this belief is felt as true on validity of cognition scale (VOC) ranging from 1 to 7.

After identifying the image, negative and positive beliefs and the VoC rating, we use the image and the negative belief to access the presently felt emotion. Then the second measurement is taken, which relates to the overall level of disturbance. This is scored on a Subjective Units of Disturbance scale (SUDs) from 0 to 10. Finally we ask where the client feels the disturbance somatically. This helps to confirm that the client is not just providing an intellectual statement, but is in touch with the disturbance.

## Phase 4: Desensitization

After the memory is activated by asking clients to think of the elements identified in phase 3, and we begin the alternating bilateral stimulation. Clients mindfully (and silently) notice what occurs during each set of bilateral stimulation. After each set of bilateral stimulation we pause, and clients tell us about what they experienced, which this may include emotions, insights, associations, physical sensations, and various changes. When the process flows effectively, therapists we will observe without interfering. When the process does not evolve or becomes blocked, when dual attention is lost, and/or clients leave the window of emotional tolerance, we will do different interventions so phase 4 can continue effectively. This phase 4 ends when the level of disturbance (SUD) reaches 0.

## Phase 5: Installation

We first verify that the positive self-belief that best fits the memory. Then we ask the client to think about the memory and the positive belief. We then add more sets of bilateral stimulation to reinforce the linkage between the memory and the positive or to process any disturbance associated with the installation of the positive belief. This phase ends when the validity of cognition (VOC) reaches 7.

## Phase 6: Body Scan

We ask clients to identify any positive or negative body sensation, continuing with sets of bilateral stimulation until they only notice positive or neutral sensations, and these are reinforced.

## Phase 7: Closure

Before ending the session, the therapist we will help clients to self-regulate, manage emotional distress, and restore stability. Even if all phases have been completed and the client feels positively, we will advise that reprocessing may continue after the session and that between sessions they may become aware of other things, feel intense emotions, and notice several changes. We ask clients to take notes, understanding these events experiences are as a continuation of the process that started in the session.

## Phase 8: Reevaluation

The effect of the reprocessing of previous targets is reevaluated, looking for residual disturbance, new material that may have come up, current triggers, anticipated future challenges, and systemic issues. If residual disturbance or new targets appear, we work on them again from phases 3 to 8. This is one of the most relevant phases of the process since it allows the adequate closing of the targets.

## The Application of EMDR in Complex Traumatization

Reading the above paragraphs, we can think that EMDR is an easily applicable method that follows these simple steps. However, it is a complex therapy, in which this basic scheme that we have described must be adjusted to every single individual and every story. The EMDR therapist must have a solid understanding of trauma, attachment, dissociation, and the various protocols and applicable modifications for special situations.

One of these special situations is in cases of severe, chronic, or early traumatization, such as those that have been associated with the development of borderline personality disorder. Here, the standard EMDR protocol, originally developed for processing memories of a traumatic experience, that is, for the response to a single trauma defined as an accident, bereavement, illness, etc., requires a number of adjustments to address the multiple defenses, dysfunctional patterns, blocks, and difficulties in regulating with which these clients present. The standard EMDR therapy principle of minimizing our intervention must be adapted here to give way to a dynamic and elaborated process of dyadic regulation, using a range of concepts and tools such as those which we describe in this book.

# Chapter 3
# Dissociation and BPD

## The Concept of Dissociation

Dissociative disorders are common in BPD, but only in the most extreme cases interventions need to resemble those for dissociative clients (Gonzalez & Mosquera, 2012). This book is oriented to the other cases of borderline presentations, but even in this group, a detailed exploration of dissociative symptoms is essential for a comprehensive phase 1 in EMDR therapy.

Dissociation can be understood as the pathology of consciousness, whose development is altered from very early stages. Consciousness of self and the world is profoundly altered by traumatic experiences, especially when these occur during sensitive periods of development (Gonzalez, 2010).

Within the alteration of consciousness, we will refer to the altered level of awareness characteristic of trance states and the qualitative alteration of consciousness of self and the environment, which gives way to the phenomena of de-realization and de-personalization. But above all, it is the impossibility of an integrated vision of oneself that will characterize the core dissociative symptoms. This view of dissociation as the lack of integration between subsystems of personality is described in detail in Chapter 14, when discussing the theory of structural dissociation of the personality.

Dissociation is a post-traumatic phenomenon (Nijenhuis, Spinhoven, Van Dyck, Van der Hart & Vanderlinden, 1998; Coons, 1994; Van der Kolk y Kadish, 1987) that has also been associated with disorganized attachment (Liotti, 1999, 2004) and is strongly influenced by the absence of maternal warmth and maternal infant play (Leeds, 2013). As we have seen, traumatic factors and early attachment disruptions are highly prevalent in borderline disorders, so it is expected that dissociation will very often be present in BPD. As we shall see in this chapter, empirical research confirms this.

Detecting the presence of dissociative symptoms is important for therapy. On one hand, it has been found that in clients with dissociative disorders, specifically addressing the related symptoms leads to greater improvement in therapy. On the other hand, EMDR therapy requires specific adaptations when we are faced with complex forms of structural dissociation (Gonzalez & Mosquera, 2012).

# What Does Research Say?

The literature speaks of high rates of dissociative symptoms among BPD clients. Some authors consider these dissociative symptoms as symptoms of a personality disorder (Linehan, 1993, 2006), while others argue that some genuine dissociative disorders have been wrongly diagnosed as borderlines (Sar, Akyuz, & Doğan, 2007; Putnam, 1997).

Various epidemiological studies report a high frequency of dissociation among clients with BPD (Galletly, 1997; Paris & Zweig-Frank, 1997; Chu & Dill, 1991). Some researchers claim that many clients with BPD also have undiagnosed dissociative disorders. These studies use a categorical approach to dissociation that, however, does not include those cases in which dissociative features do not meet all the criteria for a DSM-V diagnosis of dissociative disorder. Yet these studies show how relevant the presence of these symptoms is in borderline clients.

In an empirical study with psychiatric inpatients, Ross (2007) found that 59% of BPD patients met criteria for a dissociative disorder according to the DSM-IV, compared with 22% in non-borderline patients. Korzekwa, Dell, and Pain (2009) reviewed several studies using various diagnostic tools in different populations. They found significant dissociative symptoms in about two-thirds of individuals with borderline personality. In a non-clinical population (students), Sar, Akyuz, Kugu, Ozturk, and Ertem-Vehid (2006) examined comorbidity of dissociative disorders in clients with BPD and its relationship to a reported history of childhood trauma. Among students diagnosed as BPD (8.5%), a significant majority (72.5%) of them had a dissociative disorder, while this rate was only 18% in the comparison group. In addition, for the authors, lack of interaction between dissociative disorder and BPD, for some types of childhood trauma, does not support the view that both disorders together could be a single disorder. Watson, Chilton, Fairchild, and Whewell (2006) found that clients with BPD who had a comorbid dissociative disorder had higher rates of a reported history of childhood trauma. Zanarini, Ruser, Frankenburg, Hennen, and Gunderson (2000) found that sexual abuse was related to dissociative experiences in borderline clients. Brodsky, Cloitre, and Dulit (1995) found a relationship between dissociation, childhood trauma, and self-mutilation, while others (Zweig -Frank, Paris, & Guzder, 1994) did not find it.

Under-detection of dissociative symptoms in BPD may be partly due to the fact that many standardized tools for diagnosing mental disorders do not include dissociative symptoms or dissociative disorders. A clear example is the SCID-I (First, Spitzer, Gibbon, & Williams, 1996), the main standardized interview for diagnosing Axis I DSM-IV-TR disorders. For this reason, studies that include these interviews systematically underestimate the presence of comorbid dissociative symptoms and disorders. Perhaps, this part of the psychopathology may be detected only when instruments specifically designed to evaluate dissociative symptoms and dissociative disorders are used.

It is true that the BPD´s criterion 9 (transient paranoid ideation, stress-related, or severe dissociative symptoms) includes dissociative symptoms. But, interestingly enough, it is one of the most overlooked criteria by clinicians in their assessments (Mosquera, 2010), and it is usually reduced to just the paranoid symptoms. However, dissociative symptoms can go unnoticed by therapists unfamiliar with the exploration of this area or by clinicians who do not include dissociative symptoms in their psychopathological examination. Delusions, which sometimes may be related to atypical presentations of schizotypal or schizophrenic disorders, or substance abuse, are mixed (in criterion 9) with dissociative symptoms. Among these, it is more usual to identify symptoms such as de-personalization or trance states, than others related to mental fragmentation (such as intrusive symptoms).

The high prevalence of BPD among clients with dissociative disorders also supports a close relationship between these two disorders. According to Putnam (1997), clinical studies suggest that 30% to 70% of clients with dissociative identity disorder (DID) met criteria for BPD (among other diagnosis) more frequently than participants without a dissociative disorder (Sar et al., 2007).

There is an unresolved issue that has to do with the understanding of BPD clients that also meet criteria for DID or DDNO: should these be clearly identified as comorbid diagnoses, or should borderline traits be considered as manifestations of an underlying dissociative disorder? The theory of structural dissociation of the personality, which will be discussed in the next chapter, provides a viable way to overcome this dilemma (understood as a false choice between opposites).

## Dissociative Symptoms

We will now describe several examples of dissociative symptoms, in order to facilitate the exploration of these problems in the borderline disorder. We will not go into the description of the various psychometric instruments that measure dissociation, nor delve into this subject (to examine these concepts in depth, see the review in Gonzalez, 2010).

We will classify dissociative symptoms in five groups, following the sections in the SCID-D (Steinberg, 1994). This is the structured interview most widely used and recognized for the diagnosis of dissociative disorders.

### Amnesia

Amnesia is an inability to remember that goes beyond ordinary forgetfulness. This may refer to the past. In our sample (Mosquera et al., 2013), 52% of clients with BPD referred some type of amnesia between 5 and 15 years of age. This difficulty remembering may not be complete, and some clients who claim to have no memories are capable of completing the scale of family experiences, even if they are not able to give specific examples.

Sometimes clients have specific periods of amnesia. For example, they do not remember from 9 to 12 years old, while still being able to refer situations that happened before and after that period. This suggests that, during this period, highly traumatic events may have taken place.

In some cases, people develop a pseudo-plot to fill in their gaps. They offer a generic description of their childhood, usually with high levels of idealization, but are unable to offer any examples. Sometimes, they simply "jump over" the amnesic period when talking about their biography, which becomes evident only when there is careful interviewing of the chronology of events.

This type of remote amnesia can occur in all types of disorders, and is generally related to histories of early trauma. More specific to dissociative disorders are current memory gaps. Individuals may recognize that there are gaps in their memory, bits and pieces of the day that they do not remember and cannot be accounted for, even if they try. Sometimes, they are not even aware of these gaps; they realize it because they are doing something and do not remember what happened before, they find themselves somewhere without knowing how they got there, sometimes not even knowing what brought them to that place (micro-fugues), or they find evidence of having done things they do not remember doing. Sometimes, it is other people who tell them about these facts.

Some clients describe it like this:

> "Suddenly I appear in one place and I have no idea how I got there, or why I was going there."

> "I come home and I see cheese. And I say... I don't like cheese... And I go out shopping again. It happens many times, I find shopping items that I don't even like."

> "My handwriting changes completely. Sometimes it is deformed. Other times it's childish, like a little girl's writing. Sometimes, I find notes around the house with these handwritings and I don't remember writing them."

> "Suddenly, 'I come back', I know how I started doing what I was doing, but a while went by, I don't even know how, I kept on going on automatic pilot. But I couldn't tell you what happened in the middle."

> "My wife told me what I said, I know she is telling the truth, and I really saw she was very worried. I just remember the beginning, and I remember I was angry, and how she was reacting. But if I had not spoken to her, I would now be telling you that we had a normal discussion, without going that far. But I insulted her, my God, I even pushed her ... I had never done that, I see myself doing what my father did, that is the last thing I would want for my family. I find it hard to believe, because I can't remember everything she tells me I did..."

## Depersonalization

Clients experience a disconnection from the self or the body in various ways. They may feel like an observer of the self, or they can literally see themselves from outside the body. They may not recognize themselves in the mirror, or they may see a face that is not theirs. At times, they may not feel pain, or they may see the body, or parts of it, in different sizes.

In BPD, it is important to explore this symptom, as well as amnesia, in relation to self-harm. While many BPD clients self-injure being perfectly aware of the physical pain, seeking to leave behind the emotional pain, in other cases clients do not notice the pain, and do not remember the self-harm episode or a fragment of it.

Here are some examples:

> "When I was 12, I started playing with my consciousness, I kept it alert when I wanted and when I didn't, I turned it off, much like pressing a button voluntarily. I decided when to be aware and when not to perceive, even if I appeared to be there normally, participating in a conversation like everyone else, even if my mouth talked automatically... It's as if my mind relegated everything to the habit that my body had acquired. It's like being in a glass bubble inside my body and it acts autonomously while the other one is sleeping unaffected."

> "I left my body, I saw myself from outside, as I am seeing you now. The first time it happened, I-was a child, and then it's happened several times."

> "My head and my body are disconnected. Sometimes I see how I do things, but it's like if I was a robot. My head looks at it, but everything happens automatically."

> "Words come out of my mouth without me deciding what I say, I can't control it... Once I yelled at X and called her a "bitch" and I really don't know why I did it ... It wasn't me..."

> "It's like my body doesn't belong to me. Sometimes, I don't even feel it. Sometimes it's very distressing. I leave, I leave my body ... Then I have to cut, or burn, or hurt myself... So I can 'come back'."

> "I see myself in the mirror, but I do not see my face ... I see the face of X (an abuser from childhood) ... It's not me, it's his face (grasps her face with her hands, as if trying to shake off that feeling)."

> "I'm not paying attention to things, I'm not paying attention to life, to my life. Most of the time I feel like a robot, I follow the steps, I know them by heart, and somehow, I'm there too, watching myself. But I'm not there... I don't know how to explain it."

## Derealization

In this case, disconnection and qualitative alterations of consciousness occur in relation to the surrounding world. The feeling is strangeness. People sometimes see their surroundings as unreal, as if it were a dream or they were looking through a fog. Familiar people or places seem strange.

> "I got home, I knew it was my house, but I didn't recognize it. Nothing in that place seemed familiar. I was really scared, I was blocked. I didn't know what to do."

"For a while everything looked like a movie, like living in the middle-ages and everyone seemed like characters (literally). I also saw myself as a character."

Told by a family member: "She came to me and called me X (the father's name, who was very aggressive at times) and started hitting me, telling me to leave. She was beside herself and did not recognize me. I told her, I am me, I'm F... It took her several hours to get back to normal..."

## Identity Confusion

Identity issues are characteristic of BPD. The symptom of identity confusion is defined as a subjective feeling of uncertainty, perplexity, or conflict about identity. Clients suffering this problem are in a constant battle about who they are and what decisions to make. Identity confusion is a symptom that manifests along a spectrum of severity (Steinberg, 1994), ranging from an intermittent struggle between good and bad "parts" that appear in the absence of amnesia in personality disorders (Boon and Draijer, 1991), to persistent internal fights regarding identity, characterized by constant internal dialogues, in Dissociative Identity Disorder and Dissociative Disorders Not Otherwise Specified.

Let us see some examples:

"I don't know who I really am. It's as if I didn't have a defined identity. I constantly change my mind, I don't know what I think about anything.  I'm unable to make decisions."

"There is a struggle within me, a constant fight with myself. Different parts of me try to impose themselves. It's exhausting."

"It's like a part of me pulled to one side, and the other would want to take me to the other side, and whoever wins, I always lose... my whole self, I mean."

## Identity Alteration

Identity confusion and alteration refer to the lack of integration of the personality, identity alteration being the most severe presentation. Within identity alteration, there can be different levels of severity, depending on whether these alternate personality states take control of the behavior and their degree of development.

Clients with BPD often have marked changes in their mental state, in which they behave very differently. When someone describes them, we often hear, "She seemed like another person." These changes are sometimes very extreme, clients in one state can be amnesic for what happened in the previous state, and these states configure complex behavior patterns. When borderline clients with more dissociative profiles are in one of their behavior states, and we ask how old they are, they can surprise us by stating an age that is much lower than their chronological age.

Sometimes, in one of these states, the client believes himself to be someone else and uses a different name. This is not necessarily obvious if not explored, and it may seem to merely be extreme emotional state changes, similar to those of other clients with BPD.

Sometimes, this fragmentation of personality is not openly displayed, but operates internally. Clients may feel as if there were one or more individuals inside influencing their behavior, as if there were a child inside, a demon, a person from their biography, or simply a "force" that pushes and controls them. These parts may take the form of voices, thoughts, or egodystonic impulses that are experienced as "not me." They often claim that this feeling is so powerful that they feel like puppets in the hands of reactions or impulses that they do not understand. More than a poorly defined or confused identity, clients can go through several identities or feel great perplexity or fear of the changes they are experiencing, though they may not really feel identified with those aspects of themselves.

Here are some examples:

> "Sometimes I lose control, I get upset, and I can´t control what I do. On some occasions, I have become very aggressive... I have bits and pieces of memories of those moments, like loose parts of a movie... Then I clutch my head in my hands, I feel very embarrassed, very guilty... But I can´t help it from happening again."

> "I think there is a good Anne and bad Anne... I try to prevent bad Anne from appearing, but sometimes she completely controls me... She is very vindictive, especially with men. The other day, I saw a complaint I filed... I do not remember this... I know it was bad Anne, but can´t remember anything... Sometimes I do remember when she appears, but this time I don´t..."

> "I hear a voice that insults me, calling me a worm, he wants to control me. Sometimes he takes control, dominates me completely, and I do horrible things. It´s as if he occupies half of my brain and wants to destroy me, he wants to end it all. I try to control him all the time, but sometimes I can´t, he escapes me."

## Conversive and Somatoform Symptoms

Traumatic rupture is not only a mental phenomenon, but also a somatic one. For many authors, the body holds the basic footprint of the traumatic experience (Ogden, Minton, & Pain, 2006; Levine & Frederick, 1997).

Somatic symptoms can be quite varied. Paralysis and epileptic seizures or pseudo-seizures are best known, due to being among the classical descriptions of hysteria (Charcot, 1887/1991). However, many clients present polymorphic symptoms, sometimes episodic, sometimes changing, and sometimes chronic.

> "Sometimes I can´t walk, my legs do not respond. I become completely blocked. It can happen when something overwhelms me, but often I don´t associate it with anything. It has happened

since I was 15 years old, the first time was when my grandmother died. Sometimes it lasts for weeks, sometimes days. Then it goes away.

"I can't control these jolts (the client's whole body experiences a jolt). I've done everything to get rid of them, but it has gotten worse and worse. Now I let them be, I try to do relaxing things (new jolt), and wait for it to go way. I'm desperate."

In many of these cases, underneath these symptoms there is a system of parts that represent an identity alteration. In other cases, they may relate to somatic blockages or preverbal memories.

## Intrusions

Intrusive phenomena, such as passive influence phenomena that Schneider described as first rank factors for schizophrenia, are considered by many authors as real indicators of dissociation. Emotional dissociative parts of the personality are perceived by the individual as intrusions, which may take the form of voices, ego-dystonic thoughts, or feelings of being controlled by an external force or by "something inside me." People may feel that they are doing things without having control over what they do, they may feel like a puppet in the hands of another, or they may have emotions or physical sensations without understanding where they come from. Such experiences suggest that a part of the subject's mind works autonomously, being perceived by the rest of the mind as symptoms. Let us take a look at several examples.

"What happens is that... my hands want to hurt me, you know? I don't want them to do so, they pierce me with forks, burn me with cigarettes, scratch me... I don't feel pain, I don't notice it while it happens, I don't notice anything until after a while."

"These voices are always there, torturing me. They are like an inner voice, like the voice of my conscience. When I am more or less normal, they are there in the background. But when I'm upset, they get stronger. Then it seems like if they came from outside of me."

When asked by the therapist if the client hears voices, she admits nervously, "Yes, does that mean I'm crazy? I've always been afraid to tell psychiatrists because I thought they would want to admit me again..." When the therapist asks, "Are they telling you something now?" the client says, "Yes, they are telling me to ignore you, to not tell you things. When I was in the other therapy (at a specific center for personality disorders) the voices were silent during the session, but when I left, they'd beat me up me non-stop, they all yelled at me at once, they told me I should've kept quiet... that lasted weeks and I felt terrible." The client said nothing about this to her previous therapists, partly because they had not asked about it specifically. Stimulating the client to speak about the content of the voices in session, and trying to understand what it meant, eliminated the period of intense discomfort due to the voices that continually harassed the client.

## First-Order Factors of Pathological Dissociation

Paul Dell (2006) describes the following symptoms as indicative of pathological dissociation:

- Confusion about the self
- Aggressive intrusions (control)
- Dissociative disorientation (trance, amnesia)
- Amnesia
- Anxiety due to memory problems that prevent doing everyday tasks
- Subjective experience of the presence of dissociative parts
- De-personalization/de-realization
- Persecutory intrusions (with no experience of control)
- Trance
- Flashbacks
- Physical symptoms (loss of function and rare symptoms: change in size of body parts, parts that disappear...)
- Circumscribed loss of autobiographical memory

From the point of view of EMDR, we are also interested in understanding the connection of such manifestations to the traumatic history and the client's early attachment styles. The presence of the most severe dissociative symptomatology involves a very different therapeutic plan for working with EMDR, and we will have to use not only different protocols, but also a particular kind of approach. Clients who cannot maintain dual attention when working with traumatic memories, who have highly structured dissociative parts with, mental autonomy and strong dissociative barriers, or present marked amnesic laps need a specific preparation before being ready to access and process core traumatic memories.

Many of the concepts we use to understand the severe dissociative clinical pictures will be helpful with borderline clients, even those without high levels of dissociative symptoms. However, this book does not discuss the modifications proposed for EMDR procedures in working with dissociation, which can be found in Gonzalez and Mosquera (2012). Next, in Chapter 4 we will explore a framework for understanding and approaching the application of EMDR therapy for clients with BPD based on the theory of the structural dissociation of the personality, a model from which we can make the link between trauma, dissociation, and borderline traits.

# Chapter 4
# BPD from the Theory of Structural Dissociation of the Personality

In 2006, Van der Hart, Nijenhuis, and Steele published *The Haunted Self*, developing a theory in which knowledge of psychotraumatology and neurobiology link to classical theories on dissociation. They call their model the theory of structural dissociation of the personality. This theory provides an interesting theoretical framework for understanding BPD (Mosquera, Gonzalez, and Van der Hart, 2011), which we will describe below. Aside from the consistent clinical evidence, studies are emerging that support the basic principles of the theory of structural dissociation (e.g., Reinders et al., 2003; see Van der Hart, Nijenhuis, & Solomon, 2010, for a brief review).

To work with complex traumatization, which as we explained represents a significant portion of BPD clients, we need a map to guide us in structuring the therapy. The theory of structural dissociation of the personality provides a rich conceptualization of post-traumatic clinical pictures and also offers us intervention guidelines. In our work with EMDR, oriented toward traumatic basis and the influence of early experiences, it will be important to have a good understanding of how complex traumatization affects personality development.

## Theory of Structural Dissociation of the Personality

From this theory conceptualization includes both the traumatic events and the attachment trauma that would be in the basis of the borderline and dissociative symptomatology. These factors would not be understood as separately analyzed elements, but as part of the same psychopathological process. By including this model in the case conceptualization, we will have a more integrated view, which allows us to later apply different procedures in a structured and consistent manner.

This theory is not about dissociation understood as a symptom or disorder. The word dissociation is used here to describe a mechanism that the authors believe would be at the basis of all post-traumatic disorders. Post-traumatic clinical pictures are distributed in a psychopathological spectrum running from acute trauma and PTSD on one end, to dissociative identity disorder on the other end, as the more severe post-traumatic clinical profiles. In the middle of the spectrum we find borderline personality disorder and somatization disorders.

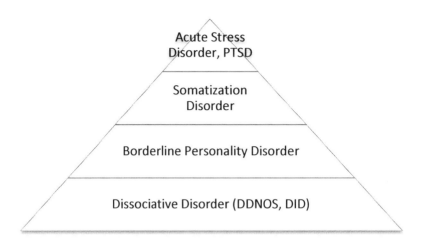

*Figure 1. The Posttraumatic Spectrum.*

## The Concept of Personality

Inspired by Allport (1981) and Janet (1907), Van der Hart et al. (2006) define personality as the dynamic organization within the individual of those biopsychosocial systems that determine characteristic mental and behavioral actions. That is, the concept of healthy personality includes the idea of integration and in that integration neurobiological, psychological, and social elements are related in a coherent, flexible, and adaptive way.

Pathology is defined by the lack of integration between these subsystems, which can operate erratically, be non-modulated, or even be in internal conflict. The various reactions and emotional states of borderline clients relate to this situation.

## Action Systems

Among the biopsychosocial systems comprising personality, psychobiologically based action systems play a major role (Lang, 1995; Panksepp, 1998; Van der Hart et al., 2006). The two main systems are defense against threat and adaptation. Both systems are organized to become instinctively activated when necessary and to give way to another system when circumstances require it. For example, when an animal is eating it is smoothly approaching an attractive stimulus, food, and all body functions are adapted to that situation. As soon as it hears a noise, this activity is interrupted and warning systems become activated. There is activation, the animal is alert, it tracks the environment. If it rules out danger, the activation disappears completely and continues eating as if nothing had happened. In this fluid way, the body keeps responding to the environment. This simple and logical mechanism may break down profoundly in response to traumatic experiences, forming what Van der Hart et al. (2006) call primary structural dissociation. From here on, things can get quite a bit more complicated.

The defense system is not characterized by a single response, but includes several methods of trying to survive an imminent threat to the integrity of the body and life itself (Fanselow & Lester, 1988). The mammalian defense action system is geared toward escape and avoidance of physical threat, as well as the associated psychological threat, and includes subsystems such as flight, freeze, fight, and total submission (Porges, 2003).

Other action systems are responsible for the interests and functions involved in daily life (Panksepp, 1998). These systems include energy regulation, attachment, care, exploration, social engagement, play, and sexuality/reproduction, and involve approximation to attractive stimuli (Lang, 1995).

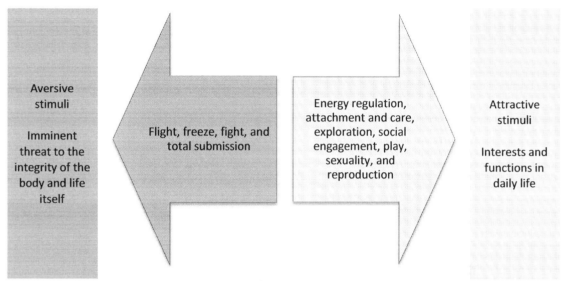

*Figure 2: Action systems*

## Dissociative Parts of the Personality

The theory of structural dissociation of the personality (TSDP) posits that in trauma – not only traumatic events that can be included in criterion A, but in situations we described when talking about attachment - the client's personality develops with two or more subsystems or dissociative (and incomplete) parts of the personality (Van der Hart et al., 2006), each mediated by action (sub) systems.

That is, defensive systems and those of everyday life stop working congruently with the environment and lose the fluid interrelation that we described. Returning to the same example, an animal that has been beaten could activate the warning system while eating, without being able to deactivate it. Thus the level of alertness persists, interfering with the feeding function. Once modulation systems are poorly adjusted, numerous variations may occur.

The human mind, with higher levels of complexity, develops various psychosocial functions associated with these neurobiological systems. If there has been a structural dissociation between defense and everyday life, the sense of self may fail to develop its integrity or may lose it with later occurring forms of PTSD. Thus, individuals in defensive mode feel in danger, establish certain interpretations about others, the environment, and the self, which they may not have at all when they are focused on everyday life. In primary structural dissociation, a characteristic of PTSD, when people are focused on the day to day and on "moving forward," they try to avoid at all costs the mental contents associated with traumatic experiences. These experiences are remembered, or rather relived, in defensive mode, with the activation of another range of biological subsystems. The system loses flexibility and its ability for dynamic adaptation. Stiffness and attempts to control replace spontaneous modulation.

These dissociative parts, also called dissociated ego states, are dysfunctionally stable (rigid) in their functions and actions, and shut off (disconnected) from one another. A subsystem of the prototypical personality is metaphorically called the *emotional part of the personality* (EP, Myers, 1940; Van der Hart et al., 2006). As EP, the client is fixated in highly emotionally charged sensorimotor reenactments, and maladaptive defensive behaviors related to traumatic experiences.

The client as EP is reliving the trauma, continues to be in the "there and then." Since for this part the threat is still active, the defensive response also continues. As mentioned, mammals are protected by several defense systems, as well as by action tendencies related to the need for attachment and attachment loss (Liotti, 1999). Fight, flight, freeze, total submission, hypervigilance, wound care, recuperation states, and attachment cry may be different subsystems in various EPs, oriented toward protection against perceived threat. In this state, clients "are continuing the action, or rather the attempted action, which began when everything happened, and they exhaust themselves in these continuous reactivations" (Janet, 1919/25, pp. 663).

It is obvious that in this state, individuals can neither continue functioning nor interacting. So, they disconnect from their emotional part and start to function from what Myers (1940) and Van der Hart et al. (2006) have called the *apparently normal part of the personality* (ANP). Mental and behavioral actions of the ANP are mediated primarily by action systems of daily living (social involvement, attachment, care, exploration, play, energy regulation, and sexuality/reproduction).

As ANP, survivors experience the EP and at least some of the actions and content of the EP as egodystonic, as something that "happens to them" but does not feel like their own, at least not completely. This ANP is set on avoiding traumatic memories and often the internal experience in general. People try to not think, not remember, not feel or come in contact with anything related to trauma and the EP, in order to go on with life. The ANP is focused and is based on action systems to function in daily life. Unable to really feel good after what happened, from the ANP, individuals try to appear normal. In order to do this, they keep the memory so isolated that they do not think about it or do not remember it, they have a narrative memory but not an emotional one. From that deep disconnection, they tell themselves "I'm over it," "It wasn't that important," or "It's not a problem in my life." Avoidance, minimization, and denial protect individuals who strive to move forward amidst the unmanageable overflow of memories. That is, they protect the ANP from the emergence of the EP.

But mental functioning is altered, and the normality of the ANP is only apparent, presenting negative symptoms of detachment, numbness, and partial, or in exceptional cases complete, amnesia for traumatic experiences. Containment of the EP is often only partial, leaving individuals, as ANP, to recurrently re-experience traumatic memories and various types of intrusions as voices, thoughts, or egodystonic sensations, which constitute EP activations.

## Primary, Secondary, and Tertiary Structural Dissociation

The TSDP suggests that the more intense, frequent, and lasting the traumatization, and the earlier its onset in life, the more complex the structural dissociation of the personality will be. The division of the personality that we described earlier between one ANP and one EP is a primary structural dissociation, and characterizes simple post-traumatic disorders, including PTSD. But when traumatic events begin early in life, are overwhelming, and/or prolonged or chronic, an elaboration of emotional parts of the personality ensues.

In secondary structural dissociation there is also one APN, but more than one EP. Different defensive subsystems characteristic of emotional parts configure the different EPs, each one based on a different response as fight, flight, freeze, or collapse. This secondary structural dissociation is mainly related to complex PTSD (Herman, 1992). Related concepts are those such as post-traumatic personality disorder (Classen et al, 2006) or the Disorder of Extreme Stress Not Otherwise Specified (Pelcovitz et al., 1997), trauma-related BPD, and dissociative disorder not otherwise specified subtype 1 (the most similar to dissociative identity disorder).

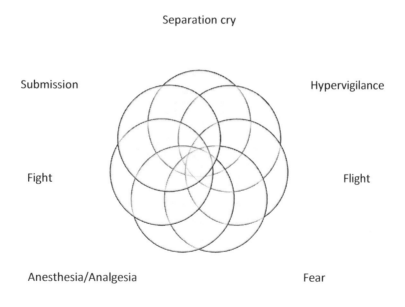

Separation cry

Submission          Hypervigilance

Fight          Flight

Anesthesia/Analgesia          Fear

*Figure 3: Different action systems*

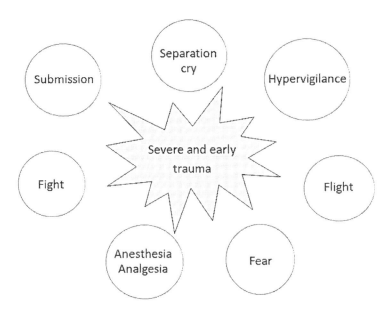

*Figure 4: Division of the personality by traumatic experiences*

Finally, tertiary structural dissociation includes not only more than one EP, but also more than one ANP. Not only are the defensive responses fragmented, disorganized and uncoordinated, but also coping with everyday life is done through the development of different mental states with a low level of integration that do not allow the individual to develop a coherent identity. Tertiary structural dissociation refers only to clients with dissociative identity disorder (DID). A few clients with DID with a very low integrative capacity, and in which the dissociation of the personality has a strong habituation, may even develop new ANPs to address minor life frustrations. Dissociation of the personality in these clients has become a lifestyle, and its prognosis is generally poor (Horevitz & Loewenstein, 1994).

Borderline clients may have a secondary or tertiary structural dissociation of the personality. The ANP and the EPs are typically fixated in a pattern of disorganized attachment that includes both approximation and defense in relationships (Steele & Siever, 2001). Both ambivalent-insecure and disorganized attachment classifications are related to inconsistent responses from the primary caregiver and lack of attunement. Some dissociated parts of the personality may be understood as the subsystems developed in order to adjust to each of these aspects in the caregiver, which often are irreconcilable. Alternation (or competition) between relational approximation and defense among these parts is a substrate of what has been called disorganized/disoriented attachment style (Liotti, 1999). The child approaches the caregiver, since the attachment is essential for survival. Biologically, everything is designed for that caregiver to be a source of protection, not the origin of the threat. When the caregiver frightens, assaults, or abuses the child, when the attachment relationship is inconsistent and unpredictable, attachment becomes disorganized. It is then that we see the highest levels of structural dissociation and more serious dissociative symptoms will be present in borderline clients.

# Dissociative Phobias

Structural dissociation is generated in trauma, but is maintained by mental actions and phobic behaviors. The core phobia is the **phobia of traumatic memories**, and from this central phobia, other phobias emerge that are directed inwards. Marilyn Van Derbur (2004), a survivor of incest, describes this very graphically:

> "I was unable to explain to anyone why I was so tied up, locked up, and disconnected from my feelings... Being in touch with my feelings would have meant opening Pandora's box... Without realizing it, I struggled to keep my two worlds separate. Without knowing why, I made sure, I made it impossible for anything to cross the barrier than I had created between the day girl (ANP) and the night girl (EP)" (pp. 26, 98).

Phobic reactions to these memories keep them isolated from everyday life, apart from other mental contents. Sometimes, this is generalized to everything that implies feeling, thinking, noticing the body, or remembering the past. Looking inward is terrifying, when there are things inside that are experienced as unmanageable and impossible to assume.

These individuals avoid any kind of self-analysis and live on the surface, in an "as if" world that sometimes alternates with uncontrolled emergence of impulses, emotions, or symptoms. This struggle to avoid inner experiences is what the theory of structural dissociation of the personality calls phobia of mental actions.

Another source of turmoil is the **phobia of dissociative parts**. There are parts of the personality that clients reject, avoid, or fear. They can assume parts of themselves, for example they can accept their loving part, being an efficient worker, or a good parent. But they are unable to assume the anger accumulated in their most aggressive part, which is focused on a fight action system, and more focused on memories of situations of aggression and abuse than other parts.

How do you accept seeing in yourself such an immense rage, so similar to the rage of the person who ruined your childhood?

When structural dissociation is more intense and those parts have more mental autonomy, more first-person perspective, clients literally feel like a different person when they function from one of them. When they return to their usual state and see what they just did, they may experience rejection, fear, or awe, "That's not me." While in one state, they may not remember what they did while in a different state. Sometimes they can be convinced that they are a different person, with a different name. These dissociative symptoms may go unnoticed if not specifically explored, as explained in Chapter 3.

# Different BPD Subgroups and Structural Dissociation of the Personality

In our opinion, the discussion of whether BPD is generated by biological or environmental factors is based on a false dichotomy. Reality is complex and science often comes to the conclusion that there are no simple explanations for complex phenomena. A truly descriptive model of BPD needs to include all the recent evidence and integrate different areas of knowledge. Currently, there is sufficient data to support a multimodal model for BPD (Mosquera et al., 2011).

The model we propose is based on a clinical perspective and it seems relevant to the conceptualization of borderline personality disorder from the EMDR therapeutic approach. BPD clients are a heterogeneous group. As Hunt (2007) states, the etiology of BPD is best explained as a combination of genetic and neurological vulnerability, combined with childhood trauma, including abuse or neglect, which leads to emotional dysregulation, cognitive distortions, deficits in social skills, and limited adaptive coping strategies.

We understand the borderline group as the product of the combination of traumatic factors (involving structural dissociation) and biological factors. The proposed classification of borderline clients in three groups is aimed at structuring treatment of these cases. On one end, we would have the most dissociative clients with borderline BPD clients (at times these clients have dissociative disorders misdiagnosed as BPD); these clients have experienced more severe trauma and have disorganized attachment. On the other end, we would place those cases of clients with BPD with a more biological basis and with co-occurring conditions such as bipolar disorder, schizophrenic psychosis, ADHD, etc. A third group with insecure attachment problems (most commonly with preoccupied but sometimes with avoidant insecure attachment) would be located between the two ends. For clinical purposes we will distinguish three BPD subgroups, in which different etiological factors have different weights (see Figure 5) and the EMDR treatment plan will need to be structured differently.

A first group consists of clients with BPD with comorbid dissociative disorder. These clients have a history of chronic traumatization and neglect in childhood, disorganized attachment, and their level of structural dissociation is greater. A second group would consist of BPD clients without a dissociative disorder diagnosis. This group overlaps with the so-called disorders of extreme stress or complex PTSD (Van der Hart, Nijenhuis, & Steele, 2005), and would be related to early and chronic trauma, neglect and environmental factors related to a dysfunctional attachment type with primary caregivers, mostly of ambivalent style. A third group of clients have BPD with a more biological comorbid disorder, such as bipolar disorder, a schizophrenia spectrum disorder, or ADHD. All these disorders may interact, in complex ways, with environmental factors, or function themselves as traumatic experiences (Goldberg & Garno, 2009). Some clients with atypical presentations of mental disorders, such as clinical pictures of the schizophrenic or bipolar spectrum, may be misdiagnosed as borderlines due to observable behaviors and symptoms (this could be the end of the spectrum, see Figure 5).

In most of these cases, however, both the biological and environmental factors would be present in varying degrees. We must take into consideration that due to their innate behavioral characteristics, children belonging to this third group are often "difficult" children that can push what would be slight to moderate disruptions in parental coping capacities to serious attunement issues. These children may demand the most from their parents or be a true challenge for some parents with similar temperaments.

As we mentioned before, some severely traumatized individuals may meet criteria for both BPD and a complex dissociative disorder. However, in some cases, symptoms interpreted as borderline manifestations may be best explained as belonging to a complex dissociative disorder and do not represent true comorbidity. For example, a client with DID had high impulsivity that manifested in self-destructive behavior, which actually was associated with the activation of an emotional part of the personality. When we worked with the internal system of dissociative parts, this symptom disappeared. After this, the client had no more impulsive reactions. In this case, we have a DID diagnosis, and the "comorbid" impulsivity symptom was only a manifestation of the dissociative disorder. In other cases, even having dissociative parts, and having worked effectively with them, impulsivity is a character trait that remains present.

Aside from these more extreme cases, most cases are based on a particular combination of factors. The model of the theory of structural dissociation of the personality serves as a conceptual framework for all subtypes, but classification framework we propose allows us to guide the treatment in a differentiated way. For example, when a biological factor is present (genetic based impulsivity, for example), the need for additional pharmacological treatment would be clearer. When dissociative symptoms are very strong, the EMDR treatment plan has to shift more toward one for dissociative disorder than one for borderline personality disorder. In the attachment group, and in many of the cases with a stronger biological basis, treatment structure will be closer to the standard procedure for EMDR work, but with the many specific changes that we will describe throughout this book.

We think it is important to consider these factors, not as opposing aspects, but as complementary and interactive. Although drawing biological and environmental factors as opposite ends of a spectrum is not a complete description of clinical reality, it gives us a reference for a differential understanding of each client, based on the predominant factors organizing the treatment plan.

We understand that there is a continuum that goes from secure attachment (right side of the arrow in Figure 5), through disruptions of attachment, all the way to severe traumatization and neglect and disorganized attachment. On a different level, biological-genetic factors may be stronger on one end, and virtually absent on the other, with an intermediate possibility where the genetically determined temperament interacts with other factors to generate character traits. It is important to remember that this representation is not exact, because there may be a strong genetic basis (at the same time) in a highly traumatic environment and quite diverse combinations of these factors.

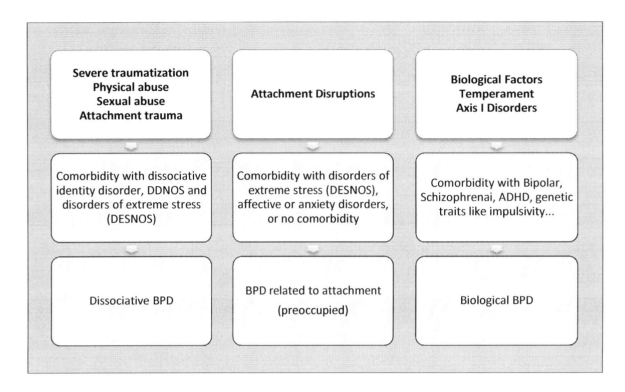

*Figure 5. Borderline Personality Disorder Groups*

The first group, **dissociative BPD**, contains borderline clients with secondary or tertiary structural dissociation, with dissociative parts of the personality that have a more developed first person perspective, and that in some cases have names and/or ages that differ from those of the main part (main ANP). Some of these parts may believe they are different people. In the intermediate group of **attachment-related BPD**, the underlying personality structure is the same (usually secondary structural dissociation), but dissociative parts have a less developed first person perspective, and the client may only notice dramatic changes in their emotions, behaviors, or cognitions, without an inner experience of "having parts," or changes in the sense of identity. The third group helps us understand the complex interaction between elements with a **more biological** base and the traumatic history, and how environmental factors and brain structure are modulated or aggravated by early attachment relationships.

In the following section, we present three clinical cases that highlight the differences between dissociative BPD, attachment-related BPD, and biological-based BPD followed by a fourth case with a mixed presentation.

**Case 1: Dissociative Borderline Personality Disorder**

Elisabeth, 28 years-old, was diagnosed with BPD and later DID, which implies a tertiary structural dissociation. She presented self-destructive behavior, anorexic traits, behavioral changes, unstable relationships, identity problems, and pseudo-psychotic symptoms (auditory hallucinations). She concealed or minimized most of her symptoms in therapy sessions. With time and a more detailed examination, it became apparent that she had significant amnesia and several dissociative parts who were responsible for different aspects of everyday life. One part was an efficient teacher (ANP-1), and from this part she could not remember anything she had done the previous weekend with her friends (when ANP-2 had been active). These parts both had a very elaborate first-person perspective. Throughout therapy, a very complex internal system of dissociative parts became apparent and many borderline symptoms could be explained as manifestations of her dissociative identity disorder. For example, her unstable relationships were related to the fact that different parts established relationships with very different people and hostile parts pushed her to associate with potentially dangerous men. Here auditory hallucinations were intrusions of various emotional parts and her self-injurious behavior represented aggressions by one part against other parts.

**Case 2: Borderline Personality Disorder Predominantly Related to Attachment**

Margaret came to therapy at age 42, without mentioning a history of severe trauma, but with an ambivalent attachment to her primary caregivers and impulsive personality traits. She suffered severe emotional dysregulation, and was prone to hyperactivation. At times she could be functional, but other times she acted more dependently and was unable to do things for herself. At such times, she behaved in a very childish way, with emotions that were connected to her early experiences of lack of affection from her parents and her anxiety due to her father's alcohol problems. Sometimes she acted like a teenager, for example, falling madly in love with different men. At those times, she had no inner experience of being a different person or having a different identity, but she described herself as acting or feeling "like a little girl" or "as a teenager." Her resources in other areas of her life were not accessible to her in those mental states, which can be understood as dissociative parts. She did not have the ability to modulate these parts of the personality or to change from one to another, and she used cocaine and alcohol to achieve those changes, for example, to reduce the feeling of loneliness connected with the "little girl part." These emotional parts were not as well defined. They had a first-person perspective less elaborate than in the previous case, but she described the behaviors that she had at those times as "alien," "I can't understand why I do this crazy stuff." This structure would be characterized by a secondary structural dissociation of the personality.

**Case 3: Biological Borderline Personality Disorder**

Lucy, 48-year-old female, was diagnosed with BPD 10 years ago. She presented mood swings with recurrent depressive states of short duration. Her interpersonal relationships were unstable. She had a troubled marriage (which she tolerated because of her fear of abandonment) and no social support. Self-destructive behaviors and suicide attempts were frequent. In therapy, she had presented a demanding and dependent attitude with her previous therapists. After several years of chronic depressive symptoms, she had a true manic episode. A later depressive episode was followed by a new manic phase with psychotic symptoms incongruent with her mood. With a combination of antidepressants, mood stabilizers and neuroleptic drugs, many personality "traits" changed. Her emotional dysregulation and self-destructive behaviors were greatly reduced. In this example, it is not easy to establish which symptoms were due to subclinical mood swings and which were due to personality traits, since so many years living with the consequences of her illness had caused a large secondary traumatization.

**Case 4: All in one**

Frank, 41 year-old male, had mood swings, high impulsivity, risky behavior, identity disorders, and unstable relationships. His family of origin was dysfunctional: his mother had been emotionally distant and often neglectful and his father was often absent, and had emotionally and physically abused him when he was home. Frank had presented behavioral problems in childhood. He met criteria for an adult attention deficit disorder (ADHD) with low sustained attention and high impulsivity and hyperactivity. His mother also met criteria for ADHD and showed an extreme lack of attention. This inattentiveness related to ADHD probably influenced her negligent care. His father was very impulsive, but with normal attention span. These factors present in both parents could have influenced the early development of the client: the negative genetic influence can be increased by attachment related patterns of parenting and the effect of physical and emotional abuse. The client showed signs of structural dissociation, alternating between an (emotional) dependent part focused on attachment, who desperately needed intimate relationships, an aggressive emotional part, facilitated by alcohol, and a depressive emotional part (EP) (linked to traits of low self-esteem), all of which alternated with a narcissistic apparently normal part (ANP). So, in addition to attachment issues, traumatic exposure and possible genetic factors for ADHD and impulsivity, Frank was characterized by a secondary structural dissociation.

## Other Approaches to the Dissociative Nature of BPD

The theory of structural dissociation of the personality (TSDP) is not the only therapeutic approach that emphasizes the dissociative features of BPD. Some authors have even described all personality disorders in terms of dissociation. Bromberg (1998), for example, states:

> "Personality Disorder" represents an egosyntonic dissociation, no matter what personality style it embodies... Dissociative disorders, themselves (...) are, from this perspective, the key to understanding all other personality disorders (pp. 201-202).

Other authors also describe concepts that are similar to those of the TSDP. Blizard (2003) and Howell (2002, 2005) conceived BPD as dissociative disorders with "a significant pattern of ego states," for example, masochistic/victim states or states of self and sadistic ego states, also called angry/perpetrator states or abusive ego states. These "states of self" are equivalent to the TSDP concept of "dissociative parts of the personality." The term "dissociative parts" is more inclusive because they can sometimes be complex and include different mental states at different times (Van der Hart et al., 2006). Lieb, Zanarini , Schmahl, Linehan, and Bohus (2004) argue that BPD clients "often move from one interpersonal reactive mood to another, with great speed and fluidity, experiencing several dysphoric states and periods of euthymia during the course of a day," a description that involves dissociation.

Some BPD models include a dissociative perspective similar to the theory of structural dissociation of the personality. Cognitive analytic theory (Ryle, 1997), for example, describes the connection between early trauma, caregiving styles, and borderline pathology. Related models of borderline functioning - the Multiple Self-States Model (MSSM) - explain many of the features of BPD in terms of alternating dominance of one small range of self-states "partially dissociated" or another (Ryle, 1997). These self-states are the equivalent of dissociative parts of the personality.

Golynkina and Ryle (1999) observed that "among these states, memory may be impaired, and there is some self-observation ability in all or some of them" (p. 431). Ryle (2007) states that borderline clients manifest significant discontinuities of their experience and behavior, and that these contribute to the difficulties that clinicians find when treating them. From this perspective, the underlying problem is a structural dissociation of the processes of the self in a small range of partially dissociated self-states, with unintentional shifts between them that can be sudden. It is obvious that this point of view has much in common with the theory of structural dissociation of the personality, which clearly emphasizes the first person perspective of dissociative parts. Some examples of the types of self-states described by Golynkina et al. (1999) are: an ideal self ("others admire me"), an angry abuser state ("I want to harm others"), a powerless victim ("others attack me and I´m weak"), and a zombie state. The theory of structural dissociation of the personality relates these different self-states or dissociative parts with different action (sub) systems, on which their function is based. For example, the angry abuser functions based on the fight defensive subsystem and the helpless victim functions based on the submission defense subsystem.

Ryle and Kerr (2006) define the reciprocal role process as a concept underlying what they call the *multiple self-states model* (MSSM). These procedures are sequences of perception, evaluation, action, and consequence analysis, which shape actions directed toward an objective. Each role is identifiable by its characteristic behavior, mood, symptoms, view of self and others, and reciprocity seeking, which links with the TSDP´s concept of first person perspective of dissociative parts.

Another orientation that links early experiences with adults symptoms and includes concepts that are very close to those from the TSDP is schema therapy (Young, Klosko, & Weishaar, 2003). Young et al. observed that clients with BPD are characterized by the existence of different "parts of the self," which they call "modes." They identify four main types: child mode, maladaptive coping mode, dysfunctional parent mode, and healthy adult mode. They state: "In clients with borderline or narcissistic disorders, modes are relatively disconnected, and the person is able to experience only one mode at a time. BPD clients switch rapidly between modes" (p. 272). This abrupt change between different modes is equivalent to the alternation between EPs and APNs such as is described by the theory of structural dissociation of the personality. In both theories, some modes or dissociative parts may in turn dissociate into subparts. One of the distinctions that Young makes belongs to the child modes: the vulnerable child, the angry child, the impulsive/undisciplined child, and the happy child. Again, the theory of structural dissociation of the personality considers that these different parts, some of which are described as EPs, are mediated by different (sub) systems, can have different levels of mental development, and contain different aspects of traumatic memories. Young distinguishes a healthy adult mode, which is distinctly different than ANP as described by Van der Hart et al. (2006). Young notes that this mode is virtually absent in many borderline clients; therefore it would be something to be achieved in the course of therapy. However, according to the theory of structural dissociation of the personality, some ANPs can be highly functional (see also Horevitz & Loewenstein, 1994), comparable to the healthy adult mode described by Young et al. But, no matter how functional the ANP appears to be, it is still a dissociative part of the personality that is not integrated with other parts. Once the personality is fully integrated, the theory of structural dissociation of the personality would speak of a healthy personality with a good capacity for self-reflection, introspection, and self-regulation.

Another important author in the conceptualization of BPD is Otto Kernberg (1993). In transference-based psychotherapy, he describes a developmental theory of borderline personality organization (Levy et al, 2006), conceptualized in terms of affects and representations of self and others, which has some similarities to dissociative parts described in the TSDP. Partial representations of self and others are associated in pairs and linked by an affect in mental units that Kernberg called object relations dyads. In borderlines, these dyads are not integrated and totally negative representations are split apart or separated from the idealized positive representations of self and others. The mechanism of change in clients treated with Transference-Based Psychotherapy is the integration of these initially polarized affective states and representations of self and others, into a more coherent whole, this integration being a shared goal with the TSDP's therapeutic approach.

Kernberg (1993) proposed various development tasks in borderline clients. They must be able to distinguish between what is the self (and their own experience) and what are the others (and their experience). This concept is present in the TSDP, which establishes the importance of differentiation and synthesis. The importance of synthesis in the TSDP is related to Kernberg's (1993) second task of development: The borderline client must relearn how to see objects as a whole, both good and bad at the same time. The similarities between the two theories are not as many as those of Ryle and Kerr (2006) and Young et al. (2003), but we can find some helpful parallels.

In addition, Fonagy et al. (2002) describe how failures in the maternal task of mirroring for the baby's emotional states affect the development of self. In some cases, the mirror may be too exact or too real, such as a mother who responds with fear to the child's fear, rather than experience a representation of the baby's fear and offer a reassuring response. In other cases, parents may improperly label the child's affect, creating a false representation of his emotion and thereby responding in a non-contingent way. For example, a mother interprets her baby's cries as manipulations and shows rejection, or shouts, or ignores her for too long. In such situations, the representations that the baby will develop of her own emotional states will be distorted. For example, she will think that if she does not cry a lot for her mother's attention, she will not come; or that she must not show her discomfort; or she will resign herself to belief that her needs will not be met. When these failures in regulation and attunement are chronic and severe, they affect the development of the child self in profound ways. The child is forced to internalize distorted mental states as if they were a part of herself. The emotional experience of the child denies essential aspects of the self, while being flooded by the parent's mental representations, as their mirroring returns the caregivers' projection and distortion. The child often internalizes the parents' hatred and aggression as her own, as a primitive way of identifying with the aggressor. These internalizations and the internal construction of mental representations arising from problems in early attachment, are similar to the idea of dissociative parts and dissociative phobias against certain parts of the personality described in the theory of structural dissociation of the personality. One element contributed by psychoanalytic theories, and which Fonagy integrates with these concepts, is the concept of projection: some internalized parts that individuals cannot assume as their own are projected onto the other.

In summary, many BPD conceptualizations can be woven into the concepts of the theory of structural dissociation of the personality. Several authors have emphasized the role of early and severe traumatization and insecure attachment in the development of BPD. They mention the switching between non-integrated mental states (dissociative parts) in borderline clients. Some of these parts can at times appear to be functional in daily life (ANPs), other parts are linked to traumatic experiences (EPs). The TSDP offers a point of view that includes all these aspects, integrating findings and insights from neurobiology and psychotraumatology.

Now that we have proposed the TSDP and the three BPD subgroups part of our framework for conceptualizing an EMDR therapy approach to the treatment of clients with BPD, we will turn our attention next to the conceptualization of BPD from the EMDR perspective.

# Part two
# Phases 1 and 2 in the Treatment with EMDR: Conceptualization and Preparation

# Chapter 5
# Understanding BPD from the perspective of EMDR Therapy

The EMDR therapy perspective helps us understand how clients´ present problems were generated by previous unprocessed experiences. What we have seen about BPD in previous chapters points to a cluster of factors in which early experiences play a key role. Not only clearly traumatic events such as abuse, but also adverse life experiences related to insecure attachment, combine with constitutional or acquired biological factors and result in borderline pathology.

As noted in Chapter 4, EMDR treatment for clients with these clinical profiles must be based on an understanding of clients' problems and their origin grounded in the AIP model. In cases of early traumatization, as it happens in many people with BPD, we need to be aware of the psychological aspects that could not develop adequately, in order to introduce them in the therapeutic process (Luber & Shapiro).

In this chapter, we will try to link two seemingly different perspectives: the classification criteria of the atheoretical DSM-V (American Psychiatric Association, 2013) and the EMDR model (Shapiro, 2001), based on etiological traumatic events and disturbing life experiences. To a greater or lesser extent, each of these criteria will be based on the cumulative effect of clients´ specific life experiences. Even when there is a high biological predisposition, the experiences and learning derived from them are what enhance or modulate a specific character trait in order to develop a disorder. The EMDR work will be to identify, access, and process such experiences.

## Understanding the DSM Criteria from the EMDR Perspective

As discussed in Chapter 1, attachment, trauma, and biology have shown their relevance in research studies related to BPD. Early experiences, especially, have been strongly associated with the development of borderline traits. We will describe, without trying to account for all possible scenarios, some possibilities for understanding each DSM V BPD criterion based on these early experiences (based on Mosquera 2010, Mosquera & Gonzalez, 2011). Other traumatic factors such as romantic relationships with elements of abuse can produce borderline symptoms, but generally, these develop from childhood and adolescence experiences characterized by dysfunctional attachment. Therefore, we will focus more on early history, which in a superficial assessment of adult clients can go unnoticed, due to their partial awareness of the relationship between their problems and their history.

The reader should not interpret this chapter as more than a description of possibilities. The many paths by which clients with BPD may arrive at similar problems cannot be covered in a single book. Each person´s life has unique characteristics and each individual is unique. In order to apply EMDR, we must understand the specific person we are working with, their history and their particular way of transitioning through life. The following are just some examples.

## Criterion 1: Frantic Efforts to Avoid Real or Imagined Abandonment

Due to the primary need for attachment, desperate efforts to avoid abandonment may be generated in a preoccupied attachment with primary caregivers fail to establish a proper differentiation of self. Children of such caregivers are not seen as autonomous beings with needs, emotions, and beliefs, but instead, are seen based on the needs of the adults. When these children grow up, they do not consider themselves able to function without others, whom they feel as inseparable parts of themselves. This may be one of the roots of emotional dependency.

Another possibility is lack of affection. In the previous paragraph, true recognition and validation of the child, of the real child, does not take place. This situation may happen in dismissing attachment, where there is an absence of affection, or in preoccupied attachment, where relationships are based on concern about the other, but not real affection. Different degrees of rejection and hostility can be present, being the attachment figure the source of danger in disorganized attachment. In all those possible situations, children have needs that are not fulfilled, or they receive conditioned affection. As adults, they may be dependent and seek attention, and they often require evidence of the love that others feel for them, as a result of their low capacity of mentalization (Bateman & Fonagy, 2004). On the other hand, a slight discrepancy, some distance, or the lack of sufficient response (it is never enough) can generate a catastrophic reaction that amplifies rather than resolves the difficulties that will arise in the relationship. Many episodes of impulsive behavior self-harm or suicide attempts will be framed in this complex relational scene.

In both cases, as adults, these children will be concerned about their bonding with others and meeting their needs for affection. Others may see them as dependents or clingy. This need for affection will never be completely fulfilled, and often requires evidence of that love, as a result of the low capacity of mentalization in people with this diagnosis (Bateman & Fonagy, 2004). On the other hand, a slight discrepancy, some distancing, or the lack of sufficient response (it is never enough) generate a catastrophic reaction that amplifies rather than resolves the difficulties that will arise in the relationship. Many episodes of impulsive behavior and suicide or self-harm attempts will be framed in this complex relational scene.

When the caregivers´ behavior is ambivalent or chaotic, the reactions of the children and future adults will not be uniform; thus they will need to develop different adaptations for the caregivers´ different emotional states. For this reason, they develop different parts of the personality, as we saw in the chapter on structural dissociation. Clients with these early experiences will have an extreme need for attachment, even stronger because they grew up subjected to intermittent reinforcement. In cases of major disorganization in early bonding, when the attachment figure is frightening or emotionally or physically harmful, often these non-integrated parts of the personality acquire a higher level of structure and independence. For example, one part may be fixed on submission responses and the search for attachment, and another part may react aggressively when approaching any possible bond. When one of the two parts is activated, the person may not have access to the other part´s mental contents, and amnesia can even occur between the two states.

## Criterion 2: Pattern of Unstable and Intense Interpersonal Relationships Characterized by Alternating Between Extremes of Idealization and Devaluation

Ambivalent or preoccupied insecure attachment and disorganized attachment, share in their effect on children the fact that the biological systems of both attachment and self-defense need to be the activated in regard to the attachment figure. Attachment is needed, but it also generates defensive reactions, which can manifest in alternating weakness and threats in reaction to perceived abandonment or distancing from another. This triggering of defensive responses with the attachment figure throughout development profoundly affects these bonds, which may thereafter show this alternation between the attachment and defense systems. Adults who have grown up in this environment will feel an intense need to bond to another and the bonding response will continue to become activated, being the only way they sense they can feel protected. But at the same time, the people to whom they bond, especially in romantic relationships, will be a direct trigger of the defensive response. This pattern can be understood as the root of the instability.

There are differences in borderline patterns between preoccupied insecure attachment (ambivalent) and disorganized attachment. In the ambivalent insecure attachment (organized), the behavioral strategy is more or less always the same: "Since I cannot predict what my caregiver will do, if I cling (crying, screaming, kicking), at least I can get her to be present." In this sense, the behavioral strategy approach is more or less stable or organized. The approaching sequence in disorganized attachment is perhaps organized and logical in dissociative structural terms, due to simultaneous activation of two action systems, which should not be activated in that way at such a time. But in terms of attachment, this is the chaotic way, precisely because the approach does not end up truly taking place. In the first case, the pattern we see in the adult will be basically dependent. In the second one, the patterns will be more shifting and unstable, not establishing a bond precisely because, that bond is a powerful trigger of the defensive fight/flight reactions. However, probably between the first and the second situation there is a gradient in which, in addition to the lack of accessibility and inconsistency of the caregiver, we can add varying degrees of hostility or overt aggression. As adults, clients from the first profile, with high emotional dependency, end up finding problems in relationships because the attention and affection received are never enough, and they finally generate rejection or hostility responses. It can also be the case that their extreme need to bond makes them initiate relationships with highly pathological people who they do not leave despite receiving serious and ongoing damage, because they cannot live without them.

Idealization is an intrinsic part of this pattern. To be able to attach to an inconsistent and aggressive parent, the child has no choice other than to idealize in order to build a parental image, which often is far from reality. Many clients tell us about perfect parents or family, denying or dissociating the elements that do not fit this image. Thus, the only possible attachment is preserved.

It is necessary to idealize the attachment figure…

…when in reality there is no possibility of bonding

When the attachment pattern is disorganized, the reactions are more changeable and extreme. The frightening aspects of the parental figure may need to be stored in a different mental state. For example, a client sexually abused by her father, who at the same time maintains a pathological idealization of him, cannot keep both types of information simultaneously in her consciousness, so automatically these mental contents dissociate to maintain a sense of coherence. Both mental states, mediated by different neurobiological structures and systems can sometimes switch seamlessly, producing extreme changes from idealization to devaluation. These situations are also frequently seen in the therapeutic relationship. Any small detail can trigger a sense of betrayal and deep pain, which is also related to fear of abandonment, imaginary in the present, but painfully real in childhood. Since the parent was often unpredictable, the warning system became permanently activated, a situation that can persist into adulthood and be associated with the hypersensitivity and susceptibility that the individual with BPD presents in interpersonal relationships.

## Criterion 3: Identity Disturbance. Markedly and Persistently Unstable Self-Image or Sense of Self

Identity could be understood as the set of features that allow us to have an image of who we are,

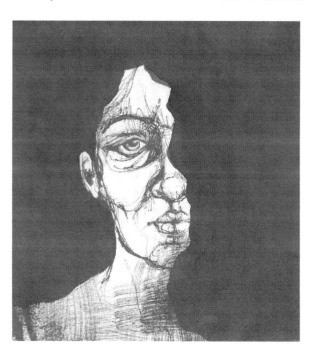

what we want, and where we are going. According to Novella and Plumed (2005), a healthy identity would include the ability to choose an appropriate path at an occupational level, to have intimate relationships and to find a place in society. In borderline clients, we will often see what Erikson (1980) defined as identity diffusion, in which there is a subjective feeling of incoherence, difficulty assuming roles and occupations, or a tendency to confuse attributes, emotions, and desires of the self with those of the other in intimate relationships, so that the fear of losing personal identity appears when a relationship ends.

Many individuals with BPD report difficulties in finding their path or finding out who they are, and are overwhelmed when they have to answer basic questions like, "How would you describe yourself?" or "What do you like to do?" Aside from this undeveloped identity, in borderline clients with a dissociative profile we will see a disorganization of identity, in which individuals present an internal conflict between alternate identities, called identity confusion and alteration (Steinberg, 1994).

Siegel & Hartzell (2004) state that secure attachment promotes individuals relating to others with curiosity, openness, acceptance, and love. Through the mindsight (Siegel, 2010) of caretakers, who realize how children are feeling and experiencing situations, they develop a sensed feeling through the connection between the prefrontal cortex and the sensorimotor areas. This connection between the different levels of experience is altered in borderline clients, as discussed in the chapter on emotional regulation.

The basic sense of security in children grows through the experience of being looked at as someone important and special for their caregivers, with a look of unconditional love (Knipe, 2008). Children accept themselves fully because they feel 100% accepted. In these children, many behaviors can be enhanced, censored, redirected, etc., without feeling questioned as individuals. If, on the contrary, children feel loved with conditions, they develop a dysfunctional belief of not being fully valid unless..., or of persistently striving to earn the love and acceptance that they can never achieve, it is never enough. As adults, this will make them more dependent on external validation, through which they define and judge themselves. Feeling unable to achieve the acceptance of others for who they really are, they develop various types of façades, which often makes them feel like a fraud. What is most frightening is that someone may get to really know them, because whenever this happens, they feel that the only possibility is rejection and contempt. What else can they think when they have seen it so many times in the face of their caregivers?

When clients do not have a distinct identity and cannot find an explanation for what happens, they often search for clues in others. Anything that allows them to explain their confusion and uncertainty, an explanation that can decrease their guilt and that, in turn, allows others to understand them. This is related to one of the aspects frequently observed in borderline patients during hospitalization: mimetization. People with diffuse identity can copy the symptoms of a group of patients, coming to see them as their own.

Some clients find a hallmark of identity in the diagnosis, which seems very valuable given their profound emptiness, inner turmoil, and difficulties connecting with their emotions and needs.

Often, clients with BPD exhibit confusion and variability around their values and these vary according to the opinions or preferences of the people with whom they interact. Winnicott (1967) explains that children who are not seen for who they really are, but as a projection of the desires and needs of their parents, will tend to internalize representations of the mental states of their parents, which they will be unable to distinguish from their own opinions, wants, and needs. This aspect is observed in many borderline clients, who will tend to repeat what others have said about them when describing themselves, especially the negative parts. For example, a client says she tries to commit suicide to draw attention. However, for this, she eats foot powder because a voice in her head tells her that she has to. She talks about this voice without giving any importance to this inner experience.

## Criterion 4: Impulsivity in at least Two Areas that Are Potentially Self-Damaging (Spending, Sex, Substance Abuse, Reckless Driving, Binge Eating...)

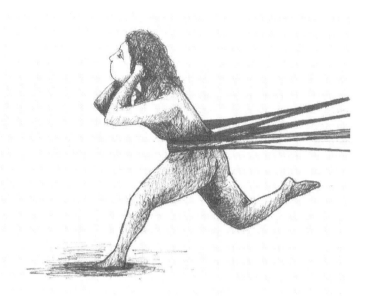

Shapiro (1965) defined impulsivity as the tendency to act, after a momentary stimulus, without a previous plan or without a clear direction or desire. People with BPD often perceive and describe themselves as impulsive, though it is unusual for them to reflect on why they behave or react that way. Often they say things like, "I´m like this, I can´t help it" or "I can´t control myself."

These behaviors sometimes have a regulatory function. The pattern of self-regulation that would have derived from a secure attachment could not be established. Therefore, regulation has to come from the outside (extreme demands for help, dependency) or from other means. A person can use drugs or alcohol led by an intense discomfort that needs to ease. At times, this is the role of self-harm (Gonzalez, 2010).

Impulsivity may also be related to the dissociation of defensive responses. Children assaulted by their caregivers learned to contain and hide their anger; otherwise the consequences were even worse. They may even have learned not to feel their own anger and they reject it even as a possibility, because they felt in their own skin how harmful it could be. Their own rage, even in its healthy expression, is associated with the aggressive parent and rejected, so this emotion cannot be integrated with the rest of mental functions. This produces an alternation between containment or the dissociation of rage, which builds up until, either by overflow or what could be a minimal trigger, it explodes in unmodulated and uncontrolled expression. The available model to express this emotion is also the one of the aggressive parent, who often has a submissive and victimized person as a partner, someone who never expresses firmness or healthy anger. The part of the personality of the client where anger builds up can have greater access to memories related to situations of aggression experienced in childhood (state-dependent memory), which in some cases are not accessible, not even partially in a calm emotional state (dissociative amnesia). This amnesia can also occur between one mental state and another. Many borderline clients do not remember or have blurred or fragmented memories of their aggressive behaviors toward self or others. They know what happened, but not the internal process, nor what they said, or what they did exactly. These phenomena may be interpreted as deliberate attempts to avoid responsibility, but often they are genuine amnesia.

Besides the obvious problem of behavioral explosions, total or partial dissociation of rage exposes the client to more negative experiences, by failing to set appropriate boundaries or not being able to stop situations that harm them. The difficulties in realizing what affects them and what they lack may also be based on early experiences with caregivers, who were so focused on their own needs (whether due to self-centeredness or their own discomfort) that they could not see and meet the needs of their children. Thus, as adults, these clients disconnect from themselves and focus on the needs of the other, or on non-core needs. The accumulated overload from withstanding negative situations is in turn what feeds the impulsive reactions.

Some clients present impulsivity more as a structural feature, being one of the aspects with a higher genetic weight. In the borderline clients with an ADHD profile, for example, impulsivity is a core symptom. In these cases, it is particularly important to correct this aspect pharmacologically, since otherwise an individual who acts first and then thinks will not be able to take advantage of the work done in therapy. It is important to look at each case on an individual basis, understanding their particular conglomerate of contributing factors.

## Criterion 5: Recurrent Suicidal Behavior, Gestures, or Threats, or Self-Mutilating Behavior

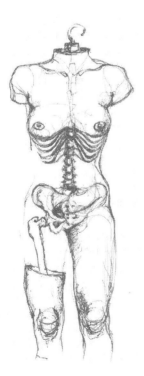

This criterion encompasses many of the reactions for which BPD clients come to the ER or are hospitalized.

Although these behaviors are often labeled as attempts at manipulation or calls for attention, underneath each one of them may be very different problems.

These problems can include: use of self-harm as the only possible emotional regulator; self-punishment for intolerable feelings of guilt; dissociated behavior in which one part of the personality attacks another one for various reasons; a profound reaction to improvement that confronts clients with a normalcy in which they see themselves unable to function; or intense desire to be annihilated or disappear due to the deep feelings of inner emptiness, lack of self-worth, or failure of behavioral strategies geared to function in the world and in relationships.

Thinking of these behaviors as "manipulation" or "calls for attention" can leave clinicians in a position of rejection, and to them feeling used or to understanding this as deliberate and conscious blackmail. What sane person would resort to this type of behavior to get the attention of others? Psychologically balanced individuals are able to establish and maintain bonds simply being who they are, knowing that they have resources and using them in an adaptive way. To help us understand this type of indirect communication, we can again examine these behaviors from the perspective of the clients' history.

Subtle aggression

Direct language often takes place in the context of secure attachment. Adults are sensitive to the needs of children and are attuned to their emotional states. They help them self-regulate. Child feel recognized and find coherent responses in adults. When they grow up in this context, they learn that they can ask for what they need and be taken care of, though they may not always receive immediate gratification. But their consistent experience is that when they suffer some frustration adults help them regain a state of balance.

In an ambivalent/preoccupied or disorganized insecure attachment, children's needs are not easily noticed. Many times, children have to shout louder or for a longer period of time in order to be noticed. As this is the usual pattern, they learn that their demands have to be flashy and insistent. When they become adults, they probably do not know how to filter who they relate to, they are used to working with people who do not take care of them, who do not care for them, or whose multiple problems make them so focused on themselves that they only respond when intensity of demand becomes extreme. In this context, self-harm may feel like the only available communication or the only one that is perceived as effective.

But let us remember that a behavior does not invariably lead to a single explanation. There are always multiple paths that can lead to the same point. Self-injury may also reflect difficulties in self-regulation and tolerating negative emotions. Cuts, burns, suicide threats, and even suicide attempts are often the only way clients have found to face difficulties (Mosquera, 2008). Clients may state that they cause themselves physical pain because it is more bearable than emotional pain. Through self-harm, they are trying to get out of an unpleasant emotion, a traumatic memory, or a depersonalization experience.

One aspect that may also play an important role in these behaviors, as we mentioned above, is the internalization of a pattern of dysfunctional self-care (Gonzalez, Seijo, & Mosquera, 2009), of which self-harm and suicide attempts are a clear expression. Clients may have not internalized an adequate self-care pattern, because the basic care received as children was deficient or inadequate (Chu, 1998).

A parenting style characterized by little or no interest in the authentic experience of the child (as opposed to demands for obedience or appearance) offers no source from which to internalize the role of self-care (Ryle & Kerr, 2002). Many clients with BPD internally reproduce comments or actions that, at some point, they received from others. When they have a problem, instead of trying to understand themselves and find practical solutions, they often beat themselves up for feeling a certain way, thus complicating things even more. We will explore self-care in more detail in Chapter 8.

## Criterion 6: Affective Instability due to a Marked Reactivity of Mood (e.g.: Intense Episodic Dysphoria, Irritability or Anxiety, Usually Lasting a few Hours and Only Rarely More Than a Few Days)

Emotional regulation is not an automatic process; it's development begins from the earliest stages of childhood through the dyadic caregiver-child relationship (Schore, 2003a, 2003b). The healthy attachment relationship is one in which adults, capable of attunement with children and consistent in their reactions, help children modulate their emotional reactions.

Healthy caregivers are not only those who are able to decrease emotional arousal when children are hyper-aroused, but also who stimulate them when they go through periods of hypo-arousal. A certain degree of discomfort is adaptive, because it helps children to learn to tolerate frustration and delay gratification. Caregivers must then help children regain balance. Thus children, and future adults, learn to keep their emotions within what has been called the window of tolerance, which implies an adequate level of activation to adapt to situations and resolve them properly (Ogden & Minton, 2000).

In people with BPD, the basic dysphoric mood (i.e., the tendency to feel sad or discouraged) is often interrupted by periods of anger, distress, or despair, and it is unusual for a state of wellbeing or satisfaction to take over. In addition, these changes can influence a marked hypersensitivity to environmental triggers, which may have, in part, a posttraumatic basis. Gestures, attitudes, expressions in another that remind clients of the caregivers' expressions in childhood can trigger reactions that may seem disproportionate and out of context in adults.

A high tone of voice, for example, produced in a client an intense reaction of feeling blocked and subsequently generated a depressed state and an intense sense of guilt. At a certain level, she could recognize that her reaction was not proportionate to the comment that her partner or a coworker had made. Her behavior, on the other hand, fit perfectly with a child's reaction to the extremely authoritarian and critical father with whom she grew up. As a child, his screaming made her feel literally paralyzed and her guilt kept a close parallel with the critical and hostile comments from her father. Since she never learned to manage her anger and completely lacked assertiveness, such reactions did not evolve to the level of other functions and capabilities. This pattern of response remained somewhat frozen in time and preserved certain features of a reaction in a girl faced with a father whom she could not confront. Even though she was now with an adult, had different options, and this person did not look too much like her father, she responded as she had as a child.

Individuals can switch from one mental system to another, resulting in a changing mood in which certain relatively constant and rigid patterns are reproduced. For example, a client defends herself against what she perceives as threatening (thinking of leaving her partner or yelling because he mistreats her), but the possibility of losing him triggers the activation of an attachment system (switching to thinking that she could not live without him or even thinking about killing herself because life without this person is meaningless).

*Sometimes, childhood experience...*

*...ends up being reenacted in the present, in the therapeutic relationship*

Mood instability is another aspect that may have a biological basis. There may be a cyclothymic pattern related to bipolar disorder or a more constitutional tendency to anxiety, depression, or activation. However, as discussed above, the presence of character traits does not invalidate the influence of life experiences in amplifying dysregulation, so we can hypothesize that processing these contributory experiences with EMDR would help with modulation.

## Criterion 7: Chronic Feelings of Emptiness

Some clients describe the feeling of emptiness as a very intense feeling that invades their whole being; others state there is nothing that fulfills them or anything that has meaning or speak of a pain that pierces them and destroys them. Others describe it as a bottomless well filled up with anguish.

In some clients, chronic feelings of emptiness seem to correspond to the absence of a secure attunement with parents during childhood. Secure attachment in children generates a sense of inner security and connection with self and others. When we ask BPD clients to think about their early life experiences associated with those feelings of emptiness, they often describe moments of feeling painfully alone, of being invisible at home, of no one realizing how they really felt. Parents, overwhelmed by their own conflicts and difficulties, may not be able to really see the children's needs or may be unable to differentiate them from their own. Caregivers are the mirror in which children see the image of who they are and, in the situation described, there is either nothing in the mirror or what there is has nothing to do with them. Making contact with this experience can be felt as emptiness.

A client described feeling this sensation since age 7. Her attachment to her mother was very extreme and she felt unprotected and incomplete since her death five years ago. She described her as a good mother, worried about her children and always working a lot for them. Her father was a usual drinker who often came home late. She recalled being in her room feeling worried, and waiting for her father to come back home. He was never physically or emotionally aggressive. When thinking about her childhood, what is most painful for her is not being able to remember a hug, and her need to be hugged has an unbearable intensity for her. She never felt that others could realize what was happening to her or how she felt. Adults were there, but there were many times when she described absolute loneliness, her mother working and her father out of the house, without expressions of affection or reinforcement. Her bonding and dependence on the mother seemed more like the expression of a need for attachment which was not entirely satisfied.

As an adult and in couple relationships, she looked for all she never had, which led her to throw herself completely into her marriage, establishing a dependent relationship in which she tolerated continued abuse for years. Sometimes, she resorted to using alcohol and cocaine to get rid of this intolerable feeling, but even after she stopped using or having problematic relationships, this feeling of emptiness was still present and intense at times, becoming particularly triggered when alone. Yet, this feeling did not motivate her to find healthy relationships, but instead paralyzed her and led her to fall into depressive states.

This feeling of emptiness is one of the aspects that is most refractory to therapeutic interventions with borderline clients and, in our clinical experience, it can be greatly modified after treatment of the memories connected with it with EMDR.

## Criterion 8: Inappropriate, Intense Anger or Difficulty Controlling Anger (e.g.: Frequent Displays of Temper, Constant Anger, Recurrent Physical Fights)

Some people with this diagnosis have unpredictable responses, consisting of abrupt mood changes or sudden emotional outbursts. These explosions can be verbal, physical, or combined.

Angry outbursts can be frightening, both for people experiencing them and for those around them. They may give the impression of being totally out of control, shaken, acting on impulses, and disregarding the consequences of their behavior. While being somewhat aware that what they are doing pushes people away, clients with BPD are not able to stop (Mosquera, 2010). When they get angry with someone, it is as if that someone stops being a person with feelings, only to become the object of their hatred and the cause of their discomfort: the enemy. They are focused on defending themselves against what they perceive as aggression. In that state of mind, what bonds them with that person, what is important for them, is not accessible or does not have enough strength to balance their behavior.

As noted before, these episodes may alternate with dependent and submissive behaviors, reflections of the world of extremes in which clients were raised. It is important not only to see the overwhelming crisis, which is most obvious, but also to pay attention to what is missing in the other stages and especially all the possible triggers immediately preceding the behavioral outburst.

Although some people with this diagnosis can be emotionally and even physically abusive, there is usually not a premeditated desire to inflict pain to others. To do this, they would have to lack the impulsivity that characterizes them and have a capacity for planning ahead. Often this reaction is triggered when something makes them feel vulnerable, frightened, or rejected. Anger gives them a feeling of strength, power, and control that they do not feel they can achieve otherwise, which can sometimes lead them to seek or cause these states. Gaining perspective of the connection between these behaviors and their own history can help prevent automatic and unreflective behaviors, but processing the memories that are the foundation of these behaviors with EMDR can have a powerful effect in removing them.

Triggers can be diverse, such as fear of abandonment, seeking acceptance or interest, or dysfunctional requests for the other person to soothe them and assure them that they will stay around and they generally express the failure of relational strategies. Expressions of anger can be followed by sorrow, remorse, and guilt and contribute to their self-perception of being bad, out of control, selfish, or freaks. However, this destructive self-criticism does not modify the behavior in the future, but instead feeds it by promoting a sense of undervaluation that often end up triggering the angry reactions. If we understand the structural dissociation behind this situation, this fact is easier to understand. When our client is blinded by anger, a part of her personality is activated, focused on the fight action system. The victimized, submissive, and vulnerable part, which blames herself for what happened, can turn what she has done around in her head many times. However, this will not be accessible to the part focused on anger and aggression the next time it becomes activated. They are stored in different compartments, which do not exchange contents. Moreover, the submissive and vulnerable part's rejection of the aggressive part's behaviors does not constitute an exercise of reflection, but just shows us the phobia that one part has toward the other. This internal conflict often reproduces the relational dynamics that the client witnessed as a child between her primary caregivers.

## Criterion 9: Transient, Stress-Related Paranoid Ideation or Severe Dissociative Symptoms

Many people with BPD are extremely vulnerable and sensitive. Some authors speak of hypersensitivity to stimuli in general, which is exacerbated when they are activated on an emotional level. From a fight action system, being defensive and thinking that others want to hurt you makes perfect sense. When this state is persistent, individuals live in a permanent state of alert.

Neither ambivalent nor disorganized attachment provides clear and consistent references regarding human behavior. As children, adults with these attachment classifications learned that relationships with others are uncertain, unpredictable and dangerous. Confusion is the norm; this is linked to Bateson´s double bind concept (Bateson, Jackson, Haley & Weakland, 1956, Bateson, 1972). In childhood, the environment was experienced as threatening, and in adulthood, gestures, words, or seemingly insignificant details may act as triggers. For example, the therapist´s (slight) insistence to work on a topic may connect with an experience of sexual abuse in which interpersonal and physical boundaries were violated, or with the intrusiveness of a very deregulated caregiver. The client´s defensive reaction, the distrust, or apparent resistance, which is incomprehensible and disproportionate in the here-and-now, takes on a new meaning when we understand it from the there-and-then.

Paranoid traits may also be associated with biological traits related to the schizophrenia spectrum, requiring antipsychotic treatment, or they may be generated or precipitated by the regular use of substances such as alcohol, cannabis, or cocaine, common in clients with BPD.

Severe dissociative symptoms are often related to early experiences and are often found in clients who have suffered traumatic events in childhood. In many cases, dissociative symptoms cannot be detected without specific exploration (Gonzalez, 2010), as discussed in the chapter on dissociation.

We can highlight auditory hallucinations that correspond to completely dissociated mental states, which are quite frequent and, in a way, act like parallel states of consciousness. At other times, the voices reproduce comments by people in the clients´ lives and are more like auditory flashbacks. Episodes of depersonalization, amnesia, and intrusions are highly frequent events in clients with BPD. These symptoms are particularly important, as we mentioned, for our work with EMDR, since they require modification of procedures in order to achieve a progressive and safe approach to the traumatic material, which usually involves a prior period of work with the internal system (Gonzalez & Mosquera, 2012).

## Case Conceptualization and Work Plan in BPD: Case Report

This extended exploration of the DSM-5 criteria for BPD offers an orientation and with the intention of opening up new perspectives for the reader. However, working with EMDR is always based on the individual. We need to address the individual client and his or her history. We must draw a map that outlines the connections between this person´s specific symptomatic pattern, the dysfunctionally stored experiences connected with this pattern, the aspects that need to be developed, the defenses that must be taken into account in order to access these memories, and the degree of structural dissociation. It is this map which will guide us in the decision making process throughout therapy. We can illustrate all of this through an example:

A 34-year-old woman came to the office with various diagnoses: amotivational syndrome, depression, depression secondary to BPD, and borderline disorder. The client had been going to therapy since she was a teenager. When she arrived at the clinic, she had just made a serious suicide attempt, after which she was in a coma for several days. She reported feeling out of control most of the time and presented high emotional dependency and all-or-nothing thoughts. In the previous 2 years, she had also experienced panic attacks several times a month. At intake, negative self-referential thoughts and persistent guilt and shame were noted. She described herself as an out-of-control paranoid with disproportionate outbursts of anger and lack of control. She also explained that she felt lonely most of the time, even when she was with groups of friends or family

Her deepest negative beliefs were: "I´m a mess," "I can´t trust anyone," "I´m useless," "I´m inadequate," "I don´t fit in," "I´m stupid," "I have no control," "I´m aggressive," "I need others to be able to function," "I´m bad," "I´m guilty," "I´m good for nothing," and "I don´t deserve to be loved."

From the perspective of the AIP model used in EMDR therapy, we explored the history of all these problems, symptoms, and dysfunctional beliefs. It emerged that the continuous negative verbalizations about herself replayed the messages she had heard at home from a very early age, especially from her mother. But even more damaging than the verbal abuse was the fact that neither her emotionally absent father, nor her mother, ever noticed how she felt. Her ongoing sense of loneliness was connected with episodes of arguments between her parents, which she often witnessed or heard without the adults being concerned about her.

Even before starting the processing of memories from which the disorder developed, the client started a process of understanding how her history and her problems were interlaced, while learning tools for emotional regulation, boundary setting, and self-care. These resources were necessary so that the client could function better in her daily life and also so that she could participate and handle the work with her early adverse experiences. She understood how this history had influenced the image she still held about herself. During these initial sessions, bilateral stimulation was introduced to reinforce insights about the link between history and her self-image and resources for emotional regulations such as boundary setting and self-care behaviors.

From session 4, we started reprocessing the memories that were at the basis of her current problems and her core negative beliefs. These memories or targets were:

1. Abandonment by parents (seeing how they went away and left her at her aunt's home).
2. Memories related to the mother, including beatings, insults, and humiliations.
3. Memories related to the father and his alcohol problem.
   - Hiding under the bed when she heard fights between her parents, feeling fear and uncertainty about what could happen.
   - Having to sit still for hours while her father yelled at them (her and her siblings).
   - Seeing how her father beat her brother up.
4. Her brother's suicide attempt.
5. Discussions with her partner.
6. Memories related to her day to day negative beliefs as a person.
7. Memories associated with being a bad mother.

Once the most obvious targets were processed, we worked with the emotional bridge from the residual symptoms (e.g., not being able to set boundaries and having to reach out to others at any price). From the feelings associated with loneliness and her difficulties with boundaries, the client connected with memories that she initially did not see as relevant and were not reflected in the list of her 10 most disturbing events, almost all related to feeling invisible and lonely. Working with these memories was particularly important in order to resolve symptoms, which in our experience are difficult to deal with from other psychotherapeutic approaches.

After processing a large number of events, the client was able to be alone and even enjoy having her own space. Suicidal ideation, self-harm, and destructive behaviors subsided. The client could become regulated even when faced with unforeseen complications. Although her relationship remained complicated, there were far fewer arguments between them and the client had enough energy to take care of her son and be attuned to his needs. In relation to her parents, with whom she continued to maintain a relationship, she was able to understand how their own history (both had traumatic histories) had influenced the way they functioned with her during her childhood.

In this example there were no relevant defenses that could interfere in the processing, but this could be crucial in other cases, as we will see in the following chapter.

# Chapter 6
# Defenses

In order to safely and effectively reprocess a memory of a traumatic experience with EMDR, some specific prerequisites are needed, which are often a therapeutic challenge in clients with BPD. Clients must realize what their problem is and often BPD clients come to therapy focused on issues that are not their real problem. For example, they may come in because of the sadness caused by the failure of their last relationship, but they do not see the dysfunctional patterns that have led them to this situation.

At other times, people with BPD have a low reflective capacity, they know they are upset and desperately need to be heard and understood, so therapy sessions turn into venting sessions that offer momentary relief but do not generate significant changes.

If we simply accept the information clients can see and talk about, we would choose the situations that are most disturbing for them as targets. But when we try to access those memories and process them with bilateral stimulation, what clients can see is not the only thing that becomes activated. So do many other elements that exist and that clients deny, ignore, minimize, or are unable to assimilate. In addition, processing may be ineffective and continue to loop. For example, a client may repeat over and over how unfair whatever they did to her was, but information about her personal contribution to these situations is blocked because it triggers a feeling of guilt that she is still unable to accept. Or the elements of idealization of the partner she believes has harmed her may be contained in a different and non-integrated emotional part, and therefore these elements do not appear during the reprocessing of the memory. Thus synthesis of these disparate elements does not take place and real awareness is not generated.

Working with EMDR also requires good self-perception and a realistic self-image. Borderline individuals have, as we will see, an incomplete development of psychic functions. They are frequently unable to identify their own emotions, thoughts, or feelings, which many of them experience as an undifferentiated and intolerable amalgam. How to identify emotion, sensation, and cognition if the very meaning of these words is still unknown? How to identify negative beliefs about the self connected to the memory if the view of the self is distorted to the point that the client has developed a false self? The dual attention that is essential when working with EMDR is difficult for a client with a very low reflective capacity, for a client who lives in the emotion but who fails to have a perspective on internal experiences. Sometimes, even the distinction between "who I am" and "who the others are" is blurred and confused.

Unable to manage their internal experiences and relationships with others, clients with BPD develop a number of defenses, which must be dismantled before we can have real access to the dysfunctionally stored material in the memory networks. Some of these defenses are related to the concept of dissociative phobias, mentioned in the chapter on the theory of structural dissociation of the personality. Clients with complex traumatization cannot easily think about their mental actions, cannot accept the most rejected or feared parts of the personality as part of their identity. They avoid approaching their traumatic memories and the emotional burden they carry. This is the case for many individuals with BPD. People who feel unable to move forward in everyday life may even experience phobia toward normal life, intimacy, healthy change, and the future.

Other difficulties are more generic and have to do with the absence of a realistic worldview, minimization, idealization, narcissistic defenses, etc. We will describe all the difficulties that borderline clients may present, understanding them as defenses and limitations. We will understand defenses as active coping behaviors (usually not fully conscious), which may interfere with the therapeutic work. Not all difficulties that are present in borderline clients have to do with active defenses; in many cases we will find insufficient development of certain mental functions, such as self-awareness, reflective capacity, and mentalization, aspects we will discuss more in depth in Chapter 7.

In moments of high intensity, people with BPD may come to perceive others as threats, even as potential enemies from whom they must protect themselves. It is common for them to address situations and problems in a way that is sometimes difficult to understand.

Broadly speaking, we can say that defenses are a type of response to situations that people have difficulty managing. They originate in experiences that could not be assimilated or digested when they happened. The role of the defense is to protect them from situations or realities they cannot cope with.

Usually, defenses are automatic mechanisms that are not the result of a thoughtful decision. Clients are not aware of them, nor do they activate them voluntarily, although they may partially notice them. In general, they are very effective in the short term, tend to be counterproductive in the medium to long term, and interfere greatly in the quality of life and in the therapeutic process for people with BPD. They are one of the most frequent interferences we will find when doing EMDR work with these clients, and they will appear not only during the processing of memories, but in each of the 8 phases that structure this therapy. We will see direct defenses that are easily identifiable and subtler manifestations that are indirectly expressed. This chapter describes some of the most common defenses (based on Mosquera 2004b, 2013b).

# Frequent Defenses

Defenses may appear during phase 1 when we explore the problem, become activated during the processing of memories in phases 3-7, or arise when analyzing the previous session in Phase 8.

## Pleasing Others

One way to avoid conflict, which is experienced as intolerable, is trying to make everyone happy. This sounds good in theory, but there is a small problem: in the real world it is impossible to please everyone. The emotional wellbeing of others does not depend on us. Their happiness or unhappiness depends mostly on what they do with their lives and their inner feelings.

Conflict is also part of life, whether we like it or not. Sometimes people focus on trying to please others to avoid problems, because they cannot deal with confrontation, yelling, or anger. It is not uncommon for people who try to avoid anger at all costs to end up being unpleasant or hostile toward others. Generally, in trying to please everyone, people become overwhelmed until they reach a certain point at which they end up causing problems to others. Subsequently, they will also feel bad about themselves, because they have ended up behaving just as they do not want others to behave toward them: aggressively or rudely.

Sometimes, accumulated resentment from always pleasing others and never thinking about oneself, about personal needs and desires, ends up creating an internal tide of resentment against others. Some clients believe that others "never step into their shoes, never think about them." When they see that other people do not respond with gratitude or do not reciprocate to the care they give, they cannot help feeling disappointed or angry. However, this does not lead them to the only possible alternative: to give less. They continue focusing on the needs of others, hoping that someday the world will return more than what they have given.

In therapy, clients who are concerned about pleasing others will not be focused on regulating what they need, they will not help the therapist to calculate the pace of the therapy or to choose what is best for them, since, of course, they are trying to please the professional. During processing, they could say what they think the therapist wants to hear or block the spontaneous flow of associations trying to be a "good client" and to relax.

## Idealizing

The tendency to idealize is included in the borderline criteria. It is usually followed by absolute devaluation, when any small detail breaks the idealized image. For example, if they meet a person, they tend to believe they have finally found a "real" friend, but when this friend inevitably fails or makes a mistake, they will feel that "he has failed me, as everyone does." Idealization is simply a screen that prevents us from seeing and accepting others as they are. Nobody can compete with an idealized image. And such an image, sooner or later, will lead to disappointment. One of the ways to suffer less, when things are not as we would like, is to change our expectations for more realistic ones. However, intermediate pathways and a balance between extremes are often deficient in borderline clients.

We can also see an idealized self-image: clients with BPD "boost themselves" to overcome their own underlying feelings of undervaluation, creating a false image of the self. If this defense is well established, clients will cling to this image at all costs, and may tend to surround themselves with those who will reflect back to them the image that they want to display. They can do this by having a partner who defines them as a successful person, relating to people with "a certain level" or "a certain style" with which they identify, or tending to always make clear how badly others do things in order to indirectly highlight their own effectiveness or worth. This artificial exaltation of the self does not allow individuals to get in touch with their true inner resources and real worth as a person.

In working with EMDR, clients who tend to idealize will give us distorted information about the reality they live in, their early history, or themselves. This makes it difficult to draw a good map from which to make good decisions in therapy. When it is time to work, this idealization may appear in the processing, e.g., with idealization of attachment figures. This idealization of attachment figures is common in insecure attachment and frequenlty blocks access to disturbing memories associated with those figures.

Another common situation, in the early stages, is the idealization of the therapist. Clients will work enthusiastically in the initial phase of therapy, but sooner or later this will change to devaluation, risking rupture or deterioration of the therapeutic relationship. The clinician must handle these changes with perspective, by bringing up these issues before they occur and by gaining perspective so as to not react to them in a personal way. There may also be an idealization of EMDR in itself and clients may consider it a magical and fast solution to all problems. If these situations are not channeled, they will interfere with psychotherapy or even make it impossible.

## Projection

Sometimes, emotion is in the air, but no one knows where it started or who generated it. We can be aware of something, but rejecting that the feeling may be ours, we attribute it to another. Projection allows a person to get rid of their discomfort and everything that is causing it, to place it outside of the self. It is as if they could place their negative thoughts, their dissatisfaction, doubts, and insecurities on another. This sometimes happens in an interaction with another person and it takes place in a sequential manner. I am angry, so I start looking for trouble, "ruffling the other person's feathers," until they finally explode. I do not like to function in this way, so when I analyze what has happened, I "omit" seeing how I contributed to the process and I just see the other person's anger and the final result, what the other person has said to me. When I tell the story, it is a rather modified version of reality: "He was furious with me.," "People always treat me badly." When we asked how it this came about, it is easier for the client with little reflective capacity to say, "He just got like that suddenly, with no reason."

## Avoidance

A common, but pernicious, psychological mechanism is avoidance. If something causes me anxiety, I avoid facing it. When I decide this, I feel immediate relief, but soon, or whenever I have to face the same problem or a similar one again, anxiety has increased a notch. Avoidance is a psychological trap, which causes exactly what we most want to avoid.

This mechanism can manifest in many ways, some very subtle. For example, every time we decide to deal with an issue, clients bring up another important problem that needs immediate attention. The emotional intensity with which borderline clients present their problems to the therapist can make him or her consider that it is essential to address it urgently. But often, one "serious crisis" is followed by another. Clients are used to living in the midst of emotional storms, but working with their inner discomfort, with the way they see themselves, or the origins of their problems can be intolerable. Crises can function as "smokescreens" that hinder therapeutic progress.

## Objecting to Everything or the "Yes, but…" Style

Focusing on what is going wrong, on how hard things are, or on why a new option will not work does not allow for possible solutions. The most typical example of this mechanism would be the "yes, but…" response to any proposal. This serves the purpose of protecting against the risk of trying some kind of change in life, although it may be for the better. It is an automatic mechanism and can lead to significant frustration in the therapist when seeing that people do not accept the help that is being provided. Clients may complain bitterly about how friends turn away from them, how their families give up on them, and how a long list of professionals threw in the towel considering them a "lost cause." But they are not aware of how they contribute to making this happen.

The fear behind the "yes, but style" may not only be the fear of failure or change, but also the fear of being helped, because that means establishing bonds and having to show their vulnerability. When the bonds from the past were painful, feeling vulnerable became synonymous with being severely hurt. So people will tend to protect themselves against any bond as an instinctive protection mechanism.

Attempting to process a memory with EMDR on a client focused on this defense can be full of obstacles or nearly impossible. We can enter into a debate about whether EMDR will really do any good, if we should work on this memory or the other, what the negative belief is, whether or not the person needs to talk... And by the time we arrive to phase 4, hopefully, end up with a "nothing comes up..." or "this doesn't work."

## Unattainable Requirements

Sometimes people ask for help, but set the bar so high that no one can "keep up." If they seek therapy, the therapist must be the most famous, the most experienced. If the professional gives any sign of ineffectiveness, fatigue, or clients feel that "he or she has failed," it will be impossible to do therapy, and thus, they will start running out of options. The same can happen with couples and friends. No one is good enough.

This can serve a defensive function. It is like when we try to sell a house but do not really want to get rid of it, so we price it exorbitantly high for the market value, not expecting anyone to pay it. If against all odds, a buyer shows up, a problem will occur to make the purchase impossible. Sometimes clients want one thing and also something opposed to it, making the dilemma impossible to solve, in order to protect themselves from feeling that they have made the wrong decision by choosing any of the options. A person who does not decide, cannot make bad decisions.

If we are able to address the processing of a memory with these clients, they will probably not recognize the relaxing effect that is visible for the therapist, the SUD will never be 0 (we will see SUD of 0.5) and during phase 8 they will state that they do not notice any effect with this therapy. It is important to understand these statements in the context of their dominant defense.

## Rationalization

Clients stay in their heads and make all kinds of interpretations, but do not really connect with what happened. They disconnect from the body and all emotions and feelings related to the subject being addressed. They can make long and elaborate analysis of what is happening to them, but there is no real awareness. If clients have previously been in cognitive or verbal therapies, this tendency can be much more pronounced. In interpersonal relationships, clients who tend to rationalize talk a lot, but do not resolve issues. They can get into long discussions with those around them that never lead to productive changes or practical solutions. They do not move forward in their lives; they have the feeling of going around and around in circles, usually along the same path, without getting anywhere.

During processing they tend to analyze everything that comes up and sometimes between sets they stop to give long explanations or ask the therapist questions. Although helping them focus on physical sensation can be useful, we believe that in this case we are not dealing with an inadequate understanding of the procedure or an alexithymia. On the contrary, it is an active defense, so helping clients to connect with their bodies could activate them more. The therapist must be aware of the development of the process.

## Conviction

Sometimes borderline clients show volatile and changing opinions or ideas about themselves, others, or the world, or are extremely insecure about their beliefs, values, or thoughts. At times, precisely because of this insecurity or lack of a defined or integrated identity, they develop extreme convictions that function as an overcompensation for their basic insecurity.

Individuals may show a strong adherence to an ideology and, defending it vehemently, often going to the extremes. At other times, as we will discuss in the chapter on beliefs, they cling to certain ideas about themselves, even though they are extremely harmful. This conviction may be learned from authoritarian or rigid environments, where influential figures function from the absolute certainty of "being right" and that their views are "the truth."

The degree to which clients are fused with their thoughts and opinions is variable and is an aspect to consider when doing our work, in order to allow change during therapy (Hayes, Strosahl, & Wilson, 2003). Clients may, for example, guide the communication in the session toward a discussion about a particular social situation in which they are involved, as a way to avoid more personal topics; but it can also be a way of feeling in control of something, given the emotional lack of control and the chaos in their own lives.

## Changing the Subject

Clients change the subject to avoid getting into what is hard for them to see. It is not always conscious and they will have difficulty understanding how this may be an interference. They are so used to relying on this defense, that they understand it as a normal thought process.

In some cases, dispersion in speech or thought is not a defense but a deficiency. Some people with BPD have ADHD traits, among which we find attentional dispersion. They jump from one topic to another, because they do not follow the conversational thread. Although this and the previous aspect can be mixed, in the first case, changing subjects can be seen as a defense because of the timing.

During processing, the transition from one topic to another can be a normal type of association. At other times, changing the subject is a disconnection from the experience that we are trying to process, or it can even be dissociation. In this case, the session may end with an apparent decrease or absence of disturbance, but the processing has been partial or only apparent.

## Denial and Evasiveness

Clients can deny to the therapist, or to themselves, the importance of an issue or an event. They can evade a question or ignore it. This evasiveness may be obvious or may be expressed with vague and imprecise responses and generalizations, such as the inability to specify with examples or the changing of focus. When we have chosen a theme to work on, clients immediately highlight the importance of another one, which will later not be considered a priority either.

Not infrequently, very significant issues are discussed after long periods of therapy, even when the therapist had initially asked about them. This may be due to the fact that, in order to reveal certain subjects, clients need to feel that the therapeutic relationship is strong enough. At other times, they cannot even tell themselves, ie., "If I don't talk about it, if I don't think about it, it's like it never happened." They may also need to become stronger with the initial therapy work in order to gather the resources they need to tackle tough or complex issues.

During the processing of a memory, the issues that are denied or that clients do not want to see are more likely to come up. Perhaps clients' difficulty in revealing them can be reduced by the effect of bilateral stimulation, as it affects both explicit and implicit information. This difficulty may, however, persist and block the processing. The therapist must always be attentive to non-verbal language and consider this possibility.

## Minimization

Experiences are recognized but are downplayed. Clients cannot assume the reality of what they have experienced, or are currently experiencing, and diminish the importance of the facts. The can say things like, "Sometimes he becomes aggressive, but he's a really good person and doesn't want to hurt me," "It's not so bad, I really think I magnify things," "This happens to everyone who has had lived through experiencies like mine, right?" Sometimes, clients tell a small part of what happened, e.g., regarding their problems with their partner. It is as if putting words to it and explaining everything would make it impossible to continue with the idealization that maintains a relationship, a relationship that is felt as indispensable.

Other times, minimization is associated with emotional disconnection. Clients speak from an apparently normal part of their personality that is not fully aware of the weight of the disturbance associated with certain memories. This discomfort is stored in an emotional part of the personality, which is at least partially disconnected. Clients may talk with conviction about terrible things, stating, "I'm completely over this." If the therapist chooses to propose the processing of these memories, bilateral stimulation can get clients in touch with such intense emotions that they may not be able to assimilate them. When clients minimize or are disconnected from their experiences, probably a therapeutic plan that starts with the processing of memories that the therapist assesses - from his knowledge of the client - as more tolerable, may be advisable.

## Laughter, Sense of Humor

With some clients, it can be really difficult to focus the session productively. Everything becomes laughable, even during EMDR processing. Phase 3 questions, eye movements, or tapping seem "funny" or "ridiculous." Other people are constantly making jokes or ironies about what they are telling, which may give the false impression that it does not affect them too much. Since many clients present with a negative, pessimist, or even victimized style, individuals who laugh about their problems can seem much more functional and stronger. But even though humor is an excellent resource, it is often a shield that protects people from getting in touch with an extremely vulnerable self.

Some people have turned to humor as the main coping mechanism for their difficulties and this becomes activated while they are telling their story. In other cases, an automatic smile protects them from showing a discomfort that had brought them negative consequences or that was not allowed in the family. It is important to see the meaning of humor in each particular individual, as well as its role in the therapeutic relationship and the treatment process.

## Somatic Symptoms

Different somatic symptoms, which the person may not necessarily understand, may appear. Clients may describe them in detail because they are annoying, but this does not make them aware of what triggers them. It is important to explore when they appear, with what inner experience they are associated and to understand what was happening just before. Somatic symptoms often are indirect communications that need to be understood.

Of special interest is the presentation of somatic symptoms during the session or in the period immediately before or after. They can sometimes give us more information than the explicit information that clients provide us verbally. It is important to be attentive when somatic symptoms occur. In the more extreme cases of structural dissociation, they may correspond with the activation of dissociative parts, of which the client may or may not be aware.

## Self-Criticism

Paradoxically, criticizing oneself harshly and constantly can sometimes prevent clients from connecting with reality. They are accustomed to being constantly hurt and, faced with the idea of connecting with their deeper self or with certain stories; they can somehow use it to "stun themselves" and not think or feel.

At other times, clients´ own criticism makes what they most fear impossible: criticism from another. Clients that are continuously putting themselves down encourage in the therapist a role of "rescuer" that tells them positive things. This, paradoxically, further reinforces their negative view about themselves. This is an interesting therapeutic trap.

In the desensitization phase of EMDR, an inner discourse full of judgment and undervaluation can interfere with or completely block the processing. Therapy can become another way to criticize and insult oneself, as discussed in the chapter on self-care patterns. They may even use the material from the therapy itself to continue putting themselves down: they will think they are doing it wrong, that they are not being good clients, that EMDR therapy does not work because they are defective, etc.

## Procrastination

When deciding generates uncertainty or fear of making a mistake, when people want to avoid the effort involved in the process, or avoid confirming that they are unable to carry it out, individuals may postpone a decision or action. The issue is that this only increases the discomfort because the problem or difficulty that originated it is not resolved. And although at times it can be useful (for example, leaving a conversation for another time if one is unable to speak calmly), in many other situations it is usually harmful.

Some people are really stuck in this mechanism, which greatly impairs their ability to function. However, individuals may not be aware, and therefore will not explain it to the therapist, unless he or she explores it. And the excuses they can give themselves can be really convincing, "Now is not the time for this, it is best to leave it for later" or "now I have to do this which is very important..."

## Complaining

Some people are focused on resentment for all the damage they suffered and for all the offenses they received. Their story is a description, filled with emotion, of how badly they have been treated by others, the world and life itself. Not all people who have been through the same kind of adversity devote their thoughts and mental energy to spinning around in their heads things like, "How can people be like this?" or "How could they do this to me?" Those who do are usually people who live in a constant state of tension and who say "they cannot stand injustice."

Although anger is absolutely natural when we have been hurt, getting stuck in that emotion ends up poisoning us and causing even more suffering, without making our life more satisfying or rewarding.

Like magical solutions, constant complaining leads people to focus on the part of the solution that is not in their hands, as if they give others the control of their life. This leaves individuals in utter helplessness, as if whatever happens does not depend on them and they were at the mercy of fate, which has turned its back on them. Somehow, this immobility may protect them from making decisions and from the everpresent possibility of making the wrong decision. Looking outside may protect individuals from looking inside. But that way, life is lived "outside the self" and people cease to be the protagonists of their own existence.

A particular risk we can take with such clients, when working with EMDR, is to take their complaints as targets to work on. Chances are that we will run into "pseudo-processing," in which sets of bilateral stimulation just momentarily interrupt the clients´ discourse, which continues at the same point where it left off when we stop each set. Although clients are able to cry or express emotions, they are not really connected with their true emotions. In some of these cases, when clients have been in therapy for a long time and finally get in touch with their pain, they sometimes state, "I think today is the first time I´ve really cried."

## Selective Mood Changes or "Letting Go of the Reins"

Obviously, mood changes cannot always be controlled, and generally, they are related to something that has happened. But, there are times when people learn that crying makes arguments stop or that only when others see how bad they really feel they stop attacking them or start caring about them. Sometimes, they realize that getting angry stops the demanding or reduces the chances that someone will oppose them and make them hear something they do not like. Symptoms are felt paradoxically as the only way, or the most effective way, to communicate something. But, obviously, this complicates things, because even if in the short term the other person ends up doing or not doing what the client wanted, it is very possible that their discomfort toward the client will increase. These situations generate rejection, hostility, distance, and many other things that are precisely what clients usually feel as most terrible. People may become caught up in a very harmful relational trap or suffer a deterioration in personal relationships, to the point of losing them.

Sometimes, people may feel an undetermined emotion or discomfort and do not make any effort to control it, not so much for achieving a purpose in interacting with another, but because in these explosions they can obtain a relief that is not easily achieved otherwise. Thus, during an argument they may not stop it or they may even "add fuel to the fire" in order to release previously accumulated tension. This mechanism is often more related to learning and therefore, it can become more conscious, though it can end up being automatic.

This tendency to let emotions run wild can occur during the processing of a memory and can take the form of an abreaction that continues to increase in intensity. This situation is different from letting an emotion or a feeling flow, which is necessary for processing. When emotions "run wild" during reprocessing, the client needs the therapist's intervention to help introduce emotional regulation.

## Magical Thinking

Magical thinking involves beliefs that a person, place, thing, or idea can make problems disappear instantly or make people feel safe and happy. This belief is something like, "If I have or get X, I will feel good," "If my mother would change, I would be fine," or "If I had money, all my troubles would be over." To think that "something" will make all our wishes come true and that the solution for our problems will come from others or the world, rather than ourselves, is a very typical childhood thought, which may persist or leave its residue in adulthood. Although we have included magical thinking as a defense, we could also see it as the permanence of a primitive thinking style, associated with the lack of development of reflective thinking and other higher order mental actions (Gonzalez & Mosquera, 2012). However, the use of magical thinking at the same time fulfills a defensive function.

The ways to solve problems from a magical thinking point of view are: "To get out of here and go to a place where people treat me well," "To find someone who understands me and really loves me," or "To be in a place where I can rest and not think about anything or anyone." Since these solutions are unfeasible, the conclusion is "there is no way out." Changes that are possible are not seen or valued, so they are discarded without trying, or at the first try. These magical solutions may end up becoming day dreams where the client takes refuge in order to leave the place they truly are with their imagination, which is another type of psychological trap, as discussed in the following section. The person may see their desire as logical, not realizing that there is no chance of that happening here and now. Seeing that the desire is not fulfilled, there is only room for frustration and disappointment. The tendency toward this type of thinking lowers people's capacity to take over the reins of their own life. Only realistic solutions, based on options that are feasible at that time and which are in our hands, will lead to real changes.

When these magical associations appear during EMDR processing, it is important not to confuse them with the connection to positive networks that appear at the end of a productive associative chain.

## Parallel Worlds

Some clients take refuge in a fantasy world where everyday life problems do not exist and which serves as an escape. These fantasies can become very elaborate (Seijo, 2012). The client may spend time dreaming of what they would want, the person they would like to fall in love with, or the life they would like to live. But this fantasy only delays or hinders taking steps to move forward in the real world, toward a truly fulfilling life.

Clients' parallel worlds may not be a dream, but a modified version of their surrounding circumstances. If there is anything I do not like, I throw some color on it. If a relationship is problematic, I deny the negative situations and amplify the few good moments until it looks like a real fairy tale in my mind. The version that clients tells their therapists is often the same one they tell themselves, but has little to do with objective facts. Those around them see things very differently, although especially in the case of the immediate family, they may also have an unrealistic and extremely skewed view of reality.

This parallel world that clients see may result from their low reflective capacity, analysis of situations based on emotional thoughts, generalizations, and unsubstantiated conclusions. But it may also exist because clients are able to avoid seeing what they really do not want to see, omitting from the story they tells themselves everything they think is their fault. Clients have to learn to tell a realistic story, based on facts, in which their participation is actual. Only with a true map of their reality, will we be able to orient ourselves in the therapeutic work.

## Perfectionism

Some clients are overly focused on doing everything right. Although it has to do with the desire to please, perfectionism is more internal. Some people cannot allow themselves to fail. Failure gets them in touch with deep feelings of undervaluation and core beliefs such as "I'm useless," "I do everything wrong," or "I'm not worth anything." Sometimes, perfectionism is based on the belief that whatever they do will never be enough, which they try to soothe unsuccessfully by doing more and more.

In some clients, perfectionism is related to control and demand, and may be directed outwardly and not just inwardly.

In any case, perfectionism interferes with processing, as it is associated with rigidity and control, contrary to the "mindful" position of observing without interfering and "letting whatever has to happen, happen," from which EMDR therapy works. Understanding where this defense comes from in each client can help therapists introduce the most appropriate interweaves to help them overcome the obstacles that arise in session.

## Learned Helplessness

Clients with a history of early traumatization often end up developing a protection mechanism known as learned helplessness. Since they know that nothing will work, they do not even try, not even when there are viable options. They have given up and caved in. Resignation, which in adverse situations protects from suffering, becomes paralyzing when circumstances have become more favorable and prevents a healthy evolution.

Clients with complex trauma, among which there are many with BPD, have difficulty using proactive fight/flight responses in adaptive ways (Levine & Frederick, 1997). They do not effectively fight for what they want and they do not know how to leave negative situations on time. Anger and fear are present, but in a maladjusted way, disproportionate to what the circumstances require at the time. Passive defensive responses, however, tend to be predominant and persistent, like submission, paralysis, or deeply regressive states based on the activation of the attachment cry (infant states). Clients must learn to "activate" themselves in an adaptive way, instead of alternating between "hypoarousal" and "hyperarousal" (going from a neglecting depressive state, to an aggressive outburst, or even to a panic attack). However, an active position involves taking risks, with the possibility of making mistakes and going out into a relational world that awakens their fears. That is why this seemingly inhospitable place of resignation and despair paradoxically works as a safe place that clients are reluctant to leave.

During the processing of a memory with EMDR, clients fixed on learned helplessness may tend to enter into hypoactivation states, in which looping occurs and is difficult to resolve. When working with a memory, it would be adaptive that, in phase 4, the whole range of responses that could become activated would appear, i.e., the entire range of emotions that it would be natural to feel. These emotions are not only sadness and despair, but also anger and fear. These two emotions are often blocked in clients with early trauma and their activation may resolve some obstacles in the reprocessing. If we have worked on emotional regulation in phase 2, we can minimize this problem and if it does appear, it would be easier to neutralize.

# Defenses and Phobias in Structural Dissociation of the Personality

The defenses described above could be understood from the theory of structural dissociation of the personality as substitute mental actions (Van der Hart et al., 2006). Given the poor development of mental functions in early neglect and traumatization and the difficulties of performing adaptive actions, individuals use "substitutes" to try to achieve their goals by other means, more or less effective, but essentially dysfunctional. In personality disorders, these substitute mental actions, as Van der Hart, et al (2006) call them, in many cases become rigid structures that shape patterns that are difficult to alter. The theory of structural dissociation of the personality has devoted more attention to the mechanisms that generate and maintain mental fragmentation than to these substitute mental actions. Given their potential for interfering in therapy, we describe them as defenses, because their function is not merely to be a substitute for other more adaptive mental actions, but also to serve as mechanisms for active protection. Through these systems, individuals protect themselves from the attachment that is implicit in the therapeutic relationship (let us remember that in BPD there is usually a dysfunctional early attachment, through which people learn that they have to protect themselves from relational bonds). In addition, they protect themselves from deep connections and painful and intolerable feelings by experiencing their self as defective.

Another set of psychological phenomena described in the theory of structural dissociation refers to the mechanisms that maintain the division of personality that was generated in traumatic experiences. As mentioned previously, structural dissociation of the personality is maintained by various types of phobias (Steele, Van der Hart, & Nijenhuis, 2005), which we will briefly describe below:

## Internal Phobias

Sometimes, thinking or feeling is scary. For some borderline clients, getting in touch with their feelings and experiences generates significant anxiety, especially when there are higher levels of dissociation. Certain aspects of the personality generate rejection, fear, or various negative reactions. Working with traumatic memories is avoided or various types of defenses are activated to prevent contact with trauma, whether clients are aware or not of the degree of discomfort that these memories still generate. Working with dissociative phobias with EMDR has been developed in more detail in Gonzalez and Mosquera (2012).

## Phobias to the External World

Relationships, intimacy, everyday life and normality changes, or the future may create uncertainty and lead clients to remain in "the devil they know." Such phobias are common in clients with complex trauma and may explain decompensation after periods of improvement, or when faced with healthy and positive challenges.

# Specific Work with Defenses in EMDR

All aspects described above are crucial for the understanding of BPD clients and good case conceptualization. In working with clients with BPD, EMDR sessions can be diverted in many ways. If we are not familiar with the most common defenses, we will have difficulties handling these situations. Defense activation can be very subtle, and clinicians unfamiliar with this disorder and its associated problems may only identify their own sense of confusion and give up, thinking that EMDR does not work with these cases or that they are not good with this type of clients. Identifying the various defenses that clients have developed over the years and offering psychoeducation about them during phase 2 is the best way to facilitate the subsequent processing of memories and to minimize problems.

In any case, when we understand that defenses are being activated, it is essential to understand their function. Focusing on removing them, without having this understanding of why clients feel they are necessary, may lead, if we succeed, to completely dismantling their containment mechanisms and leaving them exposed and helpless. Another risk with premature efforts to dismantle defenses is that symptoms exacerbate or that self-injurious behaviors or different risk behaviors occur. In many cases, if we try to demolish the defenses prematurely or with too much force, it is most likely that they will increase or multiply like a shield.

We will now describe three case examples where we work with defenses. In the first case, we target the defense itself (the urge to run away). In the second case, we target the feeling that is generated in the therapeutic relationship (based on the information provided by quick idealization and association with an authority figure). In the third case, we point out the defenses along the entire process to avoid their interference with the processing of the memory. Therefore, the procedures described below should not be used simply because we have identified a defense. If we see that the timing is right, and always helping clients to understand what we are trying to do, defenses can be used as specific targets to be processed with EMDR (Knipe, 1998, 2005).

### Example 1: Ambivalence toward EMDR Work

A 33-year-old male client is ambivalent toward the therapist and EMDR therapy. On the one hand, he is eager to know the truth about aspects of his history he does not remember clearly. On the other hand, he feels uncomfortable because he is afraid that "things may come out." He is very angry at his father, who he thinks sexually abused him, but at the same time he believes he is a bad son for thinking and saying those things. After the previous session, the client got drunk because he could not handle his emotions.

> Client: When I left the session, I had a funny feeling in my stomach... Like I wanted to cry, but I started drinking (a common way in which the client usually deals with his emotions) and the alcohol covered up those feelings.

> Therapist: Can you talk to me about those feelings?

The client explains how he feels when he is connected with his emotions.

C: Intimidation... it's like a paralyzing sensation. I know I have many defenses that are difficult to demolish.

T: It's not about demolishing defenses. I respect defenses and value them a lot... When there is internal resistance, when there is a resistant part, it's often a protective part (the client nods)... This is an important part. The idea is to reduce the internal conflict, so that you can open up and at the same time protect yourself (the client listens carefully). This can happen, not in a day or two, but we can get there.

The client nods.

T: I appreciate that you're being clear about your defenses because it's important. It's important to take it into consideration. Tell me about the feeling you have now. Do you feel unsafe here with me?

C: Yes, a little.

T: Okay, can you think of that? About feeling insecure here with me? (the client nods)

T: Don't judge anything that pops into your head (the client looks down)... this is important. Don't question what comes up. Try not to worry about what I might think, okay? (The client nods)... Here, what matters least is me. I'm here to help you; you're the only one that counts okay? (the client nods and seems more relaxed)... Try to focus on the insecurity you feel with me, just focus on that feeling, can you?

C: Yes.

Bilateral Stimulation (BLS).

T: What comes up?

C: Like I can't breathe (suffocating), I also feel that I want out of here.

T: Can you stay with that?

C: I think so.

T: Okay, good, stay with that.

BLS.

T: What comes up?

C: I want the session to end.

T: You want the session to end?

C: Yes, but it is also mixed with "I should tell her (the therapist) this and that."

T: Okay, so for me to understand, this has gotten mixed up emotionally with...?

C: More sex.

T: More sex?

C: Yes, at an early age.

T: Right now, from 0 to 10, how much do you want the session to end?

C: 70%.

T: Well, I think it is a strong enough signal; we should listen to it and stop here for today.

C: Yes.

T: Remember it is important not to force yourself. I´ll be here, I will hear everything you have to say, but it should be at a pace that you can handle (client nods).

If we had simply said "stay with that" and continued processing, probably the phobia of traumatic memories would have become activated, followed by the escape defenses and the drinking, as emergency emotional regulators. This way, we convey to the client that we will not enter into the traumatic material too quickly. Instead we will facilitate effective access to this information at a later time.

In this case, the client clearly identified his defensive reaction and, with help, was able to reveal its meaning to the therapist. In other cases, this information may be subtler and may manifest indirectly during reprocessing through symptoms such as sudden fatigue, headache, changing the subject, or comments like "nothing is coming up" or "this doesn´t work." Another indicator may be what seems like an apparently normal reprocessing, but unlike other reprocessing sessions, experienced EMDR clinicians notice that it is all too quick and easy.

### Example 2: Idealization

In the case we now transcribe, a colleague asks for supervision because therapy is stuck. The client sometimes shows up drunk and flirts with the therapist. He often teases her, makes jokes, and ends up taking control of the session. Although the therapeutic alliance is supposedly good, relational issues and defenses seem to be interfering and when the session ends, both client and therapist are frustrated and confused.

After observing one of the interactions through a one-way mirror, we explain to the client the relational dynamic and defensive reactions he is using. We point out his tendency to joke, minimize, change the subject, project, and resort to magical thinking. In the following sessions, we work directly with the client´s defenses and from the client's feelings in therapy.

The client says he feels a mix of confidence and intimidation toward the new therapist. She decides to use the feeling generated in the therapeutic relationship as a target for EMDR processing.

Therapist: Just focus on the sensation that you have towards me now, can you?

Client (patting his belly): I can.

BLS.

T: What comes up?

C: I remember that the first day you came here when I was with (his therapist), you told me, "Well, I know you're very goofy but that doesn't work here"... I was like blocked, and I think I automatically raised you to a higher category... as an authority figure, because from that moment things started to work well... when you supervised the sessions from the one-way mirror, the conversation (between his therapist and him) changed... we were more focused.

T: Then, somehow you associate me with an authority figure.

C: Yes (smiles nervously).

T: Go with that.

BLS.

T: What comes up?

Q: What comes up is that I don't completely trust that this will work, I'm feeling distrust.

T: Go with that.

C: That this lack of confidence is not because of a faulty method (meaning EMDR), that this lack of trust is because of me, because I don't do my homework, I don't do what I have to do... and that happens to me with you, with everyone, and with everything.

T: It's a problem for you, in your daily life.

C: Of course, first you think that you can do it and then you freak out, how is that?

T: Go with that.

BLS.

T: What do you get?

C: It's another boycott, another defense.

After reprocessing the relational defenses that were being activating in session, the reprocessing could flow more spontaneously with other targets.

## Example 3: Subtle defenses

When using EMDR procedures with complex trauma, the process may become blocked or stuck at many points and the therapist's intervention is required. The client we will now discuss tends to judge everything she thinks, feels and says. During EMDR reprocessing, she not only judged herself, but she also did so with those spontaneous associations that came up for her (interfering with natural reprocessing). Her self-judging was similar to the way in which her family judged her as a child. In this session, the client is working on a memory of when her grandfather screamed at her because she could not do her math homework. The memory was selected based on an emotional bridge from a current concern.

Therapist: What comes up?

Client: Stupid stuff, nothing important (self-criticism, judgment, invalidation).

T: It´s important, don´t judge anything, let it flow... (This issue was discussed in previous sessions.)

C (nodding): Okay.

T: You´re doing very well. Keep going with what comes up.

BLS.

T: What comes up?

C: Nothing (possible minimization, since it is obvious that something has come up).

T: Okay, go back to the memory, the one we are working on today (the client nods), what comes up now?

C: I don´t know... it´s... I don´t know...

The client seems to have trouble verbalizing what comes up for her. Since there are many defenses, we measure the level of disturbance, to see if she is less disturbed.

T: From 1 to 10, what level of disturbance do you notice now, when you think of that event?

C: Well... it´s not a 9 anymore (The client has trouble recognizing that the disturbance has decreased.)

T: How much would it be now?

C: It´s not a nice memory. Could it be without numbers?

T: Well, do you still notice disturbance?

C: Can I talk and not say any numbers? (Possibly related to the memory we are working on.)

Given that the client has many difficulties in her daily life saying no or setting boundaries, we feel that this is positive and we reinforce her assertiveness.

T: Of course you can.

C: Okay (relieved), it´s not a good memory... Whew!!!! (silence)... And... that´s all (denial, changing subjects, omitting information).

She is trying to verbalize what comes up, but a defense arises because she is judging what is coming up for her.

T: Okay, "it´s not a good memory..." What do you notice in your body?

C: No, it´s... I don´t notice anything... (denial, since it is obvious that the client is noticing sensations.)

We give her some time.

C: I think that there are worse things that have happened to me and... this is silly (minimizing, playing it down).

T: Okay, go with that.

We try to keep the natural processing functioning, but the client continues to judge everything that she notices: her feelings, what comes up, the memory...

T: What comes up now?

C: Bah! It´s a silly memory... This should not bother me and I don´t understand it... My grandfather was the only one who didn´t treat me so bad... My grandfather was the only one who never did anything... His only fault was to stay still, he never hit me... (minimizing, judging) Why should he come to my mind?

The client is trying to retain the only attachment figure that did not do "much harm" to her (idealization).

C: He never did anything... she (grandmother) was the one who did it.

T: If you think about that...

C: I´m very surprised about this.

Psychoeducational interweave.

T: Well, we started out with a memory that was connected to other situations in which your grandfather didn´t do anything to you directly, but you heard or saw how he fought with your father.

C: Yes, it´s true.

T: Then it makes sense; it´s not nonsense (the client nods). It´s important that you try not to put words like "silly" or "stupid" on things that are so important.

C: Yes, but he... he never... I always thought he was, excuse me, a wuss... Bah! I´m always apologizing!

T: Yes, here you don´t need to do that.

C: Let´s see, my grandfather... How I can say this? If my grandmother said, "I saw a flying donkey," he would say, "If Grandma says it happened, it happened." He never came up to me and told me, "You are stupid," he never did that. And he treated me "well." But if my grandmother said anything... it was set in stone. So when my grandmother said, "This girl is stupid," he said, "This girl is stupid." But when she was not around, he treated me all right. So I never felt for him what I felt for her, because it was never his idea, it was always hers. He just watched how my grandmother insulted me and did all these horrible things to me and he just sat there, watching TV, doing nothing.

Psychoeducation.

T: Notice the chain "she's stupid"-"she's stupid"-" I'm stupid."

C: Yes, but he never did anything, that's why I always think of him as a wuss.

T: Well, taking into consideration what you just said, let's go back to the memory. What comes up now, without judging?

C: I'm always judging everything, am I?

T: Well, that's why I'm here, to remind you.

C (smiling): Okay... Why do I do it?

T: Because you learned it.

C: To judge all the time...

T: What did they tell you all the time?

C: That I was stupid.

The therapist nods.

C: I shouldn't judge myself so much, right?

T: Ideally, you shouldn't.

C: I spend my life judging everything.

T: Yes, and you do it to yourself.

The client nods.

T: Think about the memory, keeping in mind what we just talked about.

C: Whew, okay.

T: Think about the memory. Don't judge anything that comes up. What comes up?

C: I can't stop thinking he was a wuss.

T: Go with that.

BLS.

T: What comes up?

C: That he wasn't a wuss (looking back). I'm fucked up (awareness, but with judgment, self-criticism).

T: You're not fucked up, and this is a judgment. Look at me (client does this). Go with what came up for you.

BLS.

T: What do you notice?

C (sad): That he did it because he felt it like that.

T: Notice that.

C: He was overwhelmed because of my father (drug addict) and I paid for it.

T: Go with that.

BLS.

T: What comes up now?

C: That I had no reason to know multiplication. (This was the target, the grandfather screaming at her because she could not multiply.)

T: Go with that.

BLS.

T: And now?

The client is now connecting, with tears in her eyes.

T: What is coming up?

C: That I was afraid of him.

T: Focus on that.

Too much reality, so she tries to justify it again (idealization).

C: But it was at that time... there were times... That doesn't mean that I was afraid of him during my childhood (minimization, justification).

T (with a very calm voice): Look, you don't need to clarify all this. We can talk about it later. (the client nods) Just let whatever has to come, come... I promise I will not judge anything. I'm just going to listen and help you continue with the process.

C: I'm sorry.

T: We said before that you didn't have to apologize, right?

C: Okay.

T: Think of what came up for you.

BLS.

The client is clearly processing, with tears in her eyes.

T: Very good... (without stopping BLS) What do you notice?

C: Anxiety.

At the end of the session, she places the responsibility on the adults: "They were overwhelmed with their own problems... I was just a girl... There was nothing wrong with me, I was not stupid... I was a very brave girl!"

In this session, the therapist worked with the client's tendency to judge everything she thought, including the associations that arose during reprocessing. The therapist repeatedly encouraged the client to simply observe what was coming and notice her bodily sensations without interfering. These interventions enabled the client to significantly reduce her defensive tendency to pre-judge her mental contents.

The pace and nature of these interventions were focused on improving the limited capacity of the client to emotionally self-regulate. In this session, she was able to have some awareness of the defensive idealization that she had maintained for a long time. This work on the figure of the grandfather could have been destabilizing for the client if she had not had a positive attachment nowadays with her husband and aunt. Knowing this was a relevant factor for the clinician's decision-making process in this session.

Defenses have an adaptive and protective function, even if it may not always be obvious. Clients can manage without them as they learn more possibilities for handling situations. In the therapeutic process, it is important to understand defenses as extraordinary sources of information about the individual's psychological structure, as part of our map for guiding the work. If we learn to see them as resources, they can, in fact, play a fundamental role in the progress of therapy. Defenses can also be related to lacking a clear sense of identity. Clients with a fragile identity tend to hide their vulnerabilities or sense of defectiveness behind defensive amours or *as if* modes. This will be further developed in the following chapter.

# Chapter 7
# Identity, Differentiation of Self, and Development of Mental Functions

"I have the feeling of being a deeply unstable person, because I cannot control myself. I don´t control anything: not how I feel, nor how everything and everyone affect me, nor how much I cry, nor how much I disgust myself, nor how I act. I feel like I´m swerving and tripping all over the place, like when I was a child, like when my father hit me, like when the kids at school made fun of me or beat me up and I was unable to defend myself... like when in my teens I created different masks and versions of myself to see which one worked better me for me or to see if there was any that could stabilize me. But I increasingly made more mistakes and all I was building was a bunch of characters I had to interpret. My "essence" and memories would not disappear, even if I foolishly ran away, thinking that if I escaped from this place, I would escape from myself, from all that crap I was and from the memories that hurt me so much and continued torturing me since childhood."

"I push people away from me, because I scare them, because I become addicted to them, I need them, just like I need my music. I feel that if I lose them, I will lose my connection to this world where I barely fit in, where I think there is really no place for me, because they are who make me feel "alive," if only for a moment here and there... It´s the same with music: I have no talent, but I want to keep on fooling myself as long as I can by going to my classes, believing that one day, a miracle will happen and I will be able to dedicate my life to it. I just wonder what will happen when the day comes where I can´t keep fooling myself, when others, over time, get tired of me, because even patience has a limit, and they will end up leaving my life, silently, without being able to stop it..."

"It is difficult and hard to live without knowing who you are, thinking you´re a blur, a bad or unfinished drawing. Someday, I would like to be okay with my physical appearance and find some virtue in me, something to be proud of. I don´t want to see myself like I do now when the last minute of my life arrives. I want to know who I am and how I am."

## Boundaries and the Differentiation of Self

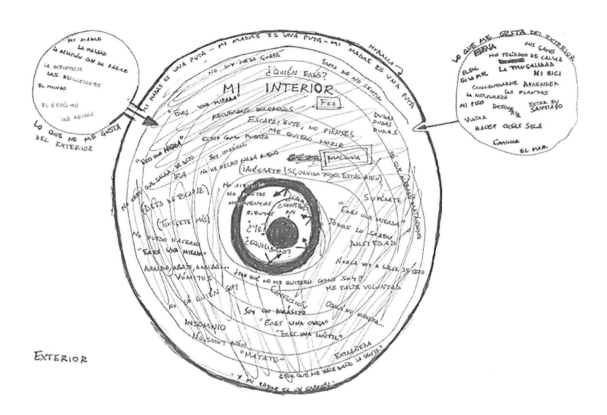

*Fig 1: On the left, she writes, "What I don´t like about the outside" (evil, the relationship with my father, injustice, arguments, abuse...). On the right, she writes, "What I like about the outside" (my cats, the sun, my calm periods). Within "herself" thoughts and beliefs pile up: my mother is a whore, I´m not pretty, try not to feel, who are you? You´re shit, ugly, painful memories, run away, don´t think, I want to die, I´m stupid, I´m shit, I do nothing good, rejoice, yes, forget everything, you´re okay, don´t feel, don´t feel, don´t feel...*

The standard protocol for EMDR work is oriented toward PTSD. When individuals who previously had acceptably healthy psychological development experience a defined trauma, the impact of the traumatic event on their current psychological functioning is the main ingredient to assess and treat.

When on the contrary, we have clients whose development has been altered by pervasive early adverse or traumatic experiences, especially when these experiences have occurred within the family context and the attachment relationship with primary caregivers, these affect psychological functioning in a much broader way. In this situation of complex traumatization, the basic EMDR protocol when we ask clients to identify a negative belief about the self, which is related to the memory and then to think about how they would like to see themselves through a positive belief about the self, we may encounter underdevelopment or dysfunction in the development of the "self" itself. Individuals may be unable to look inward, to differentiate belief from emotion or feeling, to distinguish between their own beliefs or those of others, to have an image of themselves as independent of the environment, and to see themselves as an autonomous and complete individual. To deal with a pervasive sense of emptiness and inner turmoil, they build a "false self" that acts as a substitute for a rejected, undifferentiated, or fragmented self and that stands as a screen in front for others and may be confused with having a true identity.

Asking clients with BPD for a self-referential belief may be asking for the impossible. Clients may be unable to provide a negative and positive belief, or they may give a pseudo-belief that has nothing to do with the real self, but is part of a false, defensive self. Sometimes, the beliefs they offer are deeply rooted assimilations of sentences that they heard from figures with an important psychological power over them, which were repeated many times or were pronounced at highly significant moments. Examples are the sentences that sexual abusers tell their victims and which, from then on, the victims state as their own (Salter, 2003), such as "it is your fault"- "It is my fault". Understanding when these problems are present in the development and differentiation of self and when there are defensive structures in place, is essential for achieving positive outcomes with EMDR therapy.

The concept of self as an element of the psychic structure was proposed by Freud (1923) and is part of the psychoanalytic language in a variety of orientations. In the United States, a stream of Psychoanalysis called Psychology of Self (Kohut & Wolf, 1978) focuses on this aspect and, from that basis, establishes a theory about psychological pathology. In this chapter to help the reader understand and address some of the peculiarities of working with EMDR in BPD we will use a more general concept of the self based on conceptualizations of BPD by authors of a psychodynamic origin, such as Kernberg (1967) or Bateman & Fonagy (2004).

The concept of self is diverse and complex in the history of psychology, and many perspectives have been proposed about this subject (see Harter, 1999 and Damasio, 2010). The aim of this chapter is not to delve into this conceptual debate. Instead, we want to understand how the representation of self or identity (how I describe who I am) and self-awareness (identifying feelings, emotions, and thoughts that conform the internal experience and its subjective meaning) are altered in borderline clients, and the importance of this aspect for working with EMDR.

Many authors note that the development of the self is severely impaired in BPD (Fonagy et al., 2002). Harter (1999) reviews different perspectives on the construction of the concept of self and proposes an evolutionary perspective that explains how the interaction with caregivers configures the adult representation of self.

In clients with borderline personality disorder, we can see several alterations related to self-perception and self-awareness. Reflective capacity, involved in the ability to observe one's mental actions and develop a representation of the self, is generally undeveloped or impaired in borderline clients. This is the case when there is early traumatization and we usually find a lack of development of higher-order mental functions as reflective thinking and metaconsciousness (Gonzalez &

Mosquera, 2012). With disorganized attachment and early and persistent traumatization, there is often a certain degree of psychic fragmentation, with dissociative parts that can have different levels of complexity and mental autonomy (Mosquera et al., 2011). In other cases, related to an anxious-ambivalent-preoccupied attachment style, we can see a lack of differentiation of the self (Kernberg, 1993).

Bateman & Fonagy (2004) define two primitive awareness modes of mental states. The first mode is called *psychic equivalence*. This mode equates the internal with the external: What exists in the mind must exist in the external world and what exists outside must invariably exist in the mind. Here, an aggressive fantasy is not different from a real aggression for the individual. Another primitive mode is the *as if mode*. In this mode the client's own state of mind becomes disengaged from the outer or physical reality, without recognizing that the current state of mind is connected with external events. Structurally dissociated parts of the personality or extreme emotional reactions are experienced as incomprehensible and independent of what happens outside.

## Exploring the Representation of Self

An interesting exercise with borderline clients that can help us see these aspects is to draw a circle on a blank sheet, and ask the client to draw whatever they "feel is inside of them" inside the circle. This statement is given in an open way and even when clients answer, "What do you mean?" we will just say, "Just do it however you understand it."

The difficulties that clients present with the exercise give us valuable information about their problem and the development is as important as the end result. We will see several types of clients:

### The client that sees nothing inside:

Some clients remain perplexed in front of the circle, or claim that the white circle is who they are. It is important to explore what is underneath this response. Sometimes it is due to the feeling of inner emptiness that many clients describe or to a problem defining the self without basing that definition on what others think of them. If we understand that the development of the self has its basis in the caretakers' "mindsight," (Siegel, 2011) a quality which produces awareness of how children feel and thereby is helpful for identifying, understanding and managing children's feelings, then the lack of this awareness in caretakers and the child's sense of not being seen may have a lot to do with not being able to look inside. In these cases, it is important to help clients realize what is inside, so they can become aware of their feelings, emotions, and thoughts, differentiating one from the other, realizing their needs, and making contact with their resources. All of this will be part of the preparation phase, prior to trauma reprocessing. Working with specific memories with EMDR requires this identification of psychic elements and a minimal connection with internal experience.

*Fig 2: Emptiness*

## The client that cannot even look inside

Sometimes clients do not draw anything, but the experience generates a lot of anxiety, the source of which is profound rejection of what they do see in themselves, but do not like. There may be an intense phobia of mental actions (Steele et al., 2005). Stopping to notice how they feel or what happens inside puts them in touch with emotions, thoughts, and reactions that frighten them and which they are unable to handle. This look, full of rejection and contempt for themselves, is often a reflection of the look of disapproval from primary caregivers. In this case, the self-care work that will be described later will help clients to see themselves "in a different light," with a look of complete acceptance.

*Fig 3: The client defines herself with the following words: mood swings, useless, a nuisance, weak, bothersome, slacker, boring, lazy, depression, dumb/clumsy, vulnerable, incompetent, and impulsive.*

## The client who "lives inwardly"

Some borderline clients, the more dissociative ones, draw different parts of their personality inside the circle. Some of these parts are more acceptable than others for the client, and they may not draw or may even put those aspects of themselves that they reject or fear outside of the circle. These clients may be very focused on what happens in their mind, on their symptoms and feelings, without necessarily understanding how these parts are activated in relation to external situations (representing the "as if" mode described by Bateman and Fonagy). In this case, the work implies not only the identification of parts and the reduction of conflict, but also the connection between the inner world and the outer world. For this, we will help clients become aware of which parts are activated in response to each situation and what resources they must implement to deal with everyday situations.

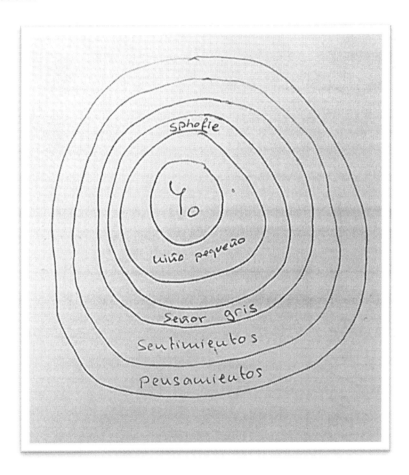

*Fig 4: Concentric circles, from the outside to the inside they read: thoughts, feelings, gray man, Sophie, small child, and inside all those layers, "Me"*

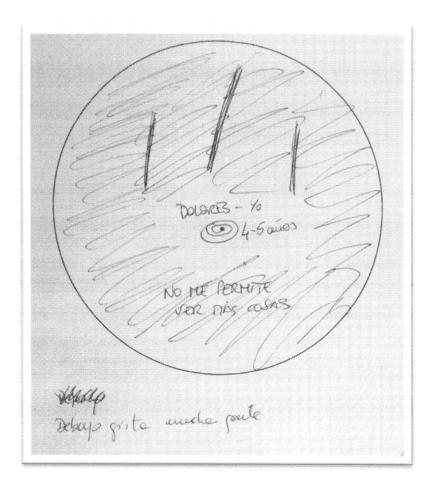

*Fig 5: Within the circle, she draws three lines, which she says are the voices in her head. There is also a 4-5 year-old self next to the name of her therapist. She then scratches it all, to represent a fog that "does not let her see more things." Outside the circle she writes: many people are shouting underneath.*

## The client who does not distinguish inside from outside

These clients draw inside the circle external figures such as parents, partners, children, or pets. They only see themselves based on those around them, they live based on others, who they feel as absolutely necessary for their existence. Sometimes, when therapists explain that these figures are very important in their life, but are not part of them, clients do not understand or react with anxiety or sadness. There is a blurring of the boundaries of the self and this speaks about an autonomy that was never developed, with invasive and worried parents who made them feel guilty for thinking or feeling differently from themselves. This situation is linked to the psychic equivalence defined by Bateman & Fonagy (2004). Some exercises to work on this differentiation and boundaries of the self are described later in this chapter.

*Fig 6: Inside the box that represents her inner world, she writes: Pain, suffering, trust, fight, I love you (next to the name of the therapist), desiring, wanting, arguing, crying, suffering, dreaming, the name of a person in her life, dad, grandpa, uncle, inferior men, manipulation, vicious circle, desire-hate, affection, coldness, anxiety.*

These situations reflect the lack of a stable sense of a representational self that feels like the agent of one´s own life. We may also see a lack of capacity for symbolic representation of mental states themselves, which Fonagy et al. (2002) consider a prerequisite for the development of a sense of identity, development that is incomplete in BPD.

This alteration in the differentiation of the self influences the implementation of EMDR procedures. Dual attention – to the memories of past within and to external sensory perceptions in the present – is an essential ingredient of the EMDR protocol for trauma processing (Lee, Taylor, & Drummond, 2006). This dual attention is extremely difficult when clients cannot differentiate themselves from the outside world. The lack of an observing self, who may have some perspective on one´s own mental actions, the lack of ability to think about why I feel this way, to give meaning to my experience, sometimes makes it impossible to establish this dual attention. Patients with BPD often identify with the emotion they feel, they are "immersed" in it. Emotions or opinions that come up often their perceptions of others and are in conflict with their own, the patient is unable to differentiate their own experience from others experiences and this confusion generate blockages.

Each individual may present different combinations of these situations that we just described.

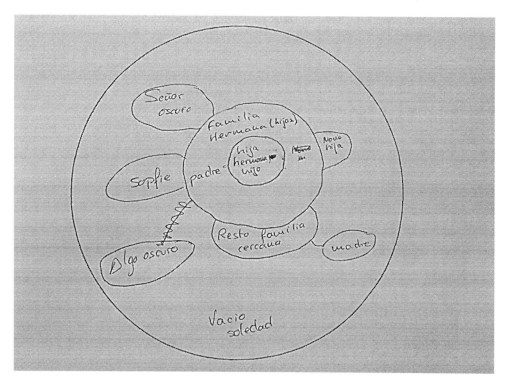

*Fig 7: Center: "daughter," "sister," "son." This central circle is surrounded by "family," "sister," "father." Further away are more distant relatives outside and the mother, who is very peripheral. In addition, in the periphery there are some dissociative parts: "dark man," "Sophie," "something dark." In the background: "emptiness," "loneliness."*

## Clinical Presentations of Identity Problems in BPD

The following section describes a variety of clinical presentations that we have encountered in our clinical practice (based on Mosquera 2004b, 2013b).

### Diffused Identity

In diffused identity, clients perceive themselves as mixed with others in such a way that it is not clear where the boundary between the self and the other person is. They do not know if what they feel is their own or if it is "absorbed," and they place emotions they are feeling onto another person. They do not know what they think or what decisions to make, because one's opinions have no value or they do not even know what they are, so they wobble at anyone's comment that "makes them doubt." They do not understand their needs. They do not "feel" what they want to do, and they lack a connection to bodily sensations, which if present, could be a source of internal security. Lacking this internal security, they desperately seek it outside.

"The feeling of emptiness, the chaos, and the uncertainty invade everything. I feel like my development had stopped when I was a child and this is how I feel most of the day. I feel I cannot be me on my own, I need others to be able to function."

In these cases, it is common that, due to their need for adaptation, they tend to behave as is expected of them and in whatever way they believe is more appropriate in order to fit into the environment they find themselves in at any given moment. They believe they need others to advise them or tell them what to do, since they rarely trust themselves and do not have a do not have distinct, clear feelings and thoughts of their own. This causes their ways of acting and feeling to vary depending on where they are and whom they are with. In turn, this leads to not knowing how to behave or what to feel in new situations or environments. While the capacity for adaptation is generally positive, in people with BPD there is a hyper-adaptation that implies a lack of psychological cohesion, along with an ignorance of their own personality, which makes them more vulnerable.

## False Identity

People with BPD often wear a mask because they lack a sense of stable identity, they become "camouflaged" behind different "roles" or costumes acquired over the years. These false identities can be mimicked from other people they know directly or indirectly. It is not uncommon, as we mentioned, that in each hospitalization, they identify with a different pathology or reproduce behaviors of famous people (Mosquera, 2004, 2013).

*Fig 8: "I feel like a clown who always plays to the gallery, I have to be okay in order not to have any problems with others; I feel I cannot express the reality of what I feel because they will not understand."*

"You look at other people and use them as a mirror to see if this way you get to feel a little more like a person. But since it's not real, you feel like a fraud."

This identification with pathology has the same function as developing an "apparent" personality. At times, individuals adopt a narcissistic mask, trying to feign a sense of security and self-esteem they are truly lacking. This might be a psychopathic appearance, which hides extreme vulnerability; or even an obsessive and rigid stance to protect themselves from inner chaos. Confusing these psychological "smoke screens" with the real underlying psychological structure can lead us to an erroneous therapeutic strategy.

## Feeling Incomplete

"It's difficult and hard to live without knowing who you are, to think that you're a blur, a bad or unfinished drawing." "It's like I am missing pieces to become a complete person."

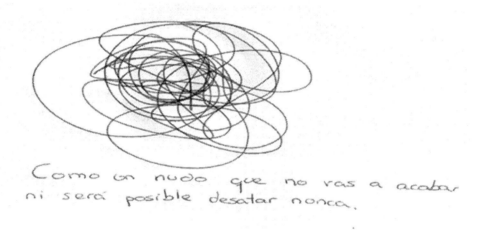

*Fig 9: "Like a knot that you will never finish or that will be impossible to unravel."*

Some people with this diagnosis feel fragile, defenseless, and incomplete, as if they are missing "something." Many feel the need to use different self-destructive behaviors to relieve their discomfort and confusion or to feel more power and control over situations and emotions. This experience may reflect that the development of the personality in borderline clients could be regarded as incomplete. People use self-destructive behaviors because they have not learned effective strategies or continue to use immature defenses, more characteristic of childhood or adolescence.

This feeling of being incomplete can also be generated in the absence of deep connection with one's own sensations, the dissociation of memories or the emotional content of some experiences, or the rejection of certain aspects of themselves.

## Fragmented Identity

Identity in BPD may also be unstable and changing because people feel divided and fragmented. They experience that their personality is made up of conflicting parts, very different from one another. In more extreme cases, the question "Who am I really?" is impossible to answer. They can change radically from one moment to the next, to the point of not remembering everything or anything they have done or said. They do or say things that they do not recognize as their own, "They are thoughts or impulses that are not mine, they are my other selves." Sometimes there are thoughts in their heads that are very different from their usual way of thinking, at times to the point of taking the form of voices. Inside, they fight with themselves, sometimes to the point of becoming completely blocked and consumed by this internal conflict. In this fight, they may feel that there are different parts inside, aspects so radically different and separate that they function "on their own" without the person being able to control what they do or what they say, but on the contrary, sometimes these parts of the personality are what control the person's thoughts, feelings, or actions.

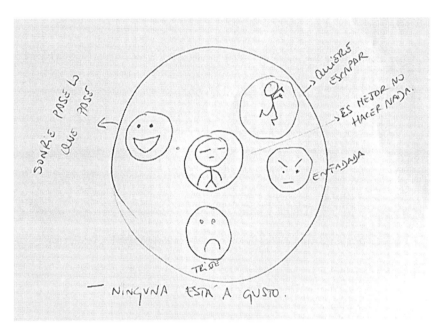

*Fig 10: Different faces: The one that smiles "no matter what" on the left. The one on the top right "wants to escape" The one in the center thinks, "It's better to do nothing." The other two faces: "mad" and "sad." "Neither one of them feels good", she concludes.*

Consciousness is affected to various degrees in BPD. In many cases, people are not fully aware of what they do or what they are generating and the apparent clarity they show at times contrasts with other moments of extreme agitation or behavioral disturbances that could, to some extent, be understood as altered states of consciousness. In cases of identity fragmentation, where ambivalence, instability, and rejection of aspects of the self are more marked, alterations of consciousness may be more apparent. Amnesia for certain periods of life or specific moments is common in many borderline clients, and the perception of the environment, the world they see, can be radically different depending on their mental state. This can be seen in a very obvious way in their descriptions of their partners when they are either in the idealization or the devaluation extremes. It can be seen, in the memory gaps they have in relation to certain behaviors: aggressive behaviors, self-harm, behaviors that are very different from their usual ones. In the chapter on dissociation we expand on these issues, and they are further discussed in Gonzalez (2010) and Gonzalez & Mosquera (2012).

## The Development of Mental Functions

Just as in severely traumatized clients, the overall development of mental functions has not taken place in many BPD clients (Gonzalez & Mosquera, 2012). The capacity for reflective thinking is limited and emotional regulation is affected in the recognition and differentiation of emotions, as well as in the connection between cognitive, emotional, and sensorimotor levels. The ability to resonate with others without getting infected with their emotional state is compromised, and they have difficulty understanding the motivations of others and seeing them as different from their own (as described in the chapter on emotional regulation).

## What Fails to Develop

First consider normal development. Fitzpatrick (1985) and Harris (1985) have shown that children develop a logical system of emotional constructs during the preoperational and operational phases (between 2 and 7 years of age). Feelings are perceived as external to oneself and are related to events. For example: joy "comes" with a gift and "goes away" when the gift is taken away or removed. Children at this age do not understand emotional responses as something internal; also, they are not able to simultaneously process positive and negative feelings (Gnepp, McKee, & Domanic, 1987; Harter & Buddin, 1987).

Between ages 7 and 12, they become able to separate feelings coming from internal aspects from those associated with external factors. At this stage, they also differentiate their own feelings from those of others (Selman, 1980).

At age 10, children are able to recognize the experience of conflicting emotions towards the same event (or toward the same person), but this ambivalence is not fully integrated until adolescence (Harter & Buddin, 1987).

As we can see, borderline clients function on an emotional level like that of very early stages of development. Emotions in BPD are seen as directly related to events, as if their internal process were not contemplated at all, "How can I not feel like this after what has happened to me?" Positive and negative feelings, emotional ambivalence, cannot be integrated and they typically swing from one extreme to the other. There is no differentiation between emotions that come from internal aspects and external factors.

The process of therapy has to resume the evolutionary development at the point where it stalled and help the client move toward a more evolved level of emotional functioning.

Semerari et al. (2005) speak of dysfunction in metacognitive skills, those restricted to the construction of integrated representations of self and others, which are needed to be able to differentiate between internal fantasies and external reality. According to the author, clients can access their emotional experience and associate it with events that caused it. In our experience, however, although the two difficulties mentioned are true, borderline clients´ access to their emotional experience lacks a meta-representative quality. Clients do not usually think about what they are feeling, in fact when they think about something emotional, they become easily immersed in that same emotion, which overwhelms them. The relationship that clients establish between their emotion and what generates it is often distorted by the mix between past and present, inside and outside, self and other.

Impulsive responses by definition lack reflective character. Impulsivity is associated with altered functioning at a prefrontal level (Spinella, 2004), and also with the development of ego functions and interpersonal relationships (Mathiesen & Weinryb, 2004).

Working on developing prefrontal functions, such as planning, delayed response, and decision making, will contribute significantly to the overall development of psychic functions.

## Distortion in Development

There are things clients could not learn, perhaps because their caregivers shared some of the same limitations in emotional and cognitive functioning. But even when this source of limitation is present, many other situations can interfere with psychological development. Some emotions are heavily censored or ignored, while others are stimulated and reinforced. Some thoughts are introduced into the inner world of the client as slogans that cannot be broken, due to countless repetitions or to the fact that they were pronounced in moments of high emotional intensity or particular significance.

If in the midst of what should be a secure foundation for the child, caregivers respond to the child with a threatening tone, generating defensive responses, which results in certain associated emotions being managed in a different way. This typically happens with fight/flight proactive responses and emotions that are consistent with these anger/fear responses.

These distortions in the emotional life need to be identified and addressed specifically for relearning of adaptive emotional responses to take place. Processing of specific memories can bring significant potential to the treatment.

## The Therapeutic Process

The process of EMDR therapy with a BPD client, as well as across the entire spectrum of complex traumatization, is not only about introducing adaptive information through psychoeducation (see chapter 11) and processing dysfunctionally stored information that is feeding the symptoms (see chapter 13). Once we overcome the multiple defenses and phobias (see Chapter 6) that these clients present, we must develop what has not been completed and restructure what is maladjusted. All these aspects must be dynamically integrated.

Some clients have developed a very convincing *as if* mode and can seem very attentive to what we say without actually doing any introspection whatsoever. Clients may appear to be excited about some of our proposals but will not be able to carry them out if they are not focused on the part of the solution that depends on them.

At each step, at each session, at every decision point, the client must participate as actively as possible. It is essential to encourage reflective thinking and to ask questions like, "What do you think?," "Does it make sense to you?," "Why does it make sense to you?," "Do you think you could accomplish what I propose?," "How could you accomplish it?" Any introspection or "insight" can be strengthened or installed with bilateral stimulation. This active engagement is crucial throughout the process.

Identity problems described in this chapter are closely related to the topic of our next chapter, self-care.

# Part Three
# Phases 3 to 8 in the Treatment with EMDR: Working with Adverse Life Experiences

# Chapter 8
# Self-Care Patterns in BPD
# A Key Element for Stabilization

The concept of self-care (Mosquera, 2004; Gonzalez, 2010; Gonzalez & Mosquera, 2012) describes the way in which individuals take care of themselves in various functional areas, including not only the physical, but also the intrapsychic and relational ones.

The pattern of self-care develops from the caregiving action of others, which is reproduced and internalized as care and warmth toward the self. The emotion of love has been identified by Panksepp (1998) as a basic emotion in mammals, and this emotion appears to become activated through the love received from others in the early stages of life. If caregivers are neglectful, abusive, or uninterested, children may internalize these attitudes toward their own inner experiences, particularly those that do not receive external validation. For example, a child who is considered good and is valued only if he is quiet and does not bother caregivers, will learn to not ask for much and not show his feelings or needs.

When children's internal experiences, particularly emotions and needs, are not recognized or are punished by caregivers, they learn to imitate and internalize the negative attitudes of the adults. And if, in addition, parents punish or ignore their feelings, thoughts, or behaviors in a selfish and unloving way, children will ignore their own needs in order to maintain the only possible bond with the caregiver. This can split children's sense of self in "a part of me that is acceptable" and "a part of me that is not acceptable" (see Chapter 7 on differentiation).

Clients with dysfunctional patterns of self-care continue to see themselves through the eyes of their early attachment figures. When caregivers functioned in a negligent or abusive manner, they learned to treat themselves in a similar way (Gonzalez & Mosquera, 2012). Many clients with BPD learned that having needs is bad, selfish, and not allowed. In many cases, the only way to get some attention (or be seen) was caring for and taking care of the needs of the adults. At other times, caregivers, functioning from concern, gave children things that they did not need, or that they did not need to such an extent, since their caregivers were looking to calm their own insecurity, reduce their guilt, or fulfill their unmet needs, instead of being attuned with the real child before them. Although the path that goes from lack of recognition of the needs of children and dysfunctional care to adult patterns is not at all simple, we can often see many parallels between "how I care for myself" and "how they cared for me."

## BPD and Self-Care Patterns

Clients with BPD often have many difficulties with self-care and it is common for them to regulate themselves through self-destructive behaviors. Many symptoms of BPD may be understood as manifestations of deficient self-care patterns.

These self-care patterns have great significance in the establishment of a therapeutic framework. Clients with BPD sometimes come to our office after a relational conflict, seeking help from a therapist in order to feel better, while at the same time doing things that are clearly harmful to themselves. They can insult, reproach, or criticize themselves harshly in front of the therapist, without this being a constructive self-analysis. They may ask themselves, "Why is this happening?" without this question being a genuine attempt to understand, but rather an inflexible demand and a reproach. They may make decisions that get them in trouble over and over again. They can focus on another person, ignoring their own needs, or they can seek immediate gratification, often through dysfunctional means. Therapy must be directed towards finding a way of looking at their problems with understanding and finding realistic solutions for them. This is often far from the clients' perspective, since they are focused on finding quick relief for their discomfort or presenting their problem to the therapist so that he or she may fix it for them. Changing the therapeutic position so that clients may work on learning how to take care of themselves in a healthy way requires modeling by the therapist regarding acceptance, realistic and constructive support, and recognition of what affects them and what they need.

## Self-Care Procedure for EMDR Therapy

The self-care procedure for EMDR therapy is inspired by Knipe's (2008) "Loving Eyes" procedure. The central aspect of this procedure involves combining bilateral stimulation with an internal image of the client looking with loving eyes into the eyes of the young child within. Based on clinical experience using this procedure, we will describe in this chapter a more elaborate protocol (Gonzalez & Mosquera, 2011; Gonzalez & Mosquera, 2012). This procedure is part of a set of interventions geared toward restoring a healthy self-care pattern in clients presenting distortions in this area.

Positive self-care can be considered as consisting of three elements: (1) an attitude or state of mind of cherishing and loving yourself, an attitude that motivates individuals to take good care of themselves; (2) an absence of self-rejection attitudes; and (3) specific beneficial actions, which make individuals grow and value themselves. Among these elements, the positive self-care attitude seems intuitively to be primary: an attitude of positive self-loves generates motivation for the other two elements of self-care.

By focusing on improving self-care, we are also working on the reorganization of the attachment system, not always accessible through specific memories. A more detailed description of the work on self-care and other interventions related to this concept may be seen in Gonzalez & Mosquera, (2012).

## Assessment of Self-Care Patterns and Preparation for the Procedure

Current areas of self-care (see table 8.1) and the client's history are thoroughly explored, without delving into traumatic experiences, in order to elaborate, collaboratively with clients, a reformulation of the presenting problem. We explain how bad they feel is one thing and a very different one is what they do about their discomfort: how they treat themselves, how they talk to themselves internally, whether they look for help or not when they feel bad, and whether or not they allow themselves to be helped. It is also important to know how they take care of themselves in general, explaining that if we do not ask for what we need and protect ourselves adequately from what hurts us, usually, sooner or later, we will feel bad.

### Table 8.1 Self-care chart

| Physical care | Needs and duties |
|---|---|
| I don´t sleep as much as I need | I can´t ask for what I need |
| I eat poorly | Duties go before pleasure |
| I don´t exercise | Other people´s needs are always more important tan mine |
| I only go to the doctor at the last minute | Things that I do have to be useful for other people |
| I miss medical check-ups that I should attend | I end up exhausted by doing things because I don´t know how to stop |
| I let myself go in personal care | There is not a balance between what I give and what I receive |
| There are always more important things than to care for my health | |

| Personal recognition | Protecting myself |
|---|---|
| Other people should be there for me when I need them | I have relationships with people that mistreat me |
| I´m always the one having to take care of others | I put up with situations or relationships that hurt me for way too long |
| No one recognizes how much I do for them | I am unable to say no |
| I always feel I am being treated unfairly and I don´t understand why | I allow people to invade my personal space |
| I get upset or angry when others don´t respond immediately to my needs | I have a hard time standing up for my rights |
| People are very ungrateful | I often feel used |
| | I can excuse anything anyone does to me |

| Accepting compliments | Time to enjoy |
|---|---|
| I don´t like compliments at all | I don´t take time for nice or fun activities |
| If I am told positive things about myself, I say something to neutralize them ("it´s no big deal") | I don´t know how to enjoy my free time |
| I mistrust people that give me compliments | I barely see my friends |
| Compliments make me feel uncomfortable | I never have time for myself |
| I believe a criticism much more easily than a compliment | I don´t have gratifying relationships |
| | I think that spending time on myself is selfish |

| Asking for help | Mistreating myself |
|---|---|
| I deal with my own problems | I do things that I know are harmful for me |
| I am unable to ask for help | I behave in self-destructive ways |
| I don´t allow myself to get help | I don´t deserve to treat myself well |
| I don´t need anyone´s help | When I´m not feeling well, I get angry at myself for feeling like this |
| I mistrust those who offer me help | I always blame myself for everything |
| I feel more comfortable helping others than the other way around | When I´m not feeling well, I do things that make me feel even worse |
| | I beat myself up internally all the time |

To improve their self-care, clients' history of attachment and trauma need to be related to different aspects of their current patterns of self-care, so that clients can understand how the most relevant problems that are seen on the scale may be related to their problem and its intensity. The Self-Care Questionnaire (SCPQ; Gonzalez, Mosquera, Leeds, & Knipe, 2012) can be used to explore the problematic areas in detail and can be downloaded in www.intra-tp.com.

Having established this as a shared goal in this phase of their therapy, we can then help clients understand *where they learned* their dysfunctional self-care patterns. We explain that, often, people who do not take care of themselves do this as a direct reflection of how they were cared for as children. We describe how with no one to realize how they felt, they learned to disconnect from their feelings or did not learn what to do with them. If when they were feeling bad or when they showed some emotion in particular, this was censored in some way, they tend to reproduce that internally throughout life. It is preferable to give concrete examples from the client's history, connecting them with the client's current self-care pattern. This way, we develop a **reformulation of the problem** with clients.

During the entire procedure, we will insist on not delving into specific memories, because the purpose of this work is to build the basis for the later processing of traumatic memories, but not to work with them directly. Clients may have trouble refraining from a detailed discussion of these memories. In this case the therapist must explain that "one thing is what happened to us and a different one is who you are. Here we are working with the image of yourself, not the bad things that happened to you." With this information, we try to reinforce differentiation. When using bilateral stimulation, during the self-care procedure we never allow a long associative chain. We always introduce information on differentiation and return frequently to target, which is looking in the child's eyes. The criterion for allowing these traumatic associations is the clinical assessment of whether or not clients can tolerate a certain degree of trauma processing at this time in the therapeutic process.

If clients have a high degree of idealization of their primary caregivers, we will never blame them about how they cared for their children. Instead we might say, "Parents do what they can. Often they do not realize how their children feel because they are not very connected to their own emotions. When the children are upset, they may become overwhelmed and feel very bad, so that the kids either become overwhelmed themselves or have to worry about regulating the adult to keep their caregiver in place. Sometimes parents may have had things happen in their own life that keep them blocked and this is triggered in the presence of their children, so they react automatically. We are not trying to judge them. We just want to help you understand how these things may have affected you, so you can learn to do things differently within you, to break that cycle."

We explain the process of secure attachment is with an example, telling the following story (with a child of the same gender as the client). For the purpose of this example and the following steps, we will choose a female client:

> *"Imagine a little girl who falls down and gets hurt. Her knee is bleeding, so she runs home. Her father looks lovingly at her (loving look in his eyes, without reproach, with proportionate concern, not anguish) and says, 'Poor thing, it hurts, right? (Recognition of the girl's suffering.) Come here (he embraces her). I'll wash the wound (making a gesture or ritual of care). Yes, of course it hurts! I'll put a band-aid on it. Come sit on my lap for a while (he consoles her through touch until she calms down).' Soon the girl will get bored and will want to go out and play. If her dad asks her if her knee still hurts, she will probably say 'no,' while walking out the door.*
>
> *Now think of another girl on the same street, a little further down, who has also hurt her knee in the same way as the other girl. She runs home, but her father tells her 'Stop crying or I'll give you a real reason to cry!' Or without being so extreme, he says, 'Nothing happened. That's nothing. Come on, don't cry.' Or her father gets very nervous and anxious when he sees the girl*

*crying. The second girl now has two problems. Her knee still hurts, but she'll feel bad if she cries or she won't think she has the right to feel bad. If she falls in the future and gets hurt again, she is not likely to go home for help. This girl can blame herself each time she feels bad (give an example of the client if this happens now with her disturbance), or tell herself that nothing is wrong, as if her suffering was not important or legitimate (give an example of the client). This makes it easier for painful emotions to accumulate and for the girl not to know what to do with them, so she may try to disconnect them or she may become overwhelmed whenever she feels them. With such early experiences, we will easily bring these same patterns into adulthood."*

Based on the information obtained from the history and the self-care scale, we search for where and when clients learned to care for themselves as they do. Clients can talk about a specific event or a time of their life. If they say, "I was always like this," we will ask for a representative example of when they were little or ask them to think of an image of themselves as a child, asking later how old they think the child is.

## Step 1: Image

Even if clients tell us about a memory, we will ask them to focus on the image of themselves, saying, "We will work so you can get over all those situations, but now we are trying to see how you see and treat yourself, that's what this exercise symbolizes. So leave aside the specific memory and focus only on the child, the image of that child. You, as an adult, sitting here in the office with me, looking at the X-year-old child you were."

"Bring to mind an image of that X-year-old child. An image of that girl who lived through these situations, just as you see her"

If clients are unable to visualize an image, we will ask them to think of any photos they may have from that age.

## Step 2: Reaction to the Image and Degree of Connection

We tell clients: "Sitting here, as the adult woman you are now, can you just look at that young girl?"

If they say yes, we ask them to describe her. We note indicators of (1) disconnection (such as the client cannot see the child; they cannot do the exercise; it's a static picture that says nothing...), which suggests dissociation or a dismissive primary attachment; (2) excessive connection or "emotional contagion" (when looking at the child, they become overwhelmed with the same emotion as in the image of the child or show signs of avoidance), which speaks of dissociation or a preoccupied primary attachment; (3) high mental autonomy in the child (the child acts in ways that surprise the client as an adult: turns around, hides, the adults says that the child does not want to talk, or describes any emotional reaction in the child that is not lived as their own), which indicates a higher level of structural dissociation. In each situation we must help the client overcome their difficulties:

a) If there is disconnection, we will help them to make contact with the child: "What do you see in this child? How do you think she could have felt? Based on her posture, what do you understand of what is happening?" (Changes, in this case, require a patient attitude of support from the therapist.)

b) If there is an extreme connection, we ask, "How could we help the child with her pain without feeling the pain that she feels?"

c) If there is a high degree of mental autonomy, we must establish negotiation processes characteristic of the work with dissociative parts (Gonzalez & Mosquera, 2012).

## Step 3: Physical Sensation and Emotion

We ask clients to look at the child in the eye, without judging, and simply to note their physical sensation and emotion when they do this . When the client feels love, affection, or any positive sensation looking at or towards the child, we reinforce it with bilateral stimulation. If there is any negative sensation, we can process it. Even when clients express rejection or claim to be unable to see the child, we ask them to find an associated bodily feeling. Sometimes the client does not initially reveal any emotional disturbance, but the bodily sensation may indicate some degree of discomfort.

The difficulties in carrying out the process are not only related to disturbance. The appearance of disturbance is a possibility: clients may feel uncomfortable looking into the eyes of the child within. This disturbance may come from a dissociative phobia, between the adult representing the apparently normal part of the personality and the child representing an emotional part, even when there is a high degree of mental autonomy. However, the disturbance may also come from a lack of differentiation of the self, which often originates in a preoccupied attachment. Discriminating this is necessary in order to introduce appropriate psychoeducation.

Sometimes, we may see a strong avoidance to the exercise. In this case, the therapist may ask, "What is good about not looking at that child?" Responding to this question, clients might say something like, "If I look away, I don't have to feel those feelings," or "If I don't look, I don't have to see how horrible it was." When the client verbalizes a defensive belief, the therapist may answer, "Think about that," followed by bilateral stimulation.

If there is an identified disturbance, it can be measured on a SUD scale from 0 to 10. But when there are connection or awareness difficulties, we may not seek this measurement. The purpose of obtaining the level of disturbance is to quantify the subjective change during the procedure, but we will omit the SUD scale when we believe that it adds an issue that may be difficult for the client to handle or may be counterproductive. The therapist should decide when to use, or not to use, specific measurements.

## Step 4: Processing Dysfunctional Elements

Anything preventing clients, as adults, from being able to look into the eyes of the children they were with acceptance and love will be processed with bilateral stimulation, in a similar way to Phase

4 of the standard EMDR protocol, starting with a focus on the associated emotional and physical sensation.

If a client begins to associate negative memories, we may decide to follow the sequence (if we are confident the client can tolerate it and the level of disturbance is mild), but without going into a long chain of associations. We are not interested in entering long associative processes at this time, so we come back often to target. Similarly, if clients go into a memory with a very high SUD, which the therapist does not consider appropriate to enter at this time of therapy, we will tell them, "This is a very important memory and we will work on it when you're ready, but now we are working with the child that you were, not with what happened to that child". Here we are stressing the differentiation between "who I am" and "what happened to me". If the level of disturbance in an associated negative memory remains inside the client's window of tolerance (Ogden & Minton, 2000), and the therapist considers it appropriate, we may continue until a positive or neutral association is reached. But with even the slightest doubt, it is best to go back to target: looking into the child's eyes with love and acceptance.

## Step 5: Reinforcing Adaptive Elements

When going back to target, we ask clients to look at the child again and tell us what they see, what is different now (promoting change), and what they are realizing now (promoting awareness and significance). We ask again to notice bodily sensation (we are interested in reinforcing getting in touch with themselves) and we continue with BLS until the SUD is 0. If we had to process the defense of avoidance, hopefully in a subsequent session we can return to the exercise, access the disturbance and process it until we reach SUD 0.

Two specific positive elements should be reinforced, mindsight (ability to realize how the child feels) and the capacity for caring. When there are early disruptions of attachment, spontaneous positive changes do not happen in most cases. These two elements must be present to repair an attachment wound, and the therapist can help introduce these positive elements whenever necessary.

### *Reinforcing Mindsight*

The therapist asks the client, as an adult, to try to realize what the child needs. When we ask the adult if the child is old enough to realize and discuss these issues, we can introduce information about what was inappropriate at some ages. For example, asking a one-year-old child what she needs would not be appropriate, but the client, who had to do many inappropriate things for her chronological age, may lack this adaptive information regarding care. In any case, the therapist will help the client as an adult to "realize" beyond what the child can see, in order to develop this mindsight. We can offer different kinds of adaptive information. For example, when a child says she does not need anything, the therapist may say, "This child is used to trying to be really strong, ignoring what she liked or needed, because adults were always so worried... But you, as an adult, can see that it would be better, as a child, not to worry about anything, just enjoy herself and let others take care of her. How could you explain all these things to a child? She has been worrying about not creating problems for adults for such a long time that it is difficult to change, but things are different with you. You could encourage her to just allow herself to enjoy herself like a kid, to just be a kid..."

### *Reinforcing the Capacity for Care in the Adult*

When clients spontaneously look at the child with unconditional love and acceptance or when the process evolves in this direction, BLS can be used to reinforce these changes. When adults have difficulty understanding and caring for the child, the therapist may actively encourage this to happen. Often, clients are able to adequately care for other people, or they like some pet animals. The therapist can help the client to activate this capacity to care for others. For example, if the client knows a child who generates a caring impulse in her, the therapist will ask the client for a detailed description of how she feels towards this child and how she takes care of her. This caregiver role will be reinforced with BLS. If the client is not a healthy caregiver for any child, we can use any caregiver role toward another adult or a pet, following the same procedure.

After strengthening the capacity in the adult for offering care to others, it will be channeled towards the client's inner child. The therapist asks the client as an adult, while feeling her ability to care for others, to look now at the child she was. After asking, we introduce a set of BLS to link the adult's caregiving networks with the image of the child. If the client informs the therapist of changes in her ability to care for that child in her imagination, it can be measured on a scale from 1 to 7, similar to the VOC level in the standard protocol, with 1 being "I do not feel capable of caring for the child I was" and 7 being "I feel completely capable of caring for that child." The subjective capacity to offer care for their inner child will be strengthened with BLS by introducing the necessary adaptive information or by going back to the healthy caring networks with other figures as needed.

Once the client, with the necessary help from the therapist, is able to identify what the child needs, the adult will try to satisfy this need in her imagination. For example, if the child needs love, the therapist will ask the adult to imagine giving the child the love she needs, in the way the adult sees fit.

The process will continue until the difficulties the client has, regarding caring for the child she was, cease to be present and she feels the capacity to do so at a level of 7. With clients who suffered serious neglect or traumatization in childhood, small improvements are to be understood as major changes and trying to complete the procedure is unrealistic and may be inappropriate. In these cases, we will avoid taking measurements if the therapist believes that these might put pressure on clients, making them feel unable or anxious.

### *Stimulating the Social Engagement System*

Porges (2003) explains how social behavior is related to self-regulation. The process of self-care is also a learning process in self-regulation and, in survivors of early trauma, the social engagement system is usually underdeveloped. Therapeutic attunement is key to restoring the capacities for social involvement. The way in which therapists interacts with clients, the style with which therapists guide clients as adults to relate to their inner child in a different way, is a powerful element in the process of self-care that cannot be fully reflected in writing.

Therapists offer clients indirect modeling, speaking in a soft and supportive tone, introducing the necessary information in each specific case: "You can see how difficult it is for that child to trust you, she has learned not to trust adults, because many of them did not care for her in a good way. You understand that she needs time, right? Can you let her notice that you're there, and that you're different from these people?" Bilateral stimulation is dynamically introduced in order to reinforce psychoeducational interventions, positive feelings toward the child, or adaptive changes. When blockages or difficulty changing toward a healthy self-care pattern appear, BLS can be used to process them.

Difficulties that may arise in working with self-care patterns can be initially overwhelming, but may become enriching acquisitions, through modeling and psychoeducation by the therapist. For example, if a client loses self-control and the therapist remains present and calm, maintains a warm and quiet tone of voice, addressing the client as a capable adult and suggests possible ways of regulating the child, the client will incorporate this pattern - a new regulation model - in her neural networks. The therapist may say, "Kids often take time to calm down, you know, and adults have patience; just by noticing that we are there, supporting them, they will regulate themselves. Sometimes we have to give them time and just be there." BLS can be introduced or not as we say these sentences, depending on the clinical judgment of the therapist (in some clients this may reinforce the assimilation of information, in others it may produce greater emotional arousal).

## Step 6: Embodying the Procedure

Since this procedure is focused on the positive connection with oneself, helping clients focus on the body will be reinforced throughout the procedure. If the process evolves to the point of reaching an adult who is able to look into the eyes of the child she was with love and unconditional acceptance, understanding her essential need and taking care of it, we will reinforce the embodiment of this critical resource.

We ask the client to locate in her body "where do you notice that child within you, where in the body would you locate her?" The client may say for example, "In my chest."

Then, we will ask her to look at her adult hand, her hands that are able to look after others, and to place her hand on the area of the body where she notices that inner child, with a gesture of taking caring of her.

We will monitor that the gesture is really of caring and that the person is not pressing or trying to "tear away" the feeling, helping the client to notice this.

If the feeling and gesture are positive, we offer more BLS.

Maintaining the gesture and the feeling, we introduce adaptive information: "Let the child realize that you are there, let her realize that you understand how she must have felt, let her notice how important she is for you..."

## Step 7: Enhancing Awareness

Throughout the procedure, clients often have interesting insights about themselves, their problems, and their self-care. At this stage, we collect these insights and also emphasize the adaptive information that the client needs to reinforce.

We also encourage reflective mental functions asking, "What did you realize by doing this exercise? What does this experience mean to you? Do you understand more about yourself now? Do you understand more about your problem or how to overcome it?" We can enhance any new awareness with BLS.

## Step 8: Closure

We continue the procedure until the client obtains significant and possible developments. The more severe the history neglect and trauma in childhood, the less ambitious the procedure should be. Clinicians should be alert never to force the client to do this procedure nor to allow the client to become overwhelmed. We must use our knowledge of clients and our clinical judgment, to decide when to stop the self-care intervention in each session.

We explain to clients that in the following days or weeks they may experience changes and that it is important to observe them and to write them down without analyzing. They may feel more intense emotions, both positive and negative, as a result of an increased contact with themselves through the image of the child within. They may feel a state of wellbeing and a positive change of the feeling towards themselves. New memories of childhood may come up, sometimes associated with a change of perspective. Sometimes, it can be seen that behaviors indicating poor self-care decrease, and adaptive self-care behaviors increase. If clients know that this work can move things inside, but that usually the effect will settle after a short time, they will be able to deal more easily with the possible disturbing sensations. We will ask them to note down these changes, without deciding whether they are good or bad, both those happening in the period immediately following the session and those taking place a few days later, once emotions are regulated and the effects are settled.

## Step 9: Re-evaluation

This exercise may need to be done over a series of sessions to strengthen the capacity of the client. It is important to check for any changes that have occurred in between sessions regarding the different self-care areas. After going over the possible changes, we return to target and see if the phobia towards the child part has decreased. We also check if both the capacity to stay present as the adult and the level of dual attention have increased. Another aspect to analyze is the adult's perceived capacity to care for the child part in a healthier way.

**Case example**

After 2 years of stabilization work mainly based on psychoeducation, the therapist is trying to process a traumatic memory. The process seems blocked, and the therapist thinks that this could be due to negative beliefs directly related to the procedure, such as, "I am incapable of explaining what I feel", "I am doing it wrong". The client lacks emotional regulation abilities and she is easily overwhelmed by her emotions.

T (after BLS): Is something different coming up for you? For a moment you stopped moving your eyes.

C: I don´t know.

T: What do you notice now?

C: The same: a lot of anguish... I don´t know... a lot... I am taking so much medication that words don´t come to me. I notice sensations, but I don´t have the words to explain them.

T: You don´t need to tell me everything that comes into your mind or to have the exact word for it, I just need an approximate description. We will do a longer set, ok?

C: Ok

BLS

T: What do you notice now?

C: I notice anguish.

BLS

T: What do you get now?

C: I'm losing concentration.

BLS

It seems that the client has difficulties following eye movements, so we change to tapping.

T: What do you get now?

C: I still notice a lot of anguish and... ugh!!! This is very difficult, I can´t.

BLS

T: What do you notice?

C: I am becoming even more anxious, because I can´t focus on anything. I am feeling useless, I can´t even do this.

T: Open your eyes, what do you think you should do now?

C: I don´t know...

T: You don't have to do anything now, you are doing fine. We are focusing on a physical sensation that you notice on a regular basis, we just want to relieve it a bit. Your mind is allowed to go wherever it needs to go. There is not a wrong way of doing this.

BLS

T: What do you get?

C: I think that if I died, many people would be relieved.

The process is not working well. Even the word "relief" that the therapist said triggers suicidal thoughts. Everything positive turns into negative.

BLS

T: What do you get now?

C: That I just want to die.

Verbal and nonverbal information do not fit together. The therapist checks in with the client.

T: How is the pressure on your chest?

C: It's the same.

T: Open your eyes (client opens her eyes) ... you say the pressure on your chest is the same, but your body has changed dramatically. Can you notice any sensation that may be different?

C: Yes

T: What do you notice?

C: It is a little bit more... more... a little bit more... more... I don't know... more... relaxed.

Even when BLS is having a positive, relaxing effect, the client's self-defeating tendencies are very intense. She has difficulties noticing improvement and she tends to focus on negative aspects

T: You are doing a big effort, and this helps you disconnect for moments at a time. Although you are feeling bad, you are still trying. You seem touched by what I am saying (client has tears in her eyes), why?

C: Because you get me. I feel that you value me. You are the only one who appreciates what I do.

The client is extremely dependent on external regulation and lacks self-regulatory capacities.

Next session: after difficulties reprocessing a memory during the past session, the therapist tries with resource development and installation (RDI).

T: Think of a time when you felt really good.

C: When I felt really good... (takes a long time to think, long silence).

T: Or when you were satisfied about something you did well.

C: It is difficult for me to feel good and to think I do something well.

T. Do you remember any time when this happened? Try to think of a situation, it would be very useful.

C: I am blocked.

When the self-care pattern is inverted, things can evolve in a reverse way. Trying to find a resource makes her feel worse, since it makes her realize how many things she is lacking. This becomes a new way of blaming herself.

T: Is it because of the question I asked?

C: Yes, because I don´t remember any.

T: Ok, so you can´t think of anything positive?

C: No.

T: What would be positive enough for you? Could you try thinking of something?

C: I don´t know how.

Self-care patterns are extremely dysfunctional. The client has an extremely negative view of herself and this interferes with any intervention attempted in therapy. Even if she is aware of the early experiences that feed her lack of self-worth, their influence does not change, neither with psychoeducational interventions, nor with EMDR processing. She has learned many emotion regulation skills and many new abilities, but she cannot use them to improve, and suicidal thoughts and acts are very present and intense. Client lacks self-regulatory capacities and is completely dependent on external reassurance (even though it does not work).

C: I don´t know, I always depend on what others say in order to value myself. I can´t do it my own, I don´t know why... I should learn to do that, to value myself.

T: And how could you learn that? (Trying to get her to think.)

C: I don´t know, I have no idea. I've never done it.

T: Where did you learn not to value yourself? Could you think about that?

C: I don´t know... I think I have never valued myself.

T: How about when you were little?

C: No.

The client does not realize the connection between rejection and hostility in her childhood family environment and her negative attitude toward herself. In order to focus on self-care patterns, the target will be the image of the child she was when the pattern was learned. Since she has no images, the target will be a picture.

T: When you look at pictures of you from when you were little, what do you feel?

C: Sadness... everyone says they would love to go back to childhood. I wouldn´t, I feel it was sad... I don´t like it at all.

T: Do you have pictures from when you were little?

C: Very few... I have one from when I was little. I took it from my mother.

T: Which picture did you take?

C: One from when I was about 1 year old. I am wearing a dress, a short one, like those where you can see the diapers.

T: Why did you choose that picture?

C: Because I had a very sweet gaze. I like her gaze.

T: When you look at this picture, what do you feel towards yourself?

C: I see a sweet child, a sad child, I don´t know... she seems unprotected. I feel like holding her.

This client does not present a relevant dissociative phobia toward this emotional part. From her adult self, a tendency to take care of this little girl spontaneously emerges. This dissociative part does not seem to have a strong mental autonomy. There are no significant barriers among the adult state and the childhood state. When she looks at the child, she is not overwhelmed by emotions. There are no elements that could need a specific intervention, so we can focus on reinforcing this positive tendency that appears.

T: It would be great if you could... I think that many of the things that you don´t understand come from there, from this sensation you already had when you were very little. If you could hold that little girl now, what would you do?

C: Hug her and cuddle her.

T: What would you say to her? Try to imagine that little girl. Look at that little girl, look at her in the eye and tell me what you would say?

C: That I will take care of her, that nothing is going to happen to her.

T: Close your eyes and notice that, think about that, let this little girl... let this little girl know how you feel.

BLS.

T: What do you get?

C: It's like I want to cry.

T: Ok, go with that and cry if you want.

BLS.

T: What do you get now?

C: I feel like holding her and protecting her.

T: Ok, let her know. What she didn´t know as a child and what you now now know as an adult: that you can protect her.

BLS.

T: What do you get now?

C: I tell her that I will cuddle her and tell her stories.

T: Go with that.

BLS.

T: And now?

C: That I will protect her, that I won´t leave her alone.

T: Ok, let her know that; it´s important. What do you get?

C: That no matter what she does, I will always support her.

T: Go with that.

BLS.

T: And now?

C: That she can always count on me.

T: Notice that.

BLS.

T: And now?

C: That I won´t bother her.

T: That´s it, very important.

BLS.

C: I will allow her to be herself.

T: Just notice... these are such important things.

BLS.

T: What do you get now?

C: I tell her that she will be able to do whatever she wants.

BLS.

T: And now?

C: I will try to make her happy.

T: Very important, notice that.

BLS.

T: What do you get?

C: That she will be the most important thing in my life.

After all these positive elements, some disturbance appears. We need to explore if it comes from the child (EP) or the adult self (ANP).

T: What do you get now?

C: I am a little disturbed.

T: Is this disturbance yours or hers?

C: Mine.

T: Go with that.

BLS.

T: What do you get now?

C: This is very strong.

T: What is?

C: The throbbing.

T: Go with that sensation.

BLS.

T: What do you get now?

C: It still is very strong.

T: Ok, go with that.

BLS.

T: And now?

C: I am disturbed, it is as if I couldn´t breathe well.

T: Can you keep going?

Client nods.

T: Take a deep breath, open your eyes. When you think about this little girl and all of the things you have told her, such important things, what are you thinking now? How did it feel to be able to say those things to this little girl?

C: It was good in a way, but I didn´t have any of that.

T: Is this why you got upset?

Client nods.

T (modeling): You can try say to this little girl that although she was so deprived of affect, you are an adult now, and you can take care of her.

C: I don´t know, because I felt a lot of responsibility.

T: Responsibility?

C: Yes, I think so.

T: What does that mean?

C: I thought, "I am saying this, but will I really be able to do it?"

T: You are very responsible, what do you think?

C: I don´t know, I don´t have children because I wouldn´t want any child to go through what I went through, to have such a sad childhood as mine, I don´t know.

When the client has difficulties imagining herself performing an adequate caregiver role with the little girl, we help the client to connect with a caregiver role in other areas of her life and then "turn" this role toward herself. Many severely traumatized people adequately take care of other people, even when they do not take care of themselves at all.

C: I don´t know if I would be able to have a child and make him happy.

T: How do you connect with your nephews (the therapist knows that they adore her)?

C: Good, but they are my nephews, they are not with me all the time.

T: I am asking how you connect with them, how they feel when they are with you.

C: Good, yes, but they are my nephews... I don´t have them the whole day.

T: But you have yourself the whole day.

C: Yes.

T: And it is important that you learn to care for yourself, to value yourself... to give yourself what you lacked as a child. Nevertheless, now you have yourself and you are doing many things to take care of yourself.

C: Yes, it´s true, I now do many things to protect myself, I do notice that.

T: Yes, that´s why I´m saying this, because now you do things to care for yourself and protect yourself, so I do think you can communicate these things to the little girl. I think it is important to "heal" that sadness from other stages of your life that has accompanied you all your life.

T: You seem calmer now.

C: Yes.

T: Why is that?

C: I don´t know, because it calms me down to listen to what you are saying.

T: Does it make sense?

Client nods.

T: I think it´s important to work with past issues, to see that you feel many sensations that you don´t quite understand, to be able to heal and learn that you have yourself, to learn to value yourself. Is this ok with you?

Client nods.

T: Does it make sense?

C: Yes.

T: The next time we meet, you will hug this little girl.

C. Ok.

T: How are you feeling now?

C: Good.

T: Will you keep protecting yourself?

C: Yes.

T: You have realized that this is important, right?

C: Yes.

T: I am glad, really glad. I didn´t expect you to say this for now.

Client nods.

T: I was waiting for you to realize this.

C: Yes (smiles) ... We are making progress.

T: Yes, we are.

In the next session, after years of pleasing other in order to be accepted, she begins to be able to set boundaries for the first time, after the therapist had worked on this issue for years. She changed from a submissive attitude to a more secure one. This also becomes obvious in her body language, she has an upright body position.

C (explaining what she said to a person who was dependent on her): So I told her, "We will talk about my illness today." I get very anxious and very sad when you tell me your problems all the time. This might be healthy for you, but it is unhealthy for me. So we must reach an intermediate point. This should be a healthy relationship for both.

T: Very good!! Very good Lisa!!

C: I will help you as much as I can, but maintaining these boundaries. She reacted well.

T: Being clear, explaining things…

C: Yes, I also told her: "If I keep tolerating this I, will be very ill and won´t be able to help you anymore. Then I would have to get away from you, and the relationship would be over, I won´t be able to help you or anybody else, and I will be ill." And she said, "No, no, I don´t want that!" And that was all.

T: You have managed this very well and you see she reacted well. The other way would be worse for both. You are setting a good example for her.

The client can focus on well-being and positive aspects. She seems not to need so much reinforcement from the therapist as before, spontaneously explaining her achievements. She is more active and her mood is fine. The previous intervention with the self-care procedure has changed how she feels and acts. It´s as if this intervention had been a turning point, which allowed the client to use all the skills she had learned in two years of therapy. From this moment on, it was possible to work with the standard protocol on traumatic issues. She could even describe the "top ten" list of traumatic events without becoming overwhelmed like she did before.

Her previous unhealthy self-care pattern was blocking improvement and, in this case, turning self-care into a positive and healthy pattern was not complicated. As we explained in this chapter, in other cases, specific interventions to overcome dissociative phobias, integrate healthy information about attachment, develop differentiation, or regulate emotions will be needed. Sometimes several sessions are needed in order to achieve changes, and healthy self-care has to be constantly interweaved into many other interventions.

This area is always a relevant issue to work on. The effect of this single intervention in this client, who presented a severe dysfunction and extremely risky suicide attempts, is a good example of this.

**Special Circumstances**

The self-care process may be very fluid in some clients and in others it may be a long process involving many sessions that must be reinforced throughout the therapeutic process. In both situations, it is usually well tolerated, compared to working with traumatic memories, and it is associated with positive changes. But, as in any possible intervention, difficulties may arise. Two circumstances should be taken into consideration:

Sometimes structural dissociation is more pronounced than expected and working with self-care triggers the emergence of hostile dissociative parts in the form of voices, thoughts, or physical sensations that are generated in the belief that the child should not be taken care of, that attention is dangerous and malicious, or that they run the risk of unveiling an unspeakable secret. This circumstance requires additional work to negotiate with the internal system.

The second are clients with extreme difficulty connecting with their own vulnerability. Their survival has been based on "being strong." These clients may experience this process as highly disruptive and become overwhelmed during or after the session. If we assess that this is the case, we should redirect the work toward self-care resource installation. That is, we will work with recent or present situations, in which clients have been able to take care of themselves in a more appropriate way, in different areas.

The most dysfunctional examples of impaired self-care are self-harming behaviors and suicide, which are frequently present in borderline clients. These problems will need special attention and will be addressed in the next chapter.

# Chapter 9
# Self-Injuries and Suicidal Ideation

*Suicide is the final manifestation of desperation.*
De Boismont, 1856

Of all the complex situations that therapy with borderline disorders may pose, self-harm and suicidal ideation are probably those which imply the greatest relational challenge for the therapist. Clients who come to therapy searching desperately for help and at the same time are self-harming are a perfect example of a therapeutic paradox.

Suicidal ideation in major depressive disorder, even in the case of a situation of high vital risk for the client, usually generates in the therapist a less ambiguous and contradictory reaction: clients who are clearly ill need someone to make decisions for them. However, clients with BPD add various ingredients that make the situation less clear for the professional. Borderline clients with suicidal ideation are more aware of reality than people with endogenous depression and are therefore more responsible for their decisions. However, the decisions they make are often irresponsible, impulsive, erratic, or harmful for themselves or others. On the other hand, while they demand a solution, it is highly unlikely that they will accept the therapist's help easily.

Dubovsky and Weissberg (1981) report a series of reactions from doctors regarding clients expressing suicidal thoughts. These reactions are based more on the myths surrounding the suicidal person than on objective data, but therapists sometimes experience, especially with personality disorders, an interesting dissociation between their theoretical knowledge and their emotional reactions toward clients. These authors explain that professionals can sometimes ignore suicidal verbalization, believing that talking about it will encourage clients to do it. They may minimize the risk, believing that "those who talk about killing themselves never do it." As a result of the frustration that the clients' attitude generates in them, and the helplessness of trying to help someone who "does not accept help," they can get angry and try to "take the idea out of their head." Other times, they provide only educational interventions, explaining to the client what they should do, in the belief that the information is enough to neutralize this type of behavior.

Emotional reactions to the possibility that clients might commit suicide can be intense, and therapists may initiate avoidance behaviors. For example, given how uncomfortable and disturbing the situation can be, they may do everything possible to end the session as soon as possible. They may feel sad and try to contain an emotion that is considered unprofessional, or fear that clients may carry out their threats and become blocked in the office, or do more than they would do in other cases, overstepping the therapeutic boundaries.

Clients´ situation of hopelessness and despair, not seeing any meaning in life, or continuing to fight, can spread to therapists, who end up asking themselves if these people are really "lost causes" and that "in the end, the best that can happen is that they kill themselves."

Some clients may attempt to place the responsibility on us. This is a particularly important point. Therapists who tend to get too involved may end up assuming responsibility for the client´s life, which will always be a dead end for the therapeutic process.

To prevent these types of responses, which are not useful for handling the situation, there are two key elements. The first one is to have sound information about the real risks in these clients. The second one is to understand and gain perspective on our own reactions. Clients who self-injure or think about killing themselves bring up a complex situation at a relational level, and for therapists to be aware of their own emotional response is a core aspect of the intervention.

Some people confuse the terms suicide and self-harm or are able to differentiate them but confuse their clients' intentions. Many people who self-harm do not want to die. In fact, this behavior sometimes helps them tolerate their suffering better and reduce their desire to die. But it is true that clients with BPD, after repeated self-destructive behaviors without intent of death, end up committing suicide. If clients do not have the resources to manage emotions or solve problems, the chances of resorting to suicide as a solution increase. The two aspects are linked but are different.

We will talk first about suicide, because the assessment of vital risk is a priority in clients with these behaviors. In the last section, we will develop a description of self-harm and its functions.

# Suicide

Schneidman (1985) talks about what he calls the 10 commonalities of suicide. Beyond the clients´ symptoms or diagnosis, these are aspects that we have to pay attention to when assessing clients:

1. The common stimulus is intolerable psychological pain.
2. The common stressor in suicide is frustrated psychological needs.
3. The common purpose of suicide is looking for a solution.
4. The common objective of suicide is to stop thinking and feeling.
5. The common emotion in suicide is helplessness-hopelessness.
6. The common internal attitude toward suicide is ambivalence.
7. The common cognitive state in suicide is constriction/narrowing.
8. The common interpersonal act is communication of intention.
9. The common action in suicide is flight.
10. Consistency: the suicidal act is consistent with coping patterns throughout life.

According to Kelly (1961), two types of extreme approaches lead individuals to consider that death makes more sense than life. The first is when the course of events seems so obvious that it makes no sense to wait for the result. The second is when everything seems so unpredictable that the only thing one can do for certain is to leave the scene. A borderline client with dependent traits had significant problems in various jobs and lived off a minimum pension, interacting only with her partner, who was becoming increasingly exhausted and overwhelmed by her situation. When, after years in the relationship, her partner decided to leave her because he could not deal with it any longer, the client desperately tried to bring him back. Understanding that this was not possible, she committed suicide, which she had attempted many times before.

Neuringer (1964) noted that highly suicidal individuals, compared with "less suicidal" ones valued life and death in a more extreme way and had a more positive view of death than life. This author argued that suicidal individuals have difficulty using and relying on internal or imagined resources, they polarize their value system more extremely than "non suicidal" people, and are more rigid in their thinking. They are also more focused on the moment, finding it difficult to project or imagine themselves in the future. Some clients with BPD idealize death because they associated it with peace and rest.

*Fig 1: Peace*

Cases with family histories of suicide, or situations in which a suicide takes place among relatives, increase the chances of individuals, who repeatedly consider the possibility of ending their lives, of going one step further.

Linehan (1993, 2006) has analyzed the issue of suicide and self-injuries specifically for borderline clients. She suggests that suicidal behavior is a coping mechanism learned to deal with intense emotional suffering. From the dialectical behavioral approach, suicidal behavior is seen as a lack of skills; i.e., people think of suicide as the solution to their suffering because they cannot think of other effective options or alternatives. According to her, factors that may contribute to these behaviors would be: adverse events, lack of social support, external and internal invalidation, and suicidal behavior observed in others.

In our experience, suicidal ideation can also work for borderline clients as an option that paradoxically keeps them alive, because it gives them a way out ("If things get worse, I can always put an end to it"), or gives them a sense of control ("I have everything I need at home, I have pills that I know would kill me, but I won´t do it. It helps just to know that all that is within my reach, that I could use it at any time.")

A key aspect of our approach is a recognition of the close connection between suicidal ideation and dysfunctional self-care patterns. Suicide would be the opposite end of a spectrum of capacities for self-care: in the worst moments of their lives, when they feel worse, annihilation is seen as the logical consequence. In those with a pattern of healthy self-care, when things are going terribly wrong they do more for themselves, they accept all the help they can get, and they continue trying to find solutions. Most deeply depressed individuals, with an intact pattern of self-care, are able to do what they can to recover with their limited strength and dreams. Intense discomfort and suicide do not necessarily go together.

## Assessment of Suicide Risk

One of the indicators for risk assessment that has been described at length is the degree of planning. The greater the degree of planning, the higher the risk. Let us see how this is presented from lowest to highest lethality (based on Perez & Mosquera, 2006):

1. **Suicidal ideation without a specific plan or method**: These individuals express the desire to die, and have suicidal ideation, but they have not elaborated how to carry out a suicide. When asked, "How have you considered killing yourself?" the answer may be "I don´t know."

2. **Suicidal ideation with a nonspecific or undetermined method**: They express the desire to commit suicide and have thought about several options or methods, without having chosen one. When asked, "How have you thought about killing yourself?" the answer may be, for example: "It doesn´t matter, hanging myself, burning myself, or jumping in front of a train."

3. **Suicidal ideation with a specific method but not planned**: They want to die, think about killing themselves, and have selected a specific method, but have not considered when to do it, where to do it, nor what precautions or measures they must take in order to commit suicide. Example: "I know that whenever I do it, I will take pills to fall asleep and not wake up."

4. **Suicide plan**: In addition to expressing a desire to end their life, they have thought about a specific method, a particular place, and the precautions they must take to not be discovered and be able to achieve the purpose of dying.

Sometimes clients do not admit explicitly to having suicidal ideation, even when therapists explore it directly. It thoughts of suicide exist, not admitting to suicidal ideation may be associated with a greater risk than when people openly talk about their thoughts, since they do not share it and keep all the pressure inside, which makes it easier to act on. The following are attitudes, comments, and behaviors that we must keep an eye on in order to identify potential suicidality (Mosquera, 2008):

- **Contradictory attitudes**: clients' moods worsen, change is noticeable, and they are irritable or sad. They downplay suicidal ideas, but make veiled comments about it, such as "don't worry about me, I'll be okay from now on," "nothing will happen."
- After a difficult period, clients are **strangely calm**. For example, they may go from being very distressed, expressing much pain and hopelessness to appearing calm, even encouraged, for no apparent reason. This may be because by making the decision to end their life, and therefore their suffering, clients feel that "they have taken a load off their shoulders," that "all their troubles are over." A classic example is the first weeks after starting antidepressant medication, when people begin to have a little more energy, but still feel miserable. In this case, medication can give them the push to take action regarding an idea that was there, but they didn't have the strength to perform before.
- Clients make **comparisons or comments about other people who have committed suicide**: "I now understand why Mary made that decision," "next week it will be one year since my friend committed suicide, I'm sure she is no longer suffering," "as it is, with today's problems, no wonder people kill themselves."
- **Contradictions between verbal and non-verbal language**. For example, a mother came to session to thank us for the service we gave to her daughter (diagnosed with borderline personality disorder and in treatment), "I needed to thank you for everything you do for us, I know that if anything happens to me, you would take care of her." (She arrived all dressed up, looking good, her tone was seemingly quiet but she had a very, very sad look in her eyes). This mother was thinking about jumping in front of a train and was subtly asking the therapist to look after her daughter. When asked if anything was going on, she denied it. When the therapist told her he had a feeling that something was up and asked if there was something she was not telling, she began to cry and talk about her plans.
- **Accumulation of drugs or purchasing the means to carry it out**. For example, a client had stopped taking her medication and her mother found a rope in her daughter's closet. A client bought poison "just in case she needs it."

## What to do when People have Suicidal Ideation?

There are a number of steps to evaluate suicidal ideation (based on Perez & Mosquera, 2006):

**First: Explore**

Regardless of how a client manifests it, it is important to explore suicidal ideation. We need to find out if suicidal ideation is passive (not wanting to live, wanting to be dead, dying) or active (wanting to kill themselves, thinking about how, planning it). Talking about it openly does not increase the risk that people commit suicide, and not doing so eliminates the possibility of intervention. Basic questions to ask would be: How? When? Where? Why? and For what and for whom?.

*How?*

This question tries to discover the suicide method. Any method can be lethal and the risk increases if the method is available.

*When?*

Through this question we explore planning, e.g., whether clients has thought of a specific time or in a certain situation, or if they are "organizing their stuff" to say goodbye (preparing a will, leaving farewell notes, starting to give away valuable things, etc.).

*Where?*

Quite often suicides occur in places that are familiar for the person (home, school, family or friends' homes...). Places that are far away and are difficult to reach, with little chance of being discovered, or that have been previously chosen for another suicide (where a relative or friend committed suicide, or places in the area that appear in the media like a bridge or a bog) carry a high risk. This does not mean that the risk is absent in other cases. Other factors may come into play, such as clients choosing their own home and planning the event for a weekend when they know they will be alone.

*Why?*

The reasons that people may have for thinking about suicide are an important aspect. Some examples are break-up, major disappointment, or family problems. The reasons are unique to each client and although they may seem unimportant or irrelevant, what counts is the subjective experiences of each individual. It is important to take into consideration that the reasons that clients are aware of may not be the most crucial, and that current factors or old memories, whose connection they do not identify, can contribute significantly to the problem.

*For what and for whom?*

It is important to discover the relational function. Sometimes, suicide is contemplated from complete isolation and serves to end psychological distress. But on many occasions, completed suicides or serious attempts have a function in relation to the environment. There may be many reasons: expressing anger (anger toward someone else or towards oneself); asking for help (not knowing how to do so otherwise); thinking that it helps others (wanting to disappear to avoid bothering their loved ones and not make them suffer); trying to express how they feel (a maladaptive way of communication); or as revenge (punishing others due to anger or disappointment). Finding these relational reasons for suicide does not reduce mortality. When suicidal intent communicates something, this communication is often desperate and can have dramatic consequences, or it can escalate if there is no response or a hostile one from the environment and the client takes "one more step."

**Second: Assess the Possibilities of Intervention**

We are interested in the answer to the following questions: Can clients make a commitment and stay safe? Has the suicidal ideation stopped after the intervention?

**Third: Take Action if Necessary**

If clients continue to present suicidal ideation, it will be important to avoid access to the methods. It is advisable to ask clients to deliver the instruments they intended to use, to avoid availability at critical times. Another advisable procedure is not to leave them alone. This should be a one-time measure, reserved for critical situations, and we should not extend it too much or a pernicious dynamic may be created. We must develop an action plan with clients, involving people who are close and always assessing these people´s availability and actual ability to help.

**Fourth: Aspects to Explore when the Crisis Has Stopped**

Self-harm episodes may be a source of learning regarding clients´ problems and resources. To analyze the triggers in detail, as well as how they are connected, can help us identify significant memories that would be interesting to process with EMDR. If something were different about this episode, if it was delayed or the behavior was not done automatically, if there were things that were helpful, or if they were able to ask for external help and benefit from it, it will be important to identify these positive coping behaviors and strengthen them. It is also important to work on the skills that need to be developed and strengthened so that the choice of suicide is not the only or the best option that clients can see. All this may be more approachable after the most acute phase of the problem.

## Working with Suicidal Clients

Some of Shneidman´s (1987) points of clinical intervention can guide us to help lower the pressure that leads to the completion of the behavior.

**Reducing pain**, either with medication or by decreasing the sources of discomfort, may be helpful. For example, clients may continue trying to do their job and caring for a family member, while being deeply affected after the breakup of a very problematic relationship. The first step is always **to use common sense to help clients reorganize their situation**. From here, we can respond to needs or think about viable answers that, in the midst of their burden and focused on the suicidal issue, they may have on hand, but may not see.

**Proposing alternatives**, while blocking this particular solution is important. Often, borderline clients are unable to identify their real needs and the source of their discomfort, and therapists must help them utilize this information, so that communication with others is not done through symptoms and dysfunctional behaviors but in more direct and adaptive ways. They also need to look at the past and the future in a different way, remembering those times when they overcame problems and thinking of new alternatives for the future. Suicidal people see the world in extremes, A and Z, and the therapist should help them see the whole range of **intermediate** possibilities.

*Fig 2: The client feels as if she was rotten inside, like a little girl crying, but she actually is an adult. She draws a broken and black heart to illustrate her pain, after many disappointments. She sees herself as a person who gives everything but barely receives anything from others. Behind the brick wall are her loved ones, in the shape of balloons, whom she feels are drifting away from her. Below, in a separate balloon (black), is where she is, feeling more and more lonely. All that is good in life shines around her (the hearts, the field with flowers, etc.), and seems very far away and hard to reach.*

## Negotiating with Clients

It is important to find ways to work with clients to solve their problems without being under the threat of suicidal gestures at the slightest setback. This requires agreements with clients, since many of the changes that would dismantle the suicidal behavior do not occur automatically. Clients with BPD, who are usually impulsive and tend to radical solutions, have an added difficulty.

The situation of responsibility is a central issue in this negotiation. The only viable treatment option is for clients take responsibility for their lives, and for the therapist to help, but without "saving them." This could be an example:

A client came to a session accompanied by her therapist, who with the best of intentions had accepted that the client keep herself alive "for her" (the therapist). After several failed sessions, in which the client accused her therapist of "forcing her to live", her therapist decided to refer the case. During the first session with her new therapist, the client reported a terrible life story, filled with emotional, physical, and sexual abuse. In addition to presenting with a borderline personality disorder, her new therapist recognized that she had a dissociative identity disorder and multiple conversion symptoms. After 40 minutes, sobbing, she asked whether her new therapist thought she could improve.

> Client: Do you think I can improve?
>
> Therapist: I think you really want that and by staying here, by staying alive... you can lead a much more positive life than the one you are leading with a lot less suffering... that is very clear...
>
> C: You're asking a lot from me...

With this "You're asking a lot," where is the client placing the responsibility for her life?

> T: I'm not going to ask anything from you now, what I'm asking is for you to let me make an assessment.
>
> C: But I don't know if I'll be able to stay alive (client lowers her head and stops looking to the therapist).
>
> T: Look at me for a second.

The client looks up and at the therapist again.

> T: I would like for you to stay alive, of course, because I trust that your situation can improve. What is clear for me, after years of working with people who have gone through very tough situations, is that a person who stays alive can improve a lot. What is also clear for me is that a person who dies doesn't, because she is no longer around.

The client listens carefully.

> T: I can't ask you for that, I'd love for you to stay alive and continue fighting to get what you'd like, but I don't want you to feel pressured. What I can convey is my trust, in the sense that a person who remains alive and fighting... and working like you're doing, can improve a lot, okay?

Client nods.

> T: That's what I wanted to tell you... I didn't want you to feel pressured with this issue...
>
> C: Okay.

It is important that the responsibility remains with the client. This does not mean that we cannot resource to external elements to help ensure their safety, but it has to be the client who considers that these are appropriate support systems. For example, if a person who usually takes pills to the point of intoxication does not have them on hand, it reduces the possibility of an impulsive act, and for ensuring this, it would be good for a friend to assist in the administration of treatment. It is important to promote the client's autonomy, but she also needs to know how to ask for help and allow herself to be helped.

## Suicide as an Expression of a Pattern of Dysfunctional Self-Care

Sometimes, clients give themselves reasons for wanting to die, which, even if they can be influential, are not as logical as they may seem. Clients can speak with such conviction that the therapist takes those reasons as realities, but deep inside, less obvious patterns are hidden. As mentioned, a common situation is for suicidal ideation to be the most extreme manifestation of a pattern of negative self-care. For example, a client spoke about her reasons for having ended up in the ER, for the seventh time, after taking pills, "I'm lonely, I was so depressed that I saw no way out." The truth was that her depression was the result of quitting her antidepressant medication which, although it did not completely solve her problems, provided significant improvement and gave her emotional stability. When she did not feel well, she tried to "cheer up" by drinking alcohol.

Therapist: Why did you stop the medication?

Client: Because I felt fine.

T: But this had already happened before, you feel well and stop taking your meds, and after a month or two, you have a relapse.

C: Yes.

T: It doesn't seem too logical.

C: No, it doesn't.

T: But it has to make sense, people don't do things just because.

C: It's that I feel so good that I think I don't need them.

T: That could be true the first two or three times, but after many attempts and always feeling bad later, you know very well that without medication you feel worse. Also, knowing it has to do with that, you could have taken it again right away.

C: Yes...

T: And yet, you resort to alcohol, which has already caused you serious problems before.

C: Yes.

T: And you don't come to see me once you feeling bad, what you do is stop coming to appointments.

C: I know.

T: Do you realize that all of this doesn't start because you feel bad, but instead just when you're at your best?

C (thoughtful): Yes.

T: Why do you think you're doing things that make you feel worse and then making so many decisions that seem to beat you up instead of helping?

C: Perhaps it's because everyone always mistreated me.

T: Do you mean your husband? (The client had a long history of physical and emotional abuse by her ex-partner.)

C: Yes.

T: And how do you remember being taken care of when you were a kid?

C: No one took care of me, I only remember that once they bought me slippers, the only time they bought anything for me, and I had to end up lending them to my sister.

The pattern of self-care learned in childhood often creeps into adulthood. Changing patterns with EMDR requires a more directed intervention and is not achieved only by processing specific experiences. Clients must learn to look at themselves through different eyes than the way they were looked at by their primary caregivers; they must pay attention to their needs and learn to care and be cared for in a balanced way.

Each client has a specific situation, which is important to distinguish in order to assess the most appropriate intervention.

For example, a 21-year-old client was in the ICU for a serious suicide attempt, which, after taking lots of pills and alcohol, caused liver failure. Against initial forecasts, she survived.

After several previous admissions, she had months of great improvement. Unfortunately, this improvement was based on a new relationship that she had hidden from the therapist, because she imagined that he would disapprove of it. For several months, she had been seeing a psychologist, who was also a professor at the college she attended, for several months and who had begun treating her in a "disinterested" way. The client was feeling a growing appreciation and, when she felt desperate, looked for this person and asked for a hug "because it was what I really needed." He gave it to her. Shortly before the suicide attempt, the situation led to a clandestine romantic relationship. When he made a certain comment, responding to the client's demands by telling her that "she was out of her mind," she decided to end her life, leaving him a note. Although the client had previously taken pills without a clear suicidal intent, this time the number of pills was 10 times higher than usual, and the concomitant consumption of alcohol was aimed at multiplying the lethal effect.

The work with this client focused on strengthening her reasons to continue living. She had a good relationship with two brothers, for whom she cared, and she did not want to make them suffer. Her therapist reminded her of the progress she had made and the resources she had. They began working intensely with EMDR on all the memories that fueled her intolerance of loneliness. Moments when she sought solitude and autonomy were enhanced and the positive feelings associated were installed as resources. A future without a partner, living by herself, was worked on as a template for the future. Suicidal behaviors did not happen again.

In a second example, a client became intoxicated with drugs after a break-up. Her boyfriend, overwhelmed by her behavior and her ups and downs, said he wanted to leave the relationship. It was probably the healthiest relationship she had had so far. When her therapist asked her about what triggered her taking the pills, she spoke about not being able to stand being alone. After the breakup her feelings of loneliness reminded her of the distress she had felt in the early stages of treatment, when she had heard voices telling her to throw herself out the window. Now the voices are not there, but there are still vague but uncomfortable feelings that she does not feel as her own.

Working with self-care procedures and EMDR, she got in touch with a little girl inside, associated with a possible sexual abuse at age 4 that had not yet been reprocessed due to major dissociative barriers. In session, when she tried to care for that child, another part showed up, which she called "the black thing." This part interferes with the care of the child, because this child represented vulnerability, and "the black thing" wanted her to be strong. This idea was connected with the figure of her father, who always wanted her to be strong, "My father wanted me to be like a rock, and I ended up being like a shell, and inside the shell there is a withered little flower." Her mother had abused alcohol for years and had not adequately cared for her. The break-up with her partner had activated this painful vulnerability, contained in this little girl, and the suicidal behavior could be understood as the reactivation of this part associated with the paternal figure, who "solved" discomfort with punishment and beat up her vulnerable part. In working through the relationship with each one of these parts, the therapist introduced information about attachment and helped change the way she looked at every aspect of herself into one of greater understanding and care. Bilateral stimulation was used in this case in a much more selective and timely manner, only to stimulate realizations or adaptive changes in patterns of self-care.

## Self-Harm and Self-Destructive Behaviors

Self-injury is an act intended to harm oneself without the intent to die. People resort to self-injury for very different reasons. Some of the most frequent self-injuries in BPD are: cuts, burns (cigarettes, lighters, etc.), scratches, beating oneself up (headbutts, punches), biting, interfering with wound healing, etc. But, in addition to the more obvious self-injuries in BPD, people often use multiple self-destructive behaviors to try to self-regulate, such as taking pills to not think or "disconnect," alcohol or drug abuse, risky behavior, and impulsive sex (Mosquera, 2008). The latter usually involves more complexity due to the connection with attachment problems and histories of sexual abuse. There may be a mix between using promiscuous sexual behavior in order to feel loved, but at the same time living it as degrading and functioning as a way of self-punishment. Often, people end up feeling bad about these behaviors and this discomfort feeds the problem.

Although some borderline clients may stop hurting themselves without much difficulty, for most people with this diagnosis, self-injury is a self-regulation resource. A security paradox takes place: "I always slept with a package of razor blades under my pillow. This gave me safety, thinking that if things got really bad, I could use them."

> "I´ve had an internal struggle for many years. As time passed, since I wasn´t finding effective solutions, I started self-harming and this was really effective. I felt better; when I thought I could not go on, that it was not worth fighting, and that life had no meaning, I resorted to cutting. It may seem strange, but I didn´t want to die, I wanted to stop suffering, I wanted to learn to tolerate the unexpected, to live without much pain... I wanted to but I couldn´t, I didn´t know how... Self-injuries were becoming stronger and I ended up "hooked," I couldn´t stop hurting myself, any situation or anything unforeseen was enough for me to hurt myself. No one noticed until I went overboard and needed an intervention, there was blood everywhere, I thought I was going to bleed out in my room and asked for help."

The reasons why people turn to self-harm are varied (based on Mosquera, 2008):

### a) Self-harm as emotional regulator

For people without effective systems that can regulate extreme and problematic emotional reactions, self-injuries can be a substitute, short-term mechanism, pathological but effective. In fact, its effect is so immediate that it may be difficult for the person to use other systems that are effective but need a little more time. Regulation can be upward or downward.

Downward regulation: Faced with emotional pain, self-harm can stop it, as clients feel that the physical pain is much more tolerable than the psychological one. It can be a way to stop a disturbing feeling, for example, to stop remembering very traumatic experiences, or to stop a depersonalization experience.

> "In my case, self-injury has a specific goal: to feel better. Whenever I cut myself, I think that I won´t do it again, that it´s not normal... I know it´s not normal but it´s like I can´t help it. I don´t always cut myself, but I think about it almost every day. Sometimes I don´t do it, and I just do other things, but there are times when the pain is so strong, so intense, and so brutal that I can´t take it any longer. It is just at those moments when I injure myself. Just after I cut myself, I feel good, relieved."

Upward regulation: When people feel empty, flat, and numb, they can use self-injury to "feel alive" or "feel real."

"Sometimes I go into a trance... I feel like I'm going crazy, that I don't exist, that I'm not real, it's like I was dead... Sometimes I burn myself just to check if I'm still alive and I still feel something."

"I can't tolerate arguments, they affect me a lot, and I can only stop them when I start to hit myself. When I hit myself, the screaming stops. It has become automatic. Sometimes I'd like to yell, 'Shut up', but I can't..."

### b) Self-harm as communication

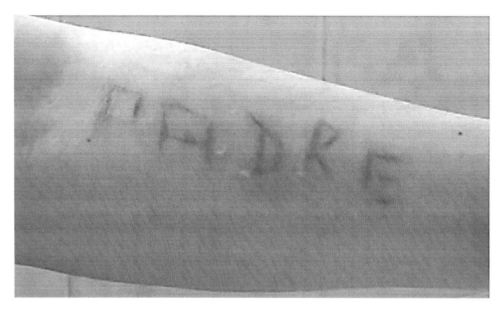

*Fig 3: "Father."*

Clients who grew up feeling that no one noticed either how they felt or their suffering may desperately need for the other to "see" or "understand." Since these behaviors often lead to rejection, frustration, and fatigue in family and friends, a pernicious dynamic can be created. Self-injuries may increase as distance or disapproval from others also increase, which enhances the others' response, without any of the participants in this vicious circle identifying the problem and being able to stop feeding it. Sometimes, when they are unable to identify or convey their discomfort, clients try to make it "visible," not only for others, but sometimes also for themselves. They may think that without these "arguments" they will not be heard nor taken seriously. Sometimes, self-harm can be a way of punishment for what situations where they saw themselves as aggressive or for a lack of interest from those around them.

"I don't know why I injure myself, some professionals have told me it's to get attention, but I don't think that's the reason. The only thing I know for sure is that after I cut myself, I feel better, calmer. Sometimes I think I do to myself what I would like to do to others, but I don't think that's the explanation either, because I wouldn't hurt anyone. I don't know, I can't answer your question."

"I spent years asking for help directly, but they only began to listen to me when I started to burn and bite my arms."

"Self-injury allowed me to keep fighting; I could take out the anger, the pain... To feel pain for a "real" reason comforted me, but it was not enough."

"It's hard to explain... I can't tell you a single reason, but I know it helps me feel better. When I hurt myself, I think, 'Now I have a real reason to suffer'... It's as if the suffering was more real, or as if I was entitled to feel it. When the pain is physical, I feel that I have the right to feel this bad and ask for help."

## c) Dissociative self-harm

Sometimes self-injuries have a dissociative basis and are associated with great internal conflict. A part of the client wants to punish her for being weak, for talking about something shameful, or for a certain behavior. People with structural dissociation often perceive the urge to self-harm as ego-dystonic, "as if it was not me." In the cases we described before, clients fully identify with the desire to cut, but in dissociative self-harm they resist it, or feel controlled by it. They can have full or partial amnesia of self-harm. For example, a client described noticing the urge to cut and feeling intense anguish because of it, and then, after a few minutes, having a very fuzzy memory of cutting herself and remembering everything clearly after she found herself in the hospital. Another client did not remember the self-harm episodes. She was just aware that they had happened when she saw the blood and looked at the cuts.

"I was hurting myself due to anguish, mental blocks, not being able to react, feeling that I was going crazy... I got very nervous. When you do these things, it seems like you're not yourself, but a completely different person. I mention this because when I self-harm I don't seem to be my "self," but a force inside that makes me do it... later you feel very guilty and very frustrated."

"Something pushes me to do it, but in this moment it's like it wasn't me... there are parts of this that I don't remember..."

## d) Self-harm as punishment

Self-inflicted injuries can be, at times, visible examples of an inverted pattern of self-care. Discomfort is unacceptable, so they punish themselves for being bad by causing themselves even more harm.

"Why do I self-harm? To get what I deserve. When I hurt myself, I think I deserve that and more. I usually self-harm when I feel guilty, when I'm angry, when I'm excited about someone and they fail me ... it can be for anything. If people fight at home, I usually cut myself because I feel very bad; I think I'm causing the arguments. They don't know what to do with me, but I can't help but think that I deserve punishment."

### e)  Other types of self-harm

Some self-injuries have more idiosyncratic and peculiar motivations. For example, clients may feel a sense of purification or cleansing: blood comes out and with it all that is bad.

## The Relational Context of Self-Harm

Hope for or past responses by the family or by the health care system (therapist, physician) can play an important role in maintaining the problem. If we explore the stories of clients who use cutting to get attention from others, it is common to find an initial idealized moment where the family, who has never seen this, mobilizes and responds with great concern. There may be demonstrations of affection (the first to seem authentic in some cases), which will remain in the client´s mind, who will then try to repeat those moments. The paradox is that, once again, those times not only are not going to happen again, but instead the family will probably start to get angry and walk away. People with BPD will intensify this "attention seeking" by getting into a situation of actual risk.

But literally interpreting the phrase "to demand attention" makes relatives - often with the advice of professionals - solve the issue by "withdrawing attention." The problem is trivialized and becomes equivalent to the response of a parent toward a child craving a lollipop before lunch. However, the issue of self-harm in borderline disorders is often framed in the midst of complex family relationships and dysfunctional attachment styles.

An example: A therapist presented the case of a 14-year-old girl, who made frequent "calls for attention," in which she hit herself against walls. According to the therapist, these behaviors were "really" only looking for the mother's attention (here "reality" is identified with the point of view of the adult - not that of the client). He explained that he has recommended to the mother that she not reinforce these behaviors and that she leave her alone when she does it. Exploring her history, we see that at the age of 9 this girl lost her father, with whom she had a good relationship, and stayed with her mother, who spent the next four years deeply depressed by the death of her husband. She recalled many times when, at the age of 9 or 10, she came home from school and had to start cooking for herself and her mother, who had not gotten out of bed. At that time, the mother did not realize what the father's death had meant for the girl and, having to deal with her mother, the girl had to bury all her pain. Now that her mother was starting to recover, the girl began to show symptoms, which she exhibited to her mother so she could not ignore them. In this case, "withdrawing attention" would be like rubbing salt in an old, deep, but still open wound.

On the other hand, it is true that reinforcing dysfunctional communication contributes to enhancing it, but often we do this without realizing it. For example, in an acute inpatient unit, we could see a client complaining, with a victimization attitude, addressing all professionals who looked at her. The staff found her tone of voice tiresome and frustrating, so inadvertently they all looked away when they ran into the client. The higher the avoidance, the greater the insistence and intrusiveness of the woman, which ended up generating frowning or people bluntly cutting her off. There came a time when the client started getting more and more annoyed and began to bang her head against the wall of her room, to the point of fracturing her skull. At that time, the entire staff fluttered around her and she had constant surveillance. In later hospitalizations, she repeated this sequence until it was identified and they attempted to strengthen healthy communication styles rather than simply censoring dysfunctional styles indirectly.

The dynamics underlying self-injury may be far from obvious. For example, self-harm behavior may be part of a pattern of victimization in which therapists can become immersed. People with a history of childhood abuse may tend to "push" therapists toward a reciprocal aggressor role, while clients take the complementary victim role. This dyad reproduces the victim-offender dyad that many of them lived through as children. Therapists must be alert to staying out of this pattern because by participating in it we do nothing but play a role in the reactivation of the clients' trauma. Gaining perspective on clients' behaviors and one's own reactions is essential in order to maintain a therapeutic function.

When self-harm is based on a lack of self-regulation skills, it is necessary to offer clients adaptive information and additional tools, in addition to working on the memories that are at the basis of such deregulation. Emotions, feelings, beliefs, and experiences of intrusive memories prior to self-harm are often connected with specific biographical events. Identifying and reprocessing these memories can bring an end to self-harming behavior. The target would not be the self-harming behavior in itself, but the circumstances surrounding the first time it happened, the origin of the negative beliefs associated with self-harm (the ones previous to it, not the ones resulting from having harmed themselves), and the memories identified through the affect bridge.

Prior work on self-care patterns, explained in previous chapters, can have a powerful influence on decreasing self-harming behaviors and suicidal ideation. In the following chapter, we will discuss emotion regulation, another area strongly related to self-harm in borderline clients.

# Chapter 10
# Emotional Regulation

An important concept when talking about emotional regulation is what Ogden & Minton (2000) have called the window of emotional tolerance. Emotions modulate our adaptation to the environment, guiding our reactions and helping us to respond to environmental circumstances. This requires not only that emotions be activated appropriately, depending on external stimulus, but also the adaptive processing of information that enables learning from experience. This processing is only effective when the intensity of activation is within the window of tolerance, which become impossible in extreme hyper and hypo activation. A useful tool to evaluate emotional regulation is the DERS scale (Gratz & Roemer, 2004), which provides a way to assess different areas of difficulties and strengths in this regard.

In humans, emotions are activated not only in direct response to internal stimuli, but also to internal triggers. Stored experiences, especially those that are not completely processed, stay in the nervous system and become part of the emotional regulation processes at different times. In EMDR, as we have explained, we look for these incompletely processed memories. Their integration into the rest of the experience is the main goal of the therapeutic intervention.

However, it is not just the accumulation of incompletely processed memories of adverse experiences that causes pathology in BPD; one's self-regulatory mechanisms are also affected. This background activation of these memories is associated with episodes of aggression, facilitated by her own alcohol abuse. In addition, she shares a biological tendency toward anxiety with her mother. She was a nervous baby and her mother was incapable of being patient with the baby's endless screams. Her mother ended up feeling desperate, losing her temper, and shouting at her to shut up. Living with the father definitely had not helped increase serenity in the client's mother. Here mother went through various depressive episodes in which she emotionally neglected her daughter and was unable to soften the effects of her father's physical abuse. It is obvious that recurrent physical abuse affects emotional regulation and, in this case, there were traumatic experiences that contributed to the development of BPD. But daily interactions are not always reported by clients when their history is explored and, in many cases, they do not identify them as traumatic, since they consider them normal or do not have a sound reference of what healthy care styles look like.

Let us see an example. One client suffered physical abuse by her alcoholic father on numerous occasions. This is associated with episodes of aggression, facilitated by her own alcohol abuse. In addition, she shares a tendency toward anxiety with her mother. She was a nervous baby and her mother was incapable of being patient with the baby's endless screams. Her mother ended up feeling desperate, losing her temper, and shouting at her to shut up. Living with the father definitely had not helped increase serenity in the client's mother. She went through various depressive episodes in which she emotionally neglected her daughter and was unable to soften the effects of her father's physical abuse. It is obvious that physical abuse affects emotional regulation and, in this case, was a traumatic event that contributed to the development of BPD. But multiple interactions with the mother, many of them preverbal, along with the absence of someone who was aware of her discomfort and could understand and regulate it, probably played a greater role in the origin of borderline traits.

We will now see possible scenarios where emotional dysregulation may be generated or promoted. These situations can be selected to be worked on with the standard EMDR protocol by introducing modifications described in the following chapters. Individuals will also need help in developing those aspects related to emotional regulation and reflective capacity that are underdeveloped, as well as acquiring skills in this regard that may help them find alternatives for managing situations that will arise.

## Understanding the sources of Emotional Dysregulation

Let us consider different problem areas, trying to outline different scenarios that may have generated or amplified emotional dysregulation. We are not trying to describe all possible links between early relational experiences and types of dysregulation in detail, but rather explain the EMDR perspective, based on an understanding of "where they learned" each problem that they present. We want to learn how to think from the adaptive information processing model.

### Lack of Emotional Recognition

When this problem is present, individuals may not perceive how they feel, may perceive it and not know how to name it or recognize what it means, or may not pay attention to what they feel. When people are upset, they may not stop to make contact with it and try to understand what happens.

In which scenarios have they learned this way of functioning? It is possible that there was insufficient attunement in attachment relationships with primary caregivers. Children learn to recognize their internal states because they have a mirror that reflects them, explains them, and responds to them (Siegel, 2010). If what this mirror shows is discordant with what the child is feeling, or there is no reflection, the inner world will not evolve toward emotional self-regulation.

*Fig 1: Can this mother regulate her baby?*

On the other hand, parents who are more focused on their own needs than on those of their children, either due to self-centeredness, a high level of discomfort, or health or life problems that take up their energy, do not offer their children enough opportunities to learn to recognize and regulate their own emotional states. It is easy for these children to develop a tendency to ignore their own needs and focus on those of others. This type of role inversion regarding care in childhood is a major source of pathology in adulthood.

Through attunement by the therapist, the therapeutic relationship can provide a new opportunity for clients to learn to pay attention, recognize, and understand their emotions. This is not just an exercise we can do in the early stages of treatment, but also something that we must strengthen throughout the therapeutic process. Whenever we work with a memory, phase 3 of the EMDR protocol is in itself a learning process in this regard.

## Understanding Personal Emotions and Needs as Important

If I can feel my emotions and know what they represent, but not value them or always consider them secondary to others' needs, I will have difficulties with emotional regulation. In times of significant distress, I may not consider myself entitled to feel this way or I may always put the needs of others before mine. For example, a client remained with her parents all the time when she visited them, ignoring the signs of overloading that were accumulating. She did not take any time for herself because she believed that her parents needed her to be there, often leading to explosions when she reached a high level of disturbance, which made her interrupt the visit prematurely and return home.

Where can this tendency come from? If parents are, as we saw earlier, focused on their own problems, they do not see the child, who ends up developing a sense of not being important. When working with these memories, we find negative self-referential beliefs (NC) of the type "I am invisible" or "I am not important." It may be because the caregivers themselves are unable to perceive their own needs (focused on material needs, not core needs), or it may be due to the role reversal we mentioned earlier, which makes the child grow up with the belief that "I am responsible for the wellbeing of others."

In the therapeutic relationship, clients can learn to take their needs into account when making decisions. We can help clients in developing this emotional regulation by encouraging clients´ participating actively in the steps we are taking in therapy, becoming aware of their sensations and starting to use them as "internal guidelines," working with self-care patterns, and through assertiveness training.

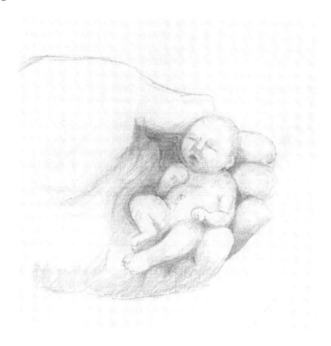

*Fig 2: The adult self relating with the inner self.*

Of special interest in borderline clients is working with interpersonal boundaries, as explained in the chapter on psychoeducation. In working with EMDR, the stop signal also requires a learning process in clients who often do not know how to say "no" to things they dislike, who give complacent responses to the therapist as they tend to do in relationships, and who have not learned to pay attention to their sensations and use them as guidelines. Any point in the session, when the clinician notices that these tendencies or difficulties arise, can be used to develop these skills. For example, when a client says "fine" to the therapist's question, "what do you notice" and the disturbance is obvious from nonverbal cues, the therapist might say the following to the client: "my sensation is that your face shows sadness, but you are saying that you are fine, you don't need to say that you are fine if you are not".

## Secondary Emotions: Feeling Bad for Feeling Bad

When I feel bad, I can multiply the degree of discomfort if, instead of trying to understand and help myself, I judge myself negatively for feeling this way. For example, I can think I am bad, weak, or inadequate for feeling this way, or that if I am feeling like this, it is my fault. If we ask clients whether, when they felt bad as children, they heard similar phrases from someone or were judged in a similar way, they often easily identify a critical or hostile primary caregiver. This attitude could have occurred toward the client or they could have witnessed how one parent humiliated, criticized, or attacked the other one. Children that grow up in this world of extremes internalize these models of *aggressor* and *victim*, and they may find themselves in the dilemma of having to decide with which to identify. The submissive response of the victimized parent can form the core identity, dissociating the aggressive response which gradually takes the form of an internal thought (or dissociative part of the personality) that endlessly "beats up" the client. Or, when they see themselves as helpless or depressed, the rejection of these memories of parental submission can generate, an extremely negative judgment based on the idea that being weak is unacceptable. "If you´re weak, you get hurt."

Working with self-care patterns and, in cases of significant internal conflict where there are more differentiated emotional parts, working with the system of dissociative parts of the personality is useful in these situations.

## Diving into Discomfort

When they feel bad, some clients think that there is nothing they can do except to let themselves become lost in that state. This may happen due to general emotional flooding or due to inability to regulate some particular emotions. This sense of emotional helplessness is common with the feelings of sadness and fatigue that characterize periods of depression and/or personal negligence into which borderline clients frequently fall. Temporary discouragement becomes a prolonged period of depression in clients who are not able to leave this state.

Often in clients´ histories, we see people with depressive profiles or a marked tendency toward negativity who amplify rather than modulate feelings of sadness. When these feelings inevitably appear, they have are no resources with which to get out of that state. All the disfunctionally stored experiences of discomfort that the child had accumulated in the sight of a chronically distressed significant person in their childhood, which no one helped them to manage, becomes reactivated now by the sight of the client´s own situation.

In the early scenarios associated with emotional and physical abuse, learned helplessness (Seligman & Maier, 1967) and the blocking of proactive responses (Levine & Frederick, 1997) of fight and flight leaves individuals with the only accessible option of abandoning themselves to that state, hoping that the passing of time will resolve it or desperately looking for an external rescuer to pull them out of it, someone who can rescue them from themselves. Therapists must be extremely careful not to assume this role, as this would take the power away from clients and undermine their possibilities of moving towards independence and regaining control of their lives (Herman, 1992). Discerning such issues is important, because, as in the previous case, while processing early memories related to a depressed caregiver may provide significant benefits, in the latter case, activation of active responses will not happen fluently and spontaneously and will need to be promoted by the therapist in order to achieve effective processing.

Clients who, when emotionally activated, "drop the reins and let go" may have also had models of major behavioral lack of control in their early history. For example, a client with BPD described how when she was about 6 years old, her mother, in the midst of a major state of agitation had attempted suicide in front of her. Although this was the most dramatic example, it was predictable that this mother, who did not contain her discomfort in front of her young daughter, would also have problems regulating herself in many other situations, of which the client was not so aware. Individuals need to learn and to remember that even if they are going down a slide, they have two hands that can slow down the descent or even stop it. If they try, they can even backtrack. Experiencing emotions like a roller coaster which the client simply rides, without access to the controls, prevents the person from managing even emotional states that are not too intense.

Another possibility is that in clients with significant problems in the development of a personal identity, as is characteristic in BPD, depression can become a substitute for a genuine identity, which they feel is unattainable. In this case, clinging to sadness is a defense that protects them from the painful contact with their inner emptiness or with what they believe to be their true self, due to which they believe they can never be recognized, valued, or loved. This situation usually has multiple facets, for example, it can be combined with a deep belief of "I do not deserve any better."

Discomfort may also function paradoxically as a safe place for people with an intense phobia towards change and normal life. No matter how unpleasant those feelings may be, everything is better than the uncertainty and panic they feel about anything new, about the circumstances of everyday life that expose them to contact with others, to bonds of intimacy, and to the failure of projects that they may start. That would be the last confirmation of their greatest fear: "When they truly know me, they'll think I'm horrible." "If I try things and don't succeed, it will confirm that I'm no good at all. I'm just as useless as my father used to say…" This clinging to the "devil we know" may explain some paradoxical decompensation following improvements, progress, or positive changes.

Some clients lose track of daily life because discomfort overrides everything. They do not complete their tasks and they cannot focus for a moment in other activities or think about other subjects. Others, at least during some of these occupations, are able to distract themselves from their negative feelings, and this works as a cushion to prevent them from completely breaking down. Although frantic activity to "not feel" may feed the problem rather than solve it, keeping a minimum of routines and activities is an important resource for borderline clients. Working with distracting activities can be useful in the stabilization phase.

## Self-Fulfilling Prophecies

Different beliefs may intensify or prolong periods of discomfort. Some have to do with experiences of helplessness or undervaluation. Others respond to negative future expectations. When these people feel bad, they are sure they are going to stay that way for a long time, which adds the anxiety about prolonged suffering that has not yet occurred to the present discomfort. As soon as they notice a disturbing feeling, these individuals predict that they will get worse and will not be able to control it. Although this is based on previous experiences of dysregulation, it leaves them without access to the more or less varied and developed resources that they do have.

Where did they learn to be pessimistic? Sometimes we can understand this from the resignation that was the only alternative in a highly traumatic environment. Childhood lasts a long time, even more from the perspective of a child. Even if a lot of time goes by, things did not only not get better, but often even became more complicated. It is not unusual for repeated experience early in life to become a prediction of what lies ahead.

Living in a dysfunctional family and expecting things to improve hurts too much, and every time the hurt is repeated, the pain is even more unbearable. For protection, individuals learn not to have expectations; they suffer less. A devastating perception of the future is a common symptom in clients with complex traumatization (Van der Kolk, et al., 2005) and it often impedes the therapeutic process. Often, clients are desperate because they do not advance, or these emotions are powerfully activated when they relapse minimally, without this feeling being related to their actual development. It is important for the therapist to be careful not to become infected with the client´s despair, which can link with feelings of ineffectiveness or undervaluation in the professional himself.

Negative anticipations can help us prepare. For example, if we have a job interview, thinking about what others could say to provoke us or sound us out, can help us think of a plan. But such strategies when carried to excess eventually stop working and, when negative anticipations increase, they block us instead of preparing us to solve situations. Thinking negatively, when the negative is recurrent, is a way to introduce predictability in a chaotic and incoherent environment. So, children who suffer repeated sexual abuse or physical abuse by a family member, and who have tried telling without being believed, end up accepting that it will happen again. They can even let it happen or look for it, because the moment after the abuse is the only moment of calmness they experience in life. People need to find patterns in the chaos, they need predictability; we are designed this way. When disorganization is omnipresent, individuals cling to anything that can give them any sense of control.

Classic work with cognitive distortions can help, as well as processing memories associated with hopelessness and working with self-care. Through a therapeutic relationship that maintains trust in clients' capabilities, even when they feel unable and without expectations, helps them to assume their responsibility in the therapeutic process in a healthy way and is the key in learning to have realistic hope.

## Relational Emotional Regulation

The borderline client tends to be dysregulated, but this is especially true in the context of interpersonal relationships. If we understand that borderline pathology originates in early attachments, we will understand that it is in interactions with others where the consequences are more obvious. This also gives us a powerful tool for intervention. Probably the most important factor in the treatment of a disorder such as BPD, characterized by high levels of dysregulation, is that the new mirror of the therapist reflects back to clients an image of calmness, firmness, consistency, and security that will help them get through the therapeutic process.

In working with EMDR, the AIP model and a clear understanding of the various origins of emotional dysregulation that we have described, can help the therapist gain perspective and not become infected with or react personally to the extreme and changing emotional reactions of the client.

Where is dysregulation learned?

*Fig 3: The client's difficulty for emotional regulation is often a reflection of the primary caregiver's inadequate regulation during childhood.*

# Neurophysiological foundations of emotional regulation

Emotional regulation is influenced by three neurophysiological areas:

1. The balance of the autonomic nervous system (ANS) and the regulation of the activation.
2. The brain mechanisms that operate in interpersonal empathy.
3. The reflective capacity or meta-consciousness. This more complex activity requires the balanced functioning of all brain structures.

Emotional regulation requires appropriate and synchronous operation of these three areas: I can regulate my emotional arousal, balance my empathic involvement, and maintain mental clarity to realize what is happening to me and why.

## 1. The ANS and Arousal Regulation

In Chapter 1, where we talked about biological factors, we saw that there may be a constitutional tendency to the activation of the ANS, presenting more anxiety reactions, and when faced with a caregiver who often shared this genetic predisposition, the trait tends to become progressively amplified rather than neutralized.

This tendency toward activation introduces a complicating factor in emotional regulation, since high levels of emotional intensity at the amygdala level is associated with low activation of prefrontal areas (Shin, et al, 2005) the activation of prefrontal areas, notably limiting regulatory capacity.

## 2. Relational Emotional Regulation

Interaction with others is an important regulatory system, which is usually affected in people with a history of early traumatization. This aspect is the one we will develop further in this chapter, as it can help us understand some of the difficulties that borderline clients often present in interpersonal relationships.

## 3. The Reflective Capacity

The tendency towards activation is just one of the areas associated with emotion regulation. We have already described in the chapter on defenses how reflective capacity, decision-making processes, and meta-consciousness are underdeveloped in clients with BPD. Activation can be increased or mitigated through various internal processes, the client may tell himself things that make him feel worse and worse, reproducing patterns learned in childhood, or he may help his own system to become rebalanced. These aspects are worked on from the procedures aimed at restoring self-care patterns, described in Chapter 8.

# Empathy, Emotional Contagion, Sympathy, Cognitive Empathy, and Regulation

These concepts have been developed by several authors, including Eisenberg (1987), Hoffman (1982), Hatfield, Cacioppo & Rapson (1993), O'Connell (1995), and Wisper (1986). We are born with the ability to participate in another's experience thanks to our mirror neurons, while at the same time we can realize that part of what we experience has to do with us. In this way we achieve a situation in which the shared emotional experience with the other does not overwhelms us through our resonance circuits.

## Mirror Neurons

The discovery of mirror neurons provided very interesting information for understanding empathy. Around 1990, a group of scientists studying the premotor area in monkeys found that when the monkey simply watched one of the researchers eating a peanut, the same neural area was activated as when the monkey ate the peanut. This only happened with circuits related to an intentional act; the monkey's brain is unresponsive if the other person's hand moves randomly. The mirror neuron system (Rizzolatti & Craighero, 2004) has come to be considered the basis for empathy in humans (Batson, 2009).

Based on this perception of the intention of the other's behavior, our human prefrontal cortex allows us to map the minds of others.

Let us see all these concepts in more detail:

## Emotional Contagion

Emotional contagion (Hatfield, Cacioppo & Rapson, 1993) is the emotional state of an observer that occurs as a direct result of perceiving the same state in someone else. It includes the expansion of any form of emotion from one individual to another (e.g., the feeling of play or fun, or discomfort or irritability in a crowd). It usually occurs with high levels of discomfort.

In true empathy, the emotional state is also shared with another, but the distinction between self and other is preserved.

Emotional contagion is self-centered: People who become overly activated are focused on their own discomfort and are no longer focused on the other person. In empathy, the focus remains on the other person and, from there, prosocial behaviors are activated.

## Sympathy

Individuals feel sorry for the other person, sensing their discomfort. It differs from empathy and emotional contagion in that there is not a shared emotional response. People are focused on another person, and this can also lead to prosocial actions to relieve their discomfort.

There is another kind of empathy called cognitive empathy (Batson, 2009; Einolf, 2012; Shamay-Tsoory, Aharon-Peretz, & Perry, 2009). In this case, people reach an understanding of the other's cognitive processes and thoughts. It necessarily implies getting perspective, standing in the other person's shoes, and being able to understand how they feel.

## Empathy and the Theory of the Mind

Empathy and theory of mind have been used as synonyms, but they represent different skills and different brain circuits.

The theory of mind (Dammann, 2003) is the ability to understand mental states such as intentions, goals, and beliefs and is based on temporal lobe and prefrontal cortex structures.

Empathy is the ability to share the feelings of others and is based on the sensorimotor cortex and the limbic and paralimbic structures (Lamm, Batson & Decety, 2007).

## Emotional Resonance

This is a broader concept that consists not only of understanding the emotion, but also the motivation of the other person. The emotional area comes into play, along with the sensorimotor and cognitive areas, in other words, all of the different structures of McLean's (1990) triune brain. This author proposed that, at an evolutionary level, three separate brains are configured, with their own subjectivity, sense of time, space, and memory.

The three brains are: the reptilian brain, the most primitive, associated with sensorimotor responses; the mammalian limbic system, associated with emotional responses; and the cortex, especially the prefrontal cortex, associated with cognitive functions. Regulation would depend not only on the limbic area, directly involved in the emotional response, but on the dynamic regulation between these three levels.

In emotional resonance (Meyer, 2008), our mirror neurons fire, our insula puts us in touch with our sensorimotor responses (people who are more in contact with their body are more empathic) and our prefrontal cortex helps us elaborate what we notice.

# Different Scenarios in Emotional Regulation

For example, if I notice that my sensorimotor responses are more activated and my mirror neurons are more attenuated, my prefrontal cortex decides that this sadness is mine, not yours. In this way, I allow my mental states to be influenced by, but not imagine they are identical to, someone else's mental states.

In emotional contagion, we feel the same or a similar emotion of another, but we cannot distinguish this from an emotion generated from our own mental processes, due to a lack of connection to the sensorimotor system. Intense emotions also act by inhibiting the prefrontal cortex, so that individuals will run on pure emotion, disconnected from the body and without cortical regulation. Clients that run "in amygdala mode" will be unable to think about what happens, make decisions, or manage their behavior. Another effect of this state is about problems connecting with others: We will be completely focused on our own responses and lose the relationship with the other person.

Another problematic possibility is the emotional activation due to the connection with implicit memories. Given an external or internal trigger, and in the absence of another's emotion with which to get infected, a traumatic memory with a significant emotional burden becomes reactivated. The presence of some level of dissociation from the memory leads to the lack of awareness that this is related to a memory, and the low prefrontal activity does not allow this reflection. If emotion is intense, prefrontal inhibition is, as we mentioned, even higher. The individual attributes this activation to what is happening in this moment. At other times, they have a sense that what is happening inside is disproportionate to what happened outside, but they "cannot help" reacting from emotion, which is what directs behavior. We are talking about the activation of an emotional part of the personality.

Disconnection from sensorimotor elements can also lead to another scenario. This activation of implicit memories occurs in the absence of a reflective capacity. The individual who usually responds in this way is used to experiencing emotional contagion in interaction with others. His emotions and those of the other probably failed to differentiate due to early bonds associated with preoccupied attachment, where the boundaries between the self and the other person never developed properly, probably because they were not established in the caregiver. According to Bateman & Fonagy (2004) this occurs at a level of psychic equivalence: What happens in the outside world has to occur within the mind, and vice versa. We feel the emotion, but the question of who is generating it, is not that simple.

Access to the sensorimotor component could provide important discriminating information and, based on this, people would notice if this emotion is theirs or not. But the connection to the sensorimotor level is not well developed or is blocked. Individuals may attribute that emotion to another or to themselves, not based on a connection with their feelings and reflective activity, but for example, depending on how familiar the emotion is or the rejection they usually feel for that kind of emotion. So familiar anxiety or sadness will be recognized as their own; but anger, charged with a much more negative connotation, may be attributed to the other person.

For example, in an argument with her partner, to which the client has contributed a great deal, she will talk about the discomfort that the words of the other person have generated in her, and how hostile and aggressive her partner got with her, without being aware of her own aggression throughout this interaction or of the discomfort that the other person could be experiencing.

These situations of emotional contagion, of lack of differentiation between my emotions and those of others, and of attributing my own emotion to the other person, are common in clients with borderline personality disorder and may lead to different situations.

For example, if clients tend to become overwhelmed in relationships, without being able to establish an appropriate differentiation from the reaction of another, they may attempt to place an empathic wall or distance themselves to avoid feeling overwhelmed by what others are feeling. They may feel so overwhelmed by their own emotions that even the minimum emotion of another will overwhelm them intolerably. Some clients become isolated as the only possible way to maintain some control over their emotional states.

Mirror neurons may not be able to establish adjusted maps because during early development there have been many inconsistent or unpredictable relational experiences ("alien" maps). Mirror neurons do not distinguish between healthy and unhealthy patterns. They only distinguish between patterns or lack of patterns. Thus, individuals will tend to give misattuned responses in interaction with others, generating situations that others cannot understand.

Given the various difficulties of understanding and managing their own activation states and of understanding the motivations and reactions of others, BPD clients, given the absence of internal references, may resort to imitation, trying to find a guide in their behavior toward others. They may function as they are told or as they see others function, generally in a rigid and stereotyped manner. Normalizing sensorimotor feedback that can tell us if what we do meets our needs and is well adapted to our situation, is not available or is not readily interpretable. Regulation from the prefrontal cortex, which can takes note of what happens and of previous experience in order to make thoughtful decisions, is not operational either. Only these behavioral clichés are left, alternating with overwhelming periods due to undetected accumulation of distress, or being abandoned since they fail to provide any internal wellbeing, without any of this being the result of conscious reflection. So when a reference is needed again, they resort once more to this copied pattern, unless they observe a new pattern they can imitate. There is no real learning or adaptive evolution if clients are unable to identify, understand, and accept their feelings, their needs, and their different emotional states.

Clients need to understand their specific problems regarding emotion regulation, and to learn new skills in order to understand and modulate their emotional states. This is a relevant aspect of psychoeducational interventions, which will be described at length in the next chapter.

# Chapter 11
# Psychoeducation

"Suddenly, the chaos begins to clear up, just like iron particles that are scattered on a surface and by the effect of a magnet become reorganized and oriented, settled and structured. This gives me peace of mind."

"I have not felt like a set of criteria selected from a manual, but like a person with 'impractical' behaviors. I have been able to identify such behaviors in myself and see it from a different angle. Now I know what is going on with me! And, with some things, I can almost understand why. I've always hated myself for this, but now that I know that this happens to many people too, it makes me feel a little less disturbed."

Psychoeducation helps clients and family members understand what is happening to them, what they can do, and what they should not do, in order to generate changes. People with borderline personality disorder need to understand what is happening to them and learn alternative responses to their destructive behaviors. For the person to be motivated to participate in therapy, having information available is one of the key elements. As they learn more about their problems, they tend to show greater motivation and adherence to treatment.

Patients with BPD can benefit from psychoeducational work, both individually and in groups with other clients, or in groups with family members. At an individual level, it helps them understand what is happening to them, the specifics of their case, and what they can do to generate changes. At a group level, a mirror effect takes place, it is easier for them to identify positive and/or negative aspects when they can see them from the outside and get feedback from others; they feel less alone with their problem and less weird. Working with their families helps them feel more included, more supported, less blamed, more loved, and also perceive more interest from their families (Mosquera, Ageitos, Bello & Pitarch, 2009).

The client will need to understand many aspects associated with BPD, like why do I have these symptoms and problems, what defenses I turn on, and how I have ended up having these problems with people. Clients will need to acquire resources to regulate themselves emotionally, so they can replace maladaptive responses. Families need to read the clients' problems in order to place themselves in a position of being able to offer productive and healthy support and to have tools for managing relational situations.

If clients are unable to do an objective interpretation of what happens to them, their "analysis" will not lead to change, but they will probably just feel overwhelmed with what they see in themselves, fueling more activation and symptoms. For example, a client describes her difficulties like this: "I'm bad, the other day I broke all of my boyfriend's books and CDs because we were fighting about the food. In that moment it's like I hate him and want to destroy what he likes the most." With psychoeducational work, she learned to see how her impulse responses are the basis of most of her difficulties and to understand which triggers activate her more. Following this work, she realized that control and invalidation by others, the point at which her activation used to skyrocket, were associated with her mother's rigid and manipulative attitude when she was a child. She could also notice that her boyfriend's attitude was often belittling, but that her own reaction to this ended up making it look like he was right and she was crazy. This helped raise the issue of interpersonal boundaries as an area to work on. Regarding the processing of specific memories, this analysis helped identify situations with the mother as dysfunctional information that fed her current reactions and, therefore, as targets for processing. In this way, the work plan starting shaping up for the next phase of therapy.

The goal of psychoeducation is to help people and their relatives understand what is happening and what they can do (or not do) to generate changes. But it is important to be careful and not turn psychoeducation into a justification for behaviors, as if they were all due to the disorder and beyond the individual's control. If clients or family excuse or tolerate any behavior, hiding behind the diagnosis, they stop taking personal responsibility for their situation, and this can be a major interference in therapy. Due to this, it will be key to emphasize the differences between person and disorder and involve the client in the active search for solutions and the development of personal autonomy (Mosquera et al., 2009).

Research has demonstrated the effectiveness of these programs in the performance of treatments by reducing relapse, raising medication compliance rates, and improving psychosocial interaction of clients and their families (Gunderson, Berkowitz, & Ruiz-Sancho, 1997; García, Junquero, Jiménez, Villegas, & Sánchez, 2009; Personality Disorders Guideline, 2011). Psychoeducation, however, must be understood as a complement to the therapeutic process. Without additional interventions, such as EMDR work on adverse and traumatic life experiences from the client's history, the person may make progress, understand what is happening, and even know how they can change it, but unresolved issues may linger in the background that continue feeding relevant problems.

As we mentioned, psychoeducational work contributes the basis for introducing other interventions. The book *Rough Diamonds II* (DB-II: Mosquera, 2004, 2013) describes a set of structured procedures, which can be applied in their entirety, or in certain problem areas, both in individual and group formats. Initially, it was developed for people diagnosed with Borderline Personality Disorder and, since then, it has been successfully applied in the treatment of other personality disorders (with variations). The program consists of 35 sessions and the contents are divided into nine sections:

1. Program introduction, goal setting
2. Possible interferences in therapy
3. Self-observation
4. Self-care, approaching self-destructive behavior, and implementing alternatives
5. Defenses
6. Boundaries and interpersonal relationships
7. Identity and differentiation
8. Emotions and emotional regulation
9. Coping techniques and maintaining improvement

## The Psychoeducational Process: Understanding Borderline Personality Disorder

The psychoeducational process is a process of personal discovery. Generated frequently in early attachment disruptions, BPD can be understood in part as emotional blindness. Parents, in many cases, had the same limitation. So, how can a blind person teach another blind person to see? The caregivers' mirror (reflecting children's emotions, giving meaning to their experiences, and putting words to them) was a mirror that was fogged up, broken, or reflected a distorted image. What primary caregivers expressed and how they interacted with the children is the origin from which individuals begin to understand both themselves and the environment, and these caregiver interactions lay the foundation for all the social experiences that come afterward. Early caregiver interactions are the original map, and the therapy process faces the challenge of rebuilding that map.

This reconstruction could fit into the metaphor of doing a puzzle. The first thing we do is spread the pieces over a wide area, put them face up, and check that they are all there and no pieces from another puzzle have slipped into this one. This reconstruction work does not start from scratch, but must try to use the maximum number of original pieces.

Borderline personality disorder, and personality disorders in general, are somewhat like disorganized, mixed up, and even in some cases incomplete puzzles. Like puzzles, the greater the number of pieces, the greater the challenge. But that is why we became therapists, right?

In many cases, the person seems "to have all the pieces of the puzzle," but the impression is that they are disorganized or "not connected." No parts of the story seem to be erased by amnesic gaps or significant fragmentation. The pieces were not put in place, perhaps because no one could read the person's emotions, feelings, and thoughts during childhood.

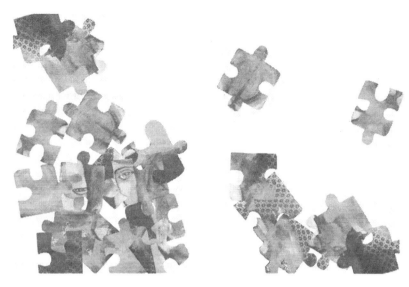

In this case, the work may be to go directly piece by piece, understanding and organizing. Like with puzzles, we look for corners and landmarks. That is, we help the client identify core-problems. To reach this goal, reviewing theoretical materials with them, providing them with information, and reflecting with them will all help them see the construction of the puzzle as something possible, interactive, and even rewarding when the pieces start falling into place. Clients identify emotions and understand their history and the process that led them to their current situation. They acquire a narrative that gives meaning to their inner experience and the story they have lived.

In other cases, when trying to put together the puzzle and starting to get an idea of the client and the current difficulties, we are left with the feeling that "parts are missing." That is, we notice that they are missing resources and skills. There are shortages and these people have great difficulty functioning effectively without harming themselves and others. Mental functions are not fully developed, the reflective capacity is scarce, and there is a lack of mentalization capacity with persistent primitive forms of thought. People may not distinguish between thought, feeling, emotion, or action. They may experience emotions as an undifferentiated amalgam, which they must learn to decipher. There may not have been an attachment figure in their history, even an accessory one, who could help generate those pieces.

In this case, psychoeducational work is based not only on knowledge, but on learning about and acquiring resources. The person will need tools for emotional regulation and social skills. The work of helping the client gain perspective and to think about what is happening, will be an essential part of the therapeutic work.

This is a more thorough job, probably slower and more progressive. It is not just sorting, but rebuilding. Clients learn to connect what happens inside, the way they think, feel, and react, with what is happening outside and in the inner world of others. The pieces of the puzzle are being prepared and also restored. It is important to be able to review everything that clients bring, regardless of how dysfunctionally they are operating initially. The aim of the psychoeducational process is not just to offer information or education, but to help clients make the most of themselves, to learn to be their "best self." In order to do this, it is crucial for them to be able to see their potential, the seed of resources that live inside.

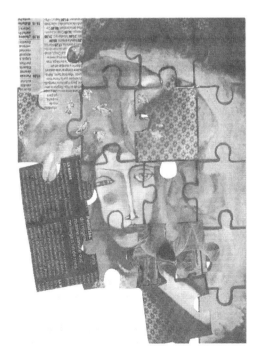

Sometimes, puzzles are mixed up and pieces from other puzzles have slipped in. These pieces are confusing and sometimes we force them to fit into the wrong place. Many borderline clients come from enmeshed families, where emotions and opinions are necessarily felt as shared, and where personal autonomy and differentiation of self is not encouraged. These clients internalize many aspects of their caregivers with preoccupied, intrusive, or controlling profiles. For example, they may live with constant internal criticism, criticism that was the soundtrack of their childhood. They may also reproduce functional patterns they absorbed from the family environment, and even if they recognize that they work in this way, somehow they feel those patterns as alien or reject them, "How can I be like this?" Often, they cannot distinguish between their own concern and another's or do not know whether

their opinions are their own or someone else´s. These extraneous pieces are from a past that remains present and continues to interfere, or they are from other current meaningful relationships, which function in a similar way.

Along these lines, sometimes the lack of a defined or acceptable identity leads them to reproduce the models of those around them, adopting styles that are not their own, sometimes changing, with the hope that they may be more acceptable for others or that this can protect them from being damaged.

In this case, the first task to address will be separating and differentiating what belongs to the self and what to another, selecting the pieces that represent their true identity, and distinguishing them from internalized or defensive reactions.

Getting to work on a puzzle without knowing whether or not the parts belong here, can lead to a dead end.

Sometimes identity, though dysfunctional, is rigidly structured. Clients´ ability to evolve in a positive way will be limited by their psychological flexibility and their ability to move in the direction of improvement. As in the more dissociative BPDs, often what we find here are parts stored in different compartments. If we realize that this is happening, putting all the pieces on the table, identifying them as part of the client, differentiating the ones that belong in other puzzles, and repositioning the whole, sometimes (only sometimes) achieves effects quickly in very disorganized clients.

When there is less fragmentation, the internal psychological structure can become well consolidated and, sometimes, it solidifies and becomes extraordinarily rigid. In such cases, it will be necessary to completely dismantle each of the pieces in order to do a really functional reconstruction.

This can be seen metaphorically as similar to when a closet is overly full, with items stuffed tightly on the shelves, and when we open the doors everything falls on us like an avalanche. The problem of therapy is how to put the entire content on the bed, select, repair, wash and place it back inside in a logical order, while the owners of the closet are determined to keep their old "order," although they have come to us for help to solve their problems. In this case, psychoeducational work should be dedicated, during the time needed, to work on clients´ defenses, to help them understand why we are interested in sorting thoroughly and what the benefit of such an expensive and long process would be (see Mosquera 2013b, for more information about the work with psychoeducation).

Even after extensive work focused on the therapeutic relationship and psychoeducation about therapy and defenses, the relocation process must be done slowly and carefully, as some parts can break easily if we are too rough in trying to break them apart.

When we finish a puzzle of over 1000 pieces, after going through all the stages of excitement, frustration, fatigue, commitment to finishing it, and starting to see the light, eventually the true image of the person we have in front of us appears. There is still work to do, but this will be a very different stage.

The processing of memories with EMDR would not only come into play after finishing this entire stage. Even with limitations and difficulties, it can be introduced early in the therapeutic process. It will help us pull parts out of the remote or recent past, reduce the influence of current situations, and dismantle defenses. It will also help develop resources (new pieces) and link them so that they will shape a coherent and consistent self-image. Many borderline clients, as discussed in Chapter 13, may tolerate the EMDR processing of early memories well, as long as the therapist introduces the necessary interventions and the procedures are modified to suit the needs and limitations of each specific client.

Psychoeducation should have a relevant place in psychotherapy with borderline clients. In order for them to participate in their healing process, they need to understand their real problems, which sometimes are very different from those presented to the therapist at the beginning of therapy. One of the significant issues to address is related to core dysfunctional beliefs, which will be discussed in next chapter.

# Chapter 12
# Core Beliefs

Positive and negative beliefs about the self are one of the elements explored in relation to working with memories in EMDR. In the AIP model, it is understood that a memory is not only associated with a disturbing sensation, but it is also dysfunctionally stored in the nervous system and it leaves a mark on the image that individuals have of themselves, affecting their view of the self.

The concept of self is severely damaged in people with BPD; it is generally underdeveloped, fragmented, or distorted. In the assessment of the target (EMDR Phase 3), when searching for a negative and positive belief, therapists often encounter particularly entrenched negative beliefs, great difficulty finding a realistic positive belief, and defensive beliefs. The view of the world and others will also be conditioned by the disorder and the biographical history that generates it, influencing clients´ attitude toward the therapist, the therapy, and their chances of recovery.

It is interesting that a disorder such as BPD, characterized by a diffuse, fragile, or fragmented identity, presents extremely rigid and entrenched self-referential negative beliefs at the same time. Some explanations are obvious. Many negative experiences in the history of clients with BPD have to do with early attachment experiences and the influence of these experiences is different from simple trauma. A time-limited event has an impact on the self, but an entire childhood growing up in a family, models and configures the self. Attachment-related experiences are not just an event, they are a set of countless repetitions of situations that take place every day, all the time. The effect of repetition, the fact that childhood and adolescence are sensitive times in psychological development, and the strong influence of primary attachment figures explain the intensity and immobility of many beliefs in BPD clients. However, there are probably more factors involved, which, along with the elements that we need to take into account in order to identify beliefs in BPD, will be described in this chapter.

## Beliefs and Schemas

Some authors, who have studied personality disorders in depth, can help us understand these aspects. Young (2003) talks about early maladaptive schemas as stable and durable themes or inferences that are generated in early childhood and are dysfunctional, determining subsequent experiences. Schemas can be inactive for a long time and at some point become activated immediately due to a specific environmental stimulus.

The main feature of early maladaptive schemas is that they are absolute beliefs about oneself in relation to the environment. They become activated with significant environmental events for each particular schema and are more closely linked to intense emotions and feelings. They seem to be the result of dysfunctional experiences with parents, siblings, and relatives in the early years of life, what we might call everyday harmful experiences, rather than being caused by defined and isolated traumatic events.

Elliot & Lassen (1997) have expanded the concept of schemas to propose a model of polarity, in which each schema would have a positive and a negative pole. According to the authors, some individuals can move in a flexible manner along the continuum between these two poles, depending on situational demands. However, others have less flexibility to change their schemas. The experiences of anxious-ambivalent (preoccupied) attachment would be associated with inflexible negative schemas. Dismissive-avoidant attachment experiences would be associated with inflexible positive schemas. Secure attachment would be characterized by flexibility (Mikulincer, 1995).

## Core Beliefs and the Family's Mental Influence

Why do these beliefs become rigid and inflexible? What processes lead to the rooting of these ideas about oneself? Why is there such an extreme adherence to these ideas that are harmful for the self?

Many factors may be involved. As we pointed out in previous chapters, some authors, such as Kernberg (1967) speak of a "lack of" development of certain mental functions, which would remain in a more primitive state. As this takes place in early stages of child development, clients will not be able to integrate the good and bad aspects of others and of the self, leading to polarized beliefs. The lack of mentalization that Bateman & Fonagy (2004) talk about may explain the absolute and simplistic nature of many beliefs, which do not reflect the nuances of human complexity and only admit the extremes of the polarity "I'm bad" – "I'm good."

However, families may also have an active role in the genesis and maintenance of these core beliefs. On one hand, many beliefs are transmitted from generation to generation as part of a more or less explicit family legacy. In other cases, clients' beliefs are direct reflections of sentences heard in the family environment, aimed at controlling them and doing away with their resistance (as in cases of abuse) or limiting their autonomy (as in enmeshed families with preoccupied attachment styles). We could also consider the existence of projective beliefs, marked by elements that parents placed on their children based on their own personal pathologies.

## Intergenerational Transmission of Beliefs

In many families, ideas about the world and human beings are unquestionable truths and they are transmitted across generations. Some families, the healthier ones, are governed by clear rules, which are also flexible and adaptable to change, allowing bonds to be established between their members while allowing personal autonomy. Other families, described as enmeshed (Minuchin,

1974), do not promote, and may even punish, autonomy of their members, establishing rigid and unshakeable rules. In families defined as chaotic, rules can be contradictory or changing. On the contrary, family systems may be based on weak affective bonding and superficial rules, the first and last scenarios being the least likely in the development of borderline pathology, where we will find especially enmeshed and chaotic families of origin.

In enmeshed and chaotic families, family beliefs will probably be more intense and more unquestionable. The enmeshed family would say, for example, "We must always think of others," creating the belief that the individuals' own needs are not important. In the chaotic family, a possible belief would be, "We must put up with it," in situations that other families would understand as intolerable, generating the belief that "I cannot protect myself."

But aside from these patterns we can often see how the effects of trauma are transmitted to several generations. For example, a client's great-grandfather was in the war and spent many years in jail, in situations of isolation and severe deprivation. When he got out of jail, he was never the same again. The client's great-grandmother, his wife, had to raise her many children during those tough times. She could not cope with the fact that, after the war ended and in the midst of the post-war economic hardship, her husband, deeply affected by his experience in prison, lived the remaining years of his life wrapped up in himself, in an awful mood, and abusing alcohol. Her beliefs about the world were that "living was a penance" and that "she was miserable" and we were "doomed to suffer." This pessimistic view of the world flooded her relationships with her children, who did not receive much affection from an overwhelmed mother and an absent father, which fed the negative and depressive mood of later generations. The personality of the client's father was marked by this story, and it all linked up with the client's intense hopelessness in therapy. She did not see that anything could change and felt "doomed by fate to suffer in this life, without being able to do anything about it." This example shows how we often have to expand the focus to include the family history, in order to understand what is happening with clients. For this understanding, it is also very useful to acquire this perspective on the origins of their beliefs, which helps to play them down.

## The Family's Mental Influence

Often, core beliefs are generated by harmful sentences said in the attachment relationship (Van der Hart et al., 2010). For example, a mother who tells her daughter things like "You're useless," "No one will love you," "You do everything wrong," "You'll never amount to anything," or "Everything is your fault," will generate deeply entrenched negative beliefs. These statements can come from parents who are not necessarily hostile or abusive, but who, even though they are concerned for their children, are affected by serious personal problems. For example, a limited and prolonged illness, depressive disorders, addictions, or any other significant psychiatric disorder, can lead a parent to be more self-centered, to be more irritable and moody, and to react to parental challenges without the necessary serenity and patience. But let us not think only of such extreme examples. When in states of fatigue, stress, or discomfort, parents who are quite functional, loving, and interested in their children may say things to them without being very aware of what they are saying or later claim that they "do not truly believe what they said." It is not uncommon to hear a father say to his son "you are stupid," "let´s see if you can do something right," "you´re bad," or "you´re lazy." If these sentences, regardless of the intent with which they are said, are repeated often in situations of high emotional intensity and with great forcefulness, their influence on the development of the self-concept can be profound.

Insights from studies on mind control and indoctrination can help us understand some aspects of mental influence on the family environment. While studies on mind control, brainwashing, and indoctrination are based on intentional control of individuals or communities by organized groups, they could explain how individuals or groups can exert an extraordinary influence on personal beliefs about the self and the world, and which factors enhance this influence. Most families do not set out intentionally planning mind control of their members; these patterns do not generally work at a conscious level. But all groups establish relationships of power and control between individuals belonging to them and, in the family, the power hierarchy is an essential part of a healthy family structure. There is a parental subsystem that has to control and have power over the children, so that their growth process takes place in a healthy way (Minuchin, 1974). Problems occur when, in some family systems, power becomes the central axis of the interaction. Authoritarianism, dominance, and extreme control exist within families more than we like to believe, and these are areas that foster the development of various pathologies in its members. There are also more subtle forms of domination and control.

Two situations are associated with a relationship of significant power and control by the family toward the younger members: enmeshed families and chaotic families. No one is easier to control than a child, vulnerable and dependent. In enmeshed families (preoccupied attachment), control is exercised to "keep the family together" and usually manifests itself more through indirect or manipulative communication. In chaotic families (disorganized attachment), power is exercised as an end in itself, intended to feed the need for absolute domination of others by any of its members. For example, a family in which there is emotional and physical abuse by a father who exercises a despotic authority in the family.

Consider an enmeshed family and preoccupied attachment. A very anxious mother is, in turn, the daughter of a woman who lived her whole life talking about how much she suffered, which made both her husband and her children revolve around her needs. The mother of the client became an insecure woman, whose mother never allowed her to follow her own desires. When she had children, her insecurity led her to try to be "the best mother" and "not let anything happen to her little girl." When her daughter made mistakes in any small chore, she took charge: "Get out of the way, baby, let me help you" (doing it for her instead of teaching her how to do it). When the girl tried to do anything outside of the family, the mother pointed out all the problems she might encounter and not be able to cope with. Conflicting messages were frequent, especially when the client had a different opinion than the mother about what she experienced as an offense from another family member: "Do whatever you want" (with an expression of disagreement on her face), "you don´t care about anyone but yourself," "you disappoint me so much, you´re so insensitive, just like your father." The client´s mother, with significant general anxiety, at times entered states of intense anxiety, in which "she said nonsense." In those states, which occurred quite frequently, she blamed everyone for her discomfort, and the daughter received comments like "You're so bad," "being like this, you'll never amount to anything," "You don't have feelings, look at how you treat your own mother." When the daughter spoke to her about those words, she diminished their importance, "They are things you say when you are angry. You can't take things like that literally." Much of the hostility that the client's mother had never been able to express toward her own mother was probably connected with the contents of these sentences.

Confusion and mixed messages define many interactions characteristic of preoccupied attachment. The content of the message may vary completely depending on the emotional intention of the communication. Someone can say, "I want the best for you," and a few moments later in the same conversation, "You only think about yourself," and later, "You always do whatever you want," and a bit later, "Do as you please. I don't want to influence you." Bateson (1972) defined the influence of the double bind, understood as a discrepancy between the explicit and the indirect message. Specialists in hypnosis intentionally use confusion to enhance suggestibility (Erickson & Rossi, 1975). In these families, message confusion is part of the communicative style and not a deliberate nor conscious strategy. However, the effect of growing up in such confusion may be relevant and could play a role in how the beliefs transmitted in that context imprint on the individual.

Taylor (2004) explains, in relation to thought control, that susceptibility to the influence of the ideas of others is higher in certain states of the brain. According to her, lack of stimulation and new experiences, lack of sleep, dogmatism, stress, the "emotional roller coaster," and various factors affecting prefrontal function facilitate simplistic and black-and-white thinking, suppression of reflective functions, fostering of intense beliefs, and the creation of pathological bonds to defend these beliefs.

If we move towards chaotic families and the environments in which emotional, physical, or sexual abuse takes place, control and power over children become core elements. The goal is not to keep the enmeshed family structure and prevent autonomy, as we described in previous paragraphs. Instead, power and control over another will be goals in themselves, generally for one of the family members. When one parent is authoritarian or dominant, the other tends to show a submissive response, and generally their ability to bond with the children is also limited. The person who exercises this despotic authority sometimes uses words to destroy the will of the other and sometimes, in the most serious cases, to destroy them as a person. Although these scenarios are more characteristic of dissociative disorders, they are present in a number of clients with BPD.

Pavlov (in Frolov, 1938) spoke of what he called transmarginal inhibition, which is the body's response to an overwhelming stimulus. Depending on his temperament, any individual enters more or less easily into a state of brain inhibition and fear paralysis as a way to protect himself when pressed beyond his resistance and when he can find no other possible response to avoid psychological damage due to extreme fatigue and stress. Pavlov gave the name of "extreme response" to what happened when the nervous system was forced beyond the limits of normal response. This produced a "rupture in the higher nervous activity."

The way to generate stress at an experimental level was to increase the painful or aversive signal, force long waits, use positive and negative signals that take place consecutively, and destabilize the physical condition. Let us think of the escalating violence between parents, of a boy waiting anxiously "once again to be the target of random verbal abuse", of the mixed messages a little girl receives when she hears, "You're my favorite" as she is abused, and of the effect of direct physical abuse. These contexts of overwhelming stress are present in many clients' childhood, including in a subgroup of borderline clients.

Behaviors following this collapse could become fixed elements of people's personality, long after the experience. When these experiences occur throughout the stages of childhood and adolescence, the permanence of these fixed patterns will logically be higher. Pavlov speaks of three phases in transmarginal inhibition. In the first or equivalent phase, as in states of extreme fatigue, there is a similar reaction to important or trivial experiences, along the lines of "I'm so tired that I don't care about anything." In the second or paradoxical phase, strong stimuli may produce fewer responses than weak ones. In the third phase, positive and negative responses are reversed.

Pavlov associated the response in animals to a condition similar to hysteria in humans. When the person is in an abnormal condition of fear, anger, or elation, and if such a state is maintained or intensified, the result is hysteria. In that state, a human being is abnormally suggestible and influences in the environment can cause a number of behavioral patterns to be replaced by others without a need for persuasive indoctrination. In states of fear or nervousness, human beings accept the broadest and most improbable suggestions. Pavlov's ideas were used by various entities for purposes of mental control, indoctrination, and torture. By debilitating the mental condition, suggestibility increased, and the person would assume any idea that was conveyed under those conditions.

Paradoxical and reverse responses to events are common in severely traumatized individuals and remind us of the paradoxical and reversed responses that borderline clients sometimes show toward positive and negative beliefs. The positive belief, as discussed later, requires additional work, since it frequently generates disturbance in itself. Regarding the negative belief, individuals sometimes seem to insist on defending a negative view of themselves.

Consider the most extreme example, associated with sexual abuse in childhood, perhaps the situation that may generate more confusion in a child. Abuse may not be mostly violent, instead it is often adorned with phrases such as the following: "I'm doing you a favor, this will help you be strong," "I do this because I love you, because you are special. You are the chosen one," "Others will do the same to you. It's better that you do it with me, I'll more careful," "You deserve it because you're bad," "You are making me do this to you, "If you behaved, I wouldn't have to do it." These are some examples of the messages that abusers transmit to their victims. All conditions for mind control are present. The abuser figure has a particular relevance for the person being abused, because it is usually a family member, a teacher, or someone important to the person.

Anna Salter (2003) conducted research with sex offenders in prison. During this study, she identified a number of cognitive distortions that operate in parallel in victim and abuser. Salter explains how some cognitive distortions are "shared." Abusers say it is the victims' fault, that they deserved it or that they were provoking him, and victims assumes it is their fault, that they deserved it, or maybe they had provoked him. If we look at these shared beliefs, there are a number of parallel aspects: a) the responsibility is placed on the victim, b) the abuser's responsibility is minimized, c) the abuse is justified, and d) they look for evidence confirming that the victim "wanted it to happen."

a)  Abusers place responsibility on the victim saying things like, "It was her responsibility to stop it, but if she said nothing it is because basically she wanted it to happen" and the victim tends to think, "I should've done something. Maybe deep inside I wanted it to happen because I never said 'no' or asked for help." This will not be prevalent in an isolated abuse, but it will be in prolonged abuse, where the abuser does an excellent job at "brainwashing" the victim, repeating these beliefs that she ultimately internalizes them.

b)  Minimization is transmitted with phrases like, "It was no big deal, just a little touching," "it happened a long time ago. It should not affect her anymore."

c)  Justification is expressed with repeated messages: "I had a problem. I drank a lot and couldn't control myself." The child and future adult repeat these messages in therapy: "My father loved me. He only did these things to me when he drank. He had an alcohol problem."

d)  The search for evidence that they wanted the abuse to happen or that they liked it is done by the most basic means: making the body respond through stimulation and then saying things like, "See how you like it?" which the adult victim will internalize as "I don't know if it really was abuse because I partly liked it."

Abusers repeat these messages at times in which clients are exposed to great confusion and are unable to use their ability to think, and victims internalize them without any filtering. Over time, they will be so internalized that victims have no doubts about it. In some cases, abuse starts so young that people are unaware that the behavior is abnormal, perhaps until something from outside makes them see it.

Since abusers externalize all responsibility and express themselves in ways that allow no rebuttal, children have no other choice but to assume what they are internalizing is something that is not questionable. Reoffending abusers know how to choose vulnerable people, especially when they are in positions of power with access to children (teachers, priests, coaches, etc..). Over time, they develop a sense of invulnerability against any possible consequences, while victims drown in pessimism and hopelessness. The abusers' narcissism, which gives priority to their own needs and ignores the needs of others, finds its perfect complementary role in victims' learned helplessness, in those who develop beliefs such as "I'm not important" or "I don't deserve anything good."

Although the above schemas are closely related to sexual abuse, it is easy to imagine that other repeated messages like "you´re useless" or "you´re good for nothing" in hypercritical environments, with verbal or physical abuse, may become internalized in a similar manner.

These scenarios are tremendously complex, and there are many factors that can contribute to the development of absolute, rigid, and inflexible beliefs about the self. Sometimes, for clients without a defined identity who are terrified at looking inward, these undervaluing claims are the only identity that saves them from vertigo and the internal void they experience. The only eyes with which they can see themselves are the ones their primary caregivers used to look at them, and there is often a great discrepancy between how they judge others and how they see themselves. Another factor that can be an influence is that devaluing the self is also a way to preserve the idealized image of the abuser (Knipe, 2009); children prefer to think "I´m bad" to not having any figure (though idealized) with whom to attach.

## Projected Beliefs

In some cases, the beliefs that are generated in children by their parents are part of a projection mechanism. Most adults do not try to control children´s autonomy or destroy them in order to dominate them, though these elements may be present. What is crucial in these cases is to keep the defensive image that adults have about themselves, a structured and rigid image. These adults want their children to be like mirrors that surround them and that continue to reflect back the constructed image to which they cling.

For example, a rigid parent with an obsessive profile will not admit any discrepancy or tolerate failures. The client will not associate her sense of "I can´t trust my judgment" with the figure of her father, but eventually she may realize, "He always needed to be right. He considered himself infallible." Narcissistic parents are likely to generate in children beliefs such as "I´m inferior," "I´m not good enough," or "I´m not worthy." In another example, a client had a constant belief of "I´m not enough," which he initially did not associate with his mother. She was always admired by all, acing everything she did. This woman, focused on her own achievements, seemed unaware of what was happening to her son, including the harassment he suffered for years at school. Her blindness to his suffering was part her need to keep the (defensive) image that she had of herself, "Only I know how to do things," "I´m perfect," "I´m well above others."

Another possibility is that parents, understanding children as projections of themselves, turn them into objects to obtain the admiration of others through their children´s achievements or extraordinary behavior. These kids are pushed by the more or less explicit requirement to fit the pattern that their parents need. Although this has more to do with the origins of narcissistic personality than with BPD, in some cases, borderline symptoms originate when people "break away" after trying for years to be the son or daughter their parents wanted them to be. These clients, as adults, will have deeply rooted beliefs of "I have to be perfect," which will alternate with "I´m not good enough."

## Common Beliefs in People with BPD

Having explored the possible origins of such beliefs in those with BPD, we will now describe the beliefs we observe most frequently in our clinic (Mosquera, 2004a):

- Thoughts of being **unwanted or defective**: "Nobody would love me if they really knew me," "No one could love someone like me," "If they truly get to know me, they will realize how terrible I am."

- Thoughts of **worthlessness** or "not being capable": "I don´t know how to do anything right," "I´m a complete disaster."

- Thoughts of **dependency**: "I can´t fend for myself, I need someone to lean on," "If you don´t accompany me, I´m sure I´ll do it wrong."

- Thoughts of being **ignored, abandoned, or forgotten**: "I´ll be alone, no one will be there for me," "If I stop cutting myself, I´m afraid they´ll forget me," "Who could remember to call someone like me?"

- Thoughts of **losing control**: "I can´t control myself," "I got carried away, it´s something beyond my control," "If I´m wrong, I´ll screw it up completely."

- **Lack of confidence in oneself** and/or one´s own decisions: "If I don´t do what others want, they´ll leave me or attack me," "If I say what I really think, they´ll think I´m stupid."

- **Distrust or suspicion in relation to other people**: "People will hurt me, attack me, or take advantage of me," "I´m sure he is good to me because he wants something from me," "I must protect myself from others."

- **Terror of being overwhelmed, deceived, or betrayed by their emotions**: "I must control my emotions or something terrible will happen," "I can´t show him how glad I was to see him again or he won´t come back," "If he knows what I really feel, he´ll think I´m crazy."

- **Self-punishment or self-sabotage**: "I´m a bad person, I deserve to be punished," "If I´m so unhappy, it´s because I deserve it," "I can just find one explanation for this discomfort I feel: I provoked it, therefore I deserve to suffer."

- **Ignoring their own needs**: "I´m not important. Who I am depends on others. I´m invisible. "

- **Extreme guilt**: "I´m responsible for everything that happens. I´m responsible for how others feel."

Some of these beliefs reflect a tendency toward dependency and a difficulty in differentiating themselves from others. Others are associated with difficulties in emotional regulation and self-care. And some are beliefs that are fed by experiences of interpersonal harm. Borderline clients need previous work in all of the areas described in the different chapters of this book as a way of preparing themselves before being able to consider and install an alternative positive belief.

## Problems with the Positive and Negative Beliefs in Phases 3 through 7 of the EMDR Protocol

As discussed in this chapter, one of the biggest difficulties is how deeply rooted many of their negative beliefs are in these clients. When asked to rate their preferred positive belief, these clients often give a VOC of "0" reflecting that they are far from believing the positive belief. Clients who see the world as follows (see picture) will have a hard time thinking "I deserve to be happy," even if that is the positive belief that fits the memory they are working on.

*Fig 1: The big eye in the sky on the left is saying, "You're useless." The one on the right is laughing.*

Often, the first modification of the standard EMDR PTSD protocol we must offer in reprocessing memories in clients with BPD is to search for a positive belief that, while still in alignment with the negative and a preferred positive belief, is a more modest, but possible, version of the positive belief. For example, introducing the PC with an "I can learn to..." facilitates change and the complete processing of each memory. Global change of beliefs generally requires full therapeutic work.

Aside from this aspect, in phase 3 of the standard EMDR protocol, we find some peculiarities when identifying negative and positive beliefs. Here are some considerations to keep in mind regarding beliefs in processing memories with EMDR in borderline clients.

## Negative Belief

Often, clients with BPD hold many negative beliefs about the self and the world. A frequent problem that occurs in the assessment of the target (Phase 3) is that, when asking clients for one negative belief about themselves, instead cascading multiple core beliefs that are lived with high emotional intensity become triggered. Helping clients to identify which one of these many beliefs is most related to the specific memory is essential for the reprocessing to be effective.

*Fig 2: Inside the head, "chaos." Thoughts are: "I´ve failed," "I made a mistake once again," "What should I do to fix my head?" and "I´ve messed up."*

Another relevant point is preventing clients from "drowning" in the negative cognition, since multiple memories open up and different beliefs become activated. With individuals who are emotionally overwhelmed, we must find a balance between helping them think, identifying a truly important belief for that memory, and facilitating the process so phase 3 does not take up the entire session and reinforce their feelings of inadequacy (see Chapter 13).

## Positive Belief

There may be several paradoxical situations in borderline clients regarding positive beliefs. For clients who have had few if any moments of shared enjoyment with or receiving praise from their caregivers, positive self-appraisals are so foreign to them that they cause discomfort. Sometimes an identified positive belief triggers a high level of disturbance when they connect with many memories that made it impossible to hold such a positive belief. Positive beliefs that clients verbalize spontaneously may be contrived products, a feature of the idealization that is so characteristic of BPD. Sometimes positive beliefs are defensive and respond to the "creation of false identities" that BPD clients often use as a substitute mechanism for missing or unavailable adaptive resources. Finally, the polarity NC-PC is too extreme, and dichotomous thinking, characteristic of borderline pathology, is obvious, but at the same time it prevents an adaptive resolution during processing.

## Lack of Positive Affect Tolerance

Sometimes the positive belief is a problem in itself. Leeds (2006) discusses the lack of positive affect tolerance as a result of emotional neglect and lack of shared positive moments with the caregiver. People experience discomfort when others say good things about them and sometimes neutralize these comments; that is, the adaptive information cannot even enter. In these cases, we can work with Leeds´s protocol for learning to tolerate and internalize the positive praise and recognition that others offer.

## When the Positive is Negative

The positive belief can generate a powerful paradoxical reaction, perhaps related to the paradoxical reactions associated with extreme stress mentioned above. For example, just the possibility of thinking "I´m worthy" triggered intense distress in a client. All the memories where she felt invalidated came to her when she thought about it. Thinking "I deserve to be well" gave her such a painful hope that she found it intolerable. There was not a model for this validation, and only when she imagined that sentence being said by another person was she able to keep it in mind. In these cases, it may be useful to reprocess the negative affect that the positive belief in itself generates. We can do this by using the positive belief as a target, enabling this adaptive network to be accessible later when the client is ready to reprocess the memory.

## Defensive PC

A client, who had a hard time throughout his school years, may have managed to complete his studies by frequently thinking "I´m strong", but this defensive belief will not help the client to resolve the aftermath of all situations of humiliation that he lived through where the NC is "I am unworthy". In this case we will need to guide this client to accept a more relevant PC such as "I am ok as I am." Another client tells herself "I´m worthy" as an artificial form of self-affirmation. This is the belief from which she begins numerous relationships in which she functions in a despotic way with her partners, whom she subsequently dumps over any little problem. When it comes to working on a memory with her, a genuine "I´m worthy" can be confused with the defensive "I´m worthy." Instead, we may select "It doesn´t affect me anymore" which can serve a similar function like the belief "I´m over it" that many clients may find helpful, when reprocessing highly traumatic experiences. We must not take a PC as valid and appropriate for reprocessing just because it appears on the list of beliefs. Instead we must consider the relationship between proposed PCs and the client's defensive beliefs.

## Positive vs. Idealized

Another problem with the selection of a positive belief is that it could be an idealized positive belief. When we ask clients with BPD what they would like to think about themselves now, we may find silence and a perplexed facial expression, along with idealized and unrealistic beliefs such as, "I´m the best," "It has not happened," "Others love me," "I can control myself" (when they have not yet learned to regulate themselves).

A client brings us an outline of what she would like her life to be like:

*Fig 3: Idealized life: Entrepreneur; home owner; cook, success; my own home; brightness; peace, love and happiness; balance; good mother; girlfriends; my car.*

Idealized goals can be useful in motivating clients, but it is important to help them focus on realistic goals that would aid in their recovery.

**The Good/Bad Polarity**

We often find, both in the negative and positive belief statement, a polarity that clients with BPD often have: "I'm bad" vs. "I'm good."

A client shares a drawing illustrating this polarity:

*Fig 4: Good/bad polarity*

Without prior psychoeducational work on this polarization, and without working with clients so their positive belief is realistic and involves a really healthy change, we are likely to have many difficulties in the spontaneous flow of the reprocessing. The negative and positive belief in BPD clients do not range from 1 to 7, they range from -100 to +100, so to speak. From this point of view, the positive belief is impossible. For example, for a client, compared to "I'm useless," the PC "I'm capable" means "I do everything right, always." "I am capable" basically means "I must be perfect," and it is actually a negative belief, not a positive one.

Prior work on core beliefs, psychoeducation, defenses, emotion regulation, and self-care can be understood as an extended preparation in phase 2, in order for the patient to process the underlying traumatic memories safely. As we will explain in next chapter on trauma processing, this does not imply that the patient should wait years until approaching traumatic memories or processing traumatic elements. This preparatory work may be strongly enhanced with procedures that include bilateral stimulation, and many clients may benefit from introducing the work on traumatic memories from the very early phases of the therapy.

# Chapter 13
# Trauma Processing

Everything described in previous chapters can be understood as preparation, which involves a somewhat complete restructuring of the personality, in order to access and process these memories. If we understand that there is a high frequency of traumatic events and adverse life experiences in BPD, the processing of these memories with EMDR will be a core element in the clients´ treatment.

However, it should not be understood that we must work on psychoeducation and emotional regulation for years until clients end up in similar conditions as individuals with simple trauma, and then start with the trauma work phase. Some BPD clients who are severely deregulated and show serious risk behaviors tolerate working on traumatic memories with EMDR very well. In some cases, we could even say that this is the most powerful stabilization maneuver we can perform.

But we can also encounter the reverse situation. Some clients become destabilized just by touching on early memories that are too painful. It could occur that even the exploration of targets to work on or the identification of the memory elements in phase 3 might make a client anxious or start a defensive response. This is not necessarily predictable based on the functional level of the individual, the presence of risk behaviors, or the degree of emotional regulation.

## What Indicators Help Us Decide when to Start Processing Memories?

Much of the information we need will proceed from a good exploration in phase 1 and prior preparation work in phase 2. It is not only working with trauma that the person may find hard or unmanageable. For many clients, who may work smoothly on the memory of a terrible beating, it can be destabilizing to connect with their own vulnerability in working with self-care, because their core defensive identity is "I am strong" and looking into the eyes of the helpless child they once were implies an intolerable intensity. Other people may process a part of the memory associated with various emotions and feelings, but the idealization of early dysfunctional attachment figures comes up amidst the processing and blocks it: it is too soon to leave that defense, which would expose individuals to assume "they had no parents" and "nobody loved them." Knowledge of clients, their history, their defenses, and their peculiarities, are the fundamental criteria that guides decision-making processes.

A specific element that does define our work style is the presence of significant dissociation. Although a certain degree of structural dissociation may be present in all clients with BPD, amnesia of the past or memory gaps in the present, marked depersonalization experiences, frequent auditory hallucinations and egodystonic thoughts, a high degree of internal conflict, phobias toward certain parts of the personality, or intense phobia of mental actions will make us switch from the intervention model described in this book to working with dissociation (Gonzalez & Mosquera, 2012). Therefore, a thorough exploration of dissociative symptoms is essential, even more in BPD, given the high prevalence of these symptoms among borderline clients. The question of which criteria the client must meet in order to begin processing trauma does not make sense if we think about it from a progressive approach. This approach was initially developed for dissociative disorders and constitutes a global perspective for the application of EMDR on different types of clients whose psychopathological complexity implies that the approach to traumatic content cannot be direct. Clients will show us their capacity to approach their history and start working on it. We will see how they respond to small initial experiments, which include bilateral stimulation in "low doses" and will allow us to explore their response to positive and negative material, old memories, and more recent memories. This work will be implemented with the client, as a joint experimentation, from which we will design a work plan tailored to the specific characteristics of the individual.

## A Progressive Approach to Nuclear Trauma

Even if biological factors or obvious traumas exist, dysfunctional early attachment is usually the foundation of most borderline disorders. Experiences of not being validated, not being seen in a real and authentic way, usually find their way into these clients´ histories. Processing these experiences means diminishing their influence as feeders of the client´s current problem, and this will be a central goal of the work with EMDR.

However, this goal does not define the quickest and safest access route to achieve it. The definition of general criteria can sometimes bring more confusion than clarity, so some exploratory work is needed prior to structuring a therapeutic plan. In this initial work, we can search for how to access the dysfunctionally stored information in each individual and in each particular organization of the individual´s personality. To find out if it may be a good time to start processing memories and if the client is ready to work directly on adverse experiences and traumatic memories, we can do small experiments. We can start with the most recent memories or current triggers, with the idea of strengthening the client´s sense of control. Working with self-care patterns (see Chapter 8) gives us information about attachment relationships, connection with the self, defensive responses, and the ability to maintain dual attention. The use of bilateral stimulation with positive elements as resources or the installation of insights during psychoeducation give us an idea about how EMDR works for clients and if they can tolerate positive affect. At the same time, it allows them to become familiar with the procedure and not associate bilateral stimulation only with working on trauma.

It is important that clients understand the purpose of these little experiments and have realistic expectations about possible outcomes. If clients find out that bilateral stimulation relieves, unblocks, and generates positive changes, we will be able to explain the effect of processing a painful memory much better.

The first full memory to be processed can also be considered a test. This first memory will be selected before deciding on the work plan, since the information provided by this session may change our previous ideas on how to proceed with each specific client. The goal of this initial processing will not be the clinical outcomes in themselves, but just having a session that will give clients a positive feeling. In this session, they will be able to see the effects of bilateral stimulation more clearly and, from their experience, understand what is different about this tool and the benefits that can be obtained by working on memories with EMDR. This idea will serve as a reference when we enter into more complex territories.

The criteria for choosing the first memory, as we mentioned, can be variable. Although we must take into account each individual client´s characteristics, in general these are perhaps the most interesting places to start (based on Mosquera, Leeds & Gonzalez, 2014):

1. **Intrusive memories and recurring thoughts and sensations** (with thoughts or feelings, we search for episodic memories connected with them in an obvious way or via the affect bridge). These memories are very present in people´s minds and it is easy for clients to connect with them during processing, even when trying to focus on a different type of memory. Also, because of their frequency, their processing will be faster and the benefit more visible to clients, increasing their subsequent motivation to work with EMDR.

2. **Targets related to risk behaviors for themselves and others or to the most debilitating or destabilizing symptoms.** If clients can tolerate working on early memories, it is interesting to go from the symptom to the target that is most closely connected with these symptoms. If we are able to work on early nuclear memories connected to current problematic behavior, the potential effect on improving clients´ situations is very high. The key here is to evaluate clients´ ability to process, without being guided by an apparent deregulation or strength, which could be more defensive than real.

3. **Current triggers** (if there are specific triggers that relate to the worsening of symptoms). We can select an uncomfortable situation of daily life, with the idea that if there is some change, clients will see the benefit in a direct and immediate way. We explain that in working with EMDR, we know it works better when we start in the past and move toward the present, because that way we first remove the roots and it will be easier to bring the tree down. However, in cases like this, starting with the roots can be counterproductive. In EMDR, when starting with the most recent issues, others from the past may come up, since the brain makes associations. We tell them that, if this occurs, it is important to communicate it to the therapist, in order to help focus the work on the present situation. We can also tell them that this work, focused on the present, is often productive, and we can keep improving things in the present; and whenever the client is recovered and feeling stronger, we can

start working on the most difficult memories. However, if many memories from the past come back, we may have to consider going there first.

4. It may also be appropriate to start with **a past event**. We can choose a memory that is not associated with a long string of difficult experiences. For example, working on the memory of a car accident may be easier than a situation that is more related to attachment, and the effect of processing such memories is more "visible." In working with memories that are part of a cluster, it is important to work with limited processing in the first few sessions, which is described in the following chapter. This way, we prevent becoming overwhelmed and opening multiple targets, which may lead to re-traumatization and later wanting to avoid EMDR work all together, or even dropping out of therapy. It is important that we facilitate, as much as possible, a good first experience with EMDR for the clients.

The central idea of all initial experiments is to present the processing of memories with EMDR as an experiment with no possibility of error. If the memory is processed, this is great, because we can improve things that are now most troublesome for the client. If the memory cannot be processed, this gives us essential information on how to structure the therapeutic work. It is not good for clients with frequent feelings of "I do everything wrong" to leave their first experience of EMDR with a confirmation of their core negative belief.

Once we have this information, we are ready to design a specific therapeutic program, with a work plan that includes a sequence of targets.

## The Therapeutic Plan

The above experiments are framed in a progressive treatment approach, along the lines defined by Gonzalez & Mosquera (2012). The selection of targets and their sequencing can be challenging for many reasons. The work plan must combine being tolerable for clients, having them feel that "this can help me" and taking steps at the pace that is most appropriate, and, at the same time, helping us dismantle the most problematic and destabilizing behaviors and symptoms as soon as possible.

In some cases, there may be many relevant targets, adverse life experiences, and unique or recurring traumatic experiences, so the therapist may struggle trying to establish an order. There may also be significant missing pieces in clients' histories, associated with amnesia that may not be too obvious, such as abuse that is not remembered but without obvious gaps in the story. Sometimes, the specific memories are clear, but the defenses (see chapter 6) do not allow us to start working on them. All these factors must be taken into consideration when deciding where to start and what path to follow.

At a very generic level, we might consider sequencing by increasing difficulty, although no sequence we may consider can be equally adapted to all types of client (based on Mosquera, et al., 2014):

1. **Psychoeducation**, explanation of EMDR work, and understanding the specific client's case. Establishing a **therapeutic relationship and a framework**. All these aspects will continue throughout the therapy process. Amid this work, we can start introducing bilateral stimulation at different points, exploring its utility to reinforce realizations during psychoeducational work, or exemplifying such explanations.

2. Using **bilateral stimulation with positive elements** such as resources and improvements in the therapy process. It is important to assess problems with positive affect tolerance, which will require specific interventions. At this point, we may assess possible positive beliefs and the emotional impact generated on clients, but working with them may not be adequate for early stages.

3. **Exploring the effects of bilateral stimulation in dysfunctional elements**. We can try with uncomfortable feelings, everyday difficulties, or specific points of discomfort that occur during the session.

4. **Targeting defenses and impulses**. It is important that clients understand the meaning of this work, and that a defense does not have to be processed just because it shows up. If this work is premature, we can leave clients helpless and too exposed, exacerbate defenses, or foster the appearance of other defenses.

5. When **differentiation of the self** is deficient, it is useful to introduce specific work on these issues.

6. When the **self-care pattern** is very dysfunctional, procedures oriented toward it can be useful and, as we said, provide important information. In most cases, working with defenses must come first. Using a cautious approach, it will be necessary to assess when working with self-care patterns provides regulation and when it brings clients closer to a vulnerability that they may not yet be able to assume.

7. When fragmentation is important, **work with parts** may be introduced using bilateral stimulation in a dynamic way to process dysfunctional elements or reinforce those that are functional. For example, using a drawing of parts representing different emotions, we can process the feeling of rejection about accepting some of them.

8. **Targeting on current triggers**. If there are specific triggers that relate to the worsening of symptoms, it is important to address them avoiding connections with associated disturbing memory chains.

9. **Targeting memories closely connected to current problems or symptoms**, relevant and problematic.

10. **Targeting memories associated with the most recurrent and disturbing nuclear negative beliefs**.

## Aspects to Be Considered in the Assessment Phase (Phase 3)

After selecting a target to process, it is important to be aware of the different signals that can become activated during phase 3. The selection of negative and positive beliefs is not always easy (see Chapter 12). Often, clients with BPD state many negative beliefs about the self and the world.

For proper processing, it will be important to help them identify which of these beliefs are related to the specific memory. At the same time, it will be important to prevent clients from drowning in their negative cognition, as it is easy to feel overwhelmed when faced with cascading negative associations. Therapists may say something like this: "I know it's difficult and many negative things are coming up for you right now, but try to leave them there and focus only on the belief that is most connected to that memory."

Having identified the negative belief, we find another challenge: the identification of a positive belief. Borderline clients are many times unable to think of something positive. As we mentioned in prior chapters, helping them find an acceptable positive cognition such as, "I can learn to accept myself" will be necessary in many cases. In other cases, the problem will be in the positive belief, because instead of thinking about adaptive positive beliefs, they will think of idealized beliefs. It is important to remember that borderline clients tend to think in extremes, in "black or white" and the gray areas are not easily discernible.

It is important to be realistic and remember that sometimes we cannot get all phase 3 elements before starting to process. If possible, it is extremely useful and it is important that therapists do not give up in advance or get carried away by the belief that clients are incapable. Helping clients to identify the different elements of the memory and understand how they relate to the vision of themselves is an important learning, which further serves to enhance reflective thinking and place clients in dual attention. However, if they begin to feel anguish, dive into the memory, or become dispersed, we must take advantage of other accessible elements and start processing. It is possible that after a period of desensitization, individuals are better able to think than at the beginning of the session.

## Processing (Phases 4 to 7)

Two of the most important aspects during phases 4 to 7 will be structure and containment. Borderline clients function in chaos and it will be necessary to keep the sessions from becoming more of the same. Sometimes, working on a disturbing memory can bring up associations or endless chains of traumatic memories that clients cannot tolerate. To prevent opening Pandora's Box in the first sessions, it is recommended to return to the target often. This way, the processing will be more contained and controlled and it may prevent clients from becoming saturated and decompensating (Mosquera et al., 2014).

Another aspect that may be necessary for clients with BPD is the introduction of interweaves to activate adaptive information. These interweaves can range from the usual interweaves that unblock a looping to psychoeducational, relational, and somatic interweaves. When there is no adaptive information, it will be necessary to introduce it and sometimes we will need to use a "continuous and dynamic interweave," in which, without entering into a constant verbal exchange, therapists will complement what is appearing spontaneously in order to keep the processing going. Generally, therapists working with BPD will be less minimalist than with simple trauma, since their more active presence may be necessary as a relational interweave: clients who during childhood did not experience anyone realizing how they felt can benefit from therapists realizing that they are more affected than they say they are. However, this does not mean that therapists should fall into "doing the work for the clients" by underestimating the ability of their system to reach adaptive resolution.

During processing sessions, it is essential to be aware of the appearance of previously explored defenses and understand why they appear when they do. These defenses may be used as a processing target, but sometimes they must be understood as a stop signal that clients are unable to express otherwise.

Another important aspect will be working with secondary emotions that borderline clients experience. Let us recall that primary emotions are the first automatic responses, the first adaptive emotion we need to feel (e.g., fearing a very loud noise or the sound of a car that runs off the road), while secondary emotions arise from learned automatic thoughts, judgments, or assumptions. They are answers that are frequently learned from others, usually from our environment. Borderline clients who have grown up in contexts with enmeshed or chaotic families have learned to respond with reproach to their most basic emotions. If my father gets nervous when I cry or get angry (primary emotion), I will learn to despise (secondary emotion) or avoid such emotion, and over time, I will react similarly to what I have learned. During processing, when the logical sadness associated with a painful memory appears, the secondary emotion of anger comes up for crying and being so weak, "I don't know why I get like this, I should be over this." Sometimes, this blocking is not so cortical, based on judgment about the primary emotion, but instead it is emotional or somatosensory: If my father's anger was associated with fear of what would come next, feeling anger in myself will generate the simultaneous activation of fear. In general, secondary emotions tend to block processing by not allowing the spontaneous flow of associations, and they require that therapists focus specifically on secondary emotions.

Finally, it is also important to be attentive to the relational aspects that can be activated during sessions. Borderline clients are very used to reading others from an extremely self-referential filter. In some cases, therapists' every gesture or word is analyzed and, when non-verbal cues of changes are identified, what happens in the clients' minds is very important. If there is a major relational problem interfering with the processing, it may be advisable to postpone working with trauma until the relational defenses are less active. Otherwise, to simultaneously address two complex challenges in BPD, such as the processing of difficult memories and the establishment of a trusting relationship with the therapist, may make both issues impossible to resolve.

## Session´s Closure and Reevaluation (Phases 7 and 8)

The basic rule for closing a session is that less is more. It is better to do a small amount of good work and end up with an incomplete session, than to force the reprocessing of a specific target too much (Mosquera et al., 2014). It is important to leave time at the end of the session in case clients need stabilization and containment. We can spend part of the session thinking, together with clients, about the material that has come up in order to promote reflective capacity and awareness.

Phase 8 is essential, since it will provide information on the effectiveness of the previous work and help us redesign the later approach. Sessions may have gone seemingly well and, in phase 8, clients may report that they have been drinking or cutting all week, which would indicate that the session was too hard for them. Significant positive changes happen in other cases, after a particularly intense session, where the SUD only lowers in one point and clients leave upset: "That night, I had a lot of nightmares, but the next day, I felt better and the rest of the week I was fairly calm, without bingeing or hurting myself."

## Dynamic Maps: A Structured yet Flexible Treatment Plan

It is important to periodically trace updated maps. Initial experiments and information from phases 1 and 2 give us the first data for our therapeutic GPS. Based on this, we will draw a road map, together with the client. We are not to trust clients´ desire to work and go straight to the core. It is expected that we will find varying degrees of disconnection, or that clients will minimize how much they are affected, "I´m over this, I am strong," or that they will try to please the therapist and do what they think he or she expects them to do. In addition, we should not trust the intense and sometimes dramatic way in which clients may tell us they do not dare to work, because sometimes this is a phobic reaction or they are speaking to us from a very childish emotional part, which has no access to their true strength. BPD clients function in extremes and, as we know, each end makes them swing to the other end. Therapists must trace a map in which the balance between desire to progress and caution must go hand in hand.

As with any GPS, data should be updated. Some streets are closed due to roadwork, new avenues are opened, and rules change. As we move forward with the processing of memories and with the additional work, the client´s structure is modified. Defenses that were previously inactive may appear, or the phobias that prevented access to certain memories may lighten up. Dissociative parts may appear in clients who had not shown apparent dissociation before. By increasing awareness, clients can access parts of their history and realize situations they had previously not remembered and had minimized, idealized, or distorted. This information must be added to the work plan and sometimes leads to rerouting. This process must be shared with clients, thus becoming partners in the therapeutic work, assuming the reins of their recovery.

Returning to the issue of balance, we must be careful that the processing does not become a chaotic trajectory with no specific direction, changing depending on what clients bring to each session and forgetting the guidelines. In many situations we will have to meet clients´ demands, crisis situations, or specific concerns, but this should not be the usual pattern. With borderline clients, not being carried away by their personal chaos is basic.

In many cases with borderline clients, we will work on standard EMDR trauma processing, introducing the necessary elements for identifying defenses, helping with emotional regulation, improving self-care, or dismantling rigid beliefs. In some sessions, specific procedures can be added to overcome particular situations, as we will describe in the next chapter

# Chapter 14
# Specific Procedures

A disorder such as BPD, with so many nuances, cannot be addressed on the basis of a protocol or a set of procedures. The best strategies will be of little use if we do not have a global view of the problem. Most of the sessions in the treatment of borderline personality disorder will be based on working with psychoeducation, defenses, self-care, and emotional regulation; processing memories following the standard protocol outline; and dynamically introducing all strategies to regulate and channel the process. The use of specific protocols and procedures will take up a very small amount of that time. However, in this chapter, we present some interventions that, at certain times, we have found useful to facilitate or unblock the work.

Some procedures have been previously described in *EMDR and Dissociation: The Progressive Approach* (Gonzalez & Mosquera, 2012), such as working with parts, self-care patterns, and the processing of dissociative phobias, and they can be applied in the BPD treatment when appropriate. In this chapter, we will focus on different or modified proposals.

## Resources

Installation of resources in BPD treatment does not differ from the one proposed by Leeds (2001). However, the material to be installed deserves a separate section. Given the distorted view of the borderline client, what people identify as a resource is often a defense. In a way, defenses may be understood as the only way that individuals, so far, have been able to manage their internal processes and the external world.

For example, a client who had not been able to find a safe place says the only place she feels safe is at the gym, where she goes for an hour each day. She has had numerous plastic surgeries and she is extremely concerned about her physical care. Although the therapist is aware that this is not a true resource, she explores what might happen with the installation. The client defines her sensation when running on the treadmill at the gym as feeling energetic. After the first set of bilateral stimulation, the association is negative, and she starts thinking about her sense of emptiness, of which she is more aware just after "the rush." The therapist goes back to the target of the gym, and the client now describes a different, less intense sensation, but she doubts about its quality, since it does not seem completely bad. The therapist decides to go on, and after another set of BLS, the client says, "It would be great if I could keep feeling this; what I feel in the gym is so strong that the downturn always comes later." After another set, this idea is reinforced, discovering a previously unlikely possibility: to "feel something like this outside of the gym."

The therapist returns to the target of the gym situation, and the feeling seems to continue "settling." The client says, "It's like before, but... it's lower, but more... solid...? It's like it's more real." The therapist says, "Can you imagine now noticing that situation in your day to day?" The client says yes and chooses a situation of being alone, since during the first part of the session they had done psychoeducational work on the importance of learning to be alone. They add the new sensation to an image of being at home alone, quietly doing her things, and she ends with a very positive feeling.

In this case, resource installation became the processing of a defense and, following the client's process, brought a new perspective to her situation.

Certain situations are especially significant resources for BPD clients, which would probably never be selected as such: situations in which they could have been alone or done things alone; moments in which they have shown a non-extreme reaction with issues that typically make them go from one extreme to the other; times when they have been able to handle their discomfort; sentences along the lines of self-care or self-regulation; times when they have cared for themselves properly; situations in which they have established healthy boundaries, etc. This resource installation is introduced in the initial psychoeducational work, since there the client is improving her understanding of what the exercise means and we add reflective and awareness work. Installation of resources also strengthens psychoeducational work.

# Defenses

Jim Knipe (2005) has developed several procedures for working with defenses and, although these were not intended for borderline disorders, they are totally applicable. Since the number of defenses in borderline clients is very large, we must pay special attention to the selected targets. For example, the fantasy defense requires slow preparation, since clients will be reluctant to leave their wonderful imaginary world. In order to let go of the dream world, clients must have another planet to arrive to, and they must consider it fairly habitable. Thus, we will have to process the disturbance associated with situations that represent living in reality and install alternative resources to escaping to the fantasized world at times of distress. It is useful, at the right time, to add self-statements that represent the change of perspective, such as "I can live in reality." Below, we mention some thoughts on this change in perspective for each defense, to be understood as illustrative, and to be raised only when the client does not have an adaptive response to the question "What could you say that would help you in this situation?"

| Defense | Possible sentences |
| --- | --- |
| Pleasing | I also matter<br>I don't have to please everyone<br>Other people's wellbeing is not solely my responsibility<br>I can be loved just as I am<br>Healthy relationships are balanced |
| Idealizing | Everything has its pros and cons<br>There is not just black and white, there are many shades of gray<br>I don't need people to be wonderful<br>Not everything has to be fantastic |
| Projection | I always have 50% of participation in my relationships with others<br>It is important that I see my part in the problems<br>I can assume the things I don't like about my behavior |
| Avoidance | I can face things<br>I have resources<br>I can learn to manage situations |
| Seeing problems with everything or "yes, but…" | I can try it<br>If I don't try, I'll never make it<br>If I don't try, I'll never know if it really works |
| Unattainable demands (toward others and the world) | Situations or people don't have to be perfect<br>Not everything has to be perfect<br>I can accept things as they are<br>I can take the part that interests me<br>I have to choose between the possible options<br>I can make a pact with reality |
| Rationalization | I can connect with my emotions<br>I can feel (this sentence needs the additional work of paying attention to somatic sensations and staying with them)<br>There are things that can be understood only by reasoning<br>I can trust my sensations/intuition |
| Changing subjects, denial, minimization, laughter, sense of humor | I can tolerate discomfort<br>I can confront difficult things<br>It is important to see things as they are<br>We can only solve things when we accept that they are there |
| Somatic symptoms | I can understand my reactions (they need help from the therapist to explore what is underneath the symptom)<br>The body is wise, it is important to listen to it and try to understand what it is telling us |
| Self-criticism | I can look at myself with understanding<br>I do what I can<br>If people do what they can, we can't ask for more<br>I can learn to value myself |

| | Criticism helps when it's constructive |
| --- | --- |
| | I can learn to improve without beating myself up |
| Procrastination | The sooner, the better |
| | If I do it now, I am saving myself hours or days of anguish |
| | I will feel better if I do it soon |
| Complaining | Everyone makes mistakes |
| | We all have flaws |
| | The world is at it is, but even so, it's worth it |
| | Complaining gets me stuck and doesn't let me see the way out |
| | Complaining doesn't solve problems, it just blocks me |
| Selective mood changes or "letting go of the reins" | I can handle my emotions |
| | I can slow down and have self-control |
| | Taking the reins of my behavior will make me feel better |
| | I can achieve things in a different way |
| Magical thoughts | It is important that I focus on what depends on me |
| | I can always resort to what is at hand |
| | I don't want to leave the control of my decisions to others |
| | Magic doesn't exist |
| | What can't be, can't be and it's also impossible |
| | Regardless of how much I want the sun to disappear, it won't, so I can just decide which hat to wear |
| Parallel worlds | In the real world, there are many things that are worthy |
| | Things are how they are |
| | I can use my creativity in the real world |
| Perfectionism | I don't have to be perfect |
| | I have the right to make mistakes, like everyone else |
| | We learn from our mistakes |
| Learned helplessness | I can learn to protect myself |
| | I can confront things (this often requires behavioral activation exercises) |
| | The past is behind me, now I have more resources |
| Internal phobias | I can accept myself just as I am |
| | I can assume everything that has happened to me |
| | The past is gone |
| | Everything inside of me has its function and its meaning |
| Phobias of the external world | Change is worth it, even if it's scary |
| | The devil you know has the problem that it's the devil |
| | I can lead a satisfactory life |
| | I can manage life situations |
| | The past doesn't have to repeat itself |
| | I can learn |

# Differentiation

Differentiation requires a specific type of work, and it is an example of a process that, without being actively channeled by the therapist, does not tend spontaneously toward adaptive resolution with bilateral stimulation. The following sections describe different ways to work with differentiation.

## Drawing the Circle of the Self

The exercise we proposed in the chapter on differentiation, drawing a circle in which clients symbolically represent what they feel inside, provides rich exploratory material and also allows the implementation of specific interventions. For example, if clients draw inside the circle other people who are not themselves, we ask them to make a new drawing placing those people outside the circle and focusing on putting only who they are inside the circle. The discomfort coming from this change will be processed with bilateral stimulation. We can help clients realize their healthy resources, draw them inside the circle, and become aware of them, reinforcing this connection with BLS. We may ask clients to be aware of their boundaries and see if they need to be reinforced somehow, designing "filters" so things from the outside do not get inside directly, doors they can open or close depending on what the issue is and all the variants that may arise, in order to strengthen the boundaries of the self and the awareness of an autonomous self.

## Differentiation of Self Procedure

Differentiation requires a specific type of work, and it is an example of a process that, without being actively channeled by the therapist, does not tend spontaneously toward adaptive resolution with bilateral stimulation. In this section we will describe a way of working on differentiation, based on the proposal of Litt (2007). The author describes an interesting exercise to be used as interweave, which we have redesigned as a differentiation protocol.

1. We explain to the client that with a specific person, for example her mother, she failed to establish complete differentiation, how this connects with the mixture of her own and other people's emotions that she notices internally, and the problems this causes.

2. We ask her to stand in front of a wall, leaving some space in between.

3. We give the indication that she lean on the wall "as if pushing a very heavy weight."

4. We now tell her to visualize her mother, but before that, she must rename her and call her by her first name (let us say her mother's name is Rose). We explain that when children grow up they no longer see their parents as parents, and come to relate to them as adults and see them as any other person, with their full name.

5. We ask the client to look at Rose and notice how many of the emotions and sensations she feels are truly hers and how much has she absorbed from Rose.

6.  Noticing the absorbed emotions and sensations, we ask that she push the wall really hard, sending over to Rose's side what belongs to Rose and noticing how she keeps only what belongs to Mary (the client's name).

7.  We ask the client to focus on the physical sensation that goes from the location of the emotions and sensations that she feels are Rose's to her hands pushing the wall, and we do BLS on the client's shoulders, while we stand at her side, after asking for permission.

8.  We ask, "What comes up?" after a set of BLS, and we introduce psychoeducation if necessary. For example, it is common for the client to say, "I can't burden my mother with all that worry." The therapist explains that worry is not measured in weight, and the fact that she has carried Rose's worry around has not turned Rose into a less worried woman. In the style of classical cognitive interweaves, when the client shows signs of assimilating new information, we repeat another set of BLS.

9.  After three rounds of BLS following the same procedure, the disturbance associated to "putting things in place" usually decreases, and the client begins to experience relief. During the second or third set, it is important to add specific instructions on "opinions," asking the client, "Notice which of your opinions are inherited or absorbed from Rose and which ones you feel are really yours... push Rose's views over to Rose's side, notice your hands pushing..."

10. We also install boundaries: "Notice the wall, notice the boundary where Rose ends and Mary begins." This indication often brings up guilt in preoccupied attachment, as if understanding that we are different people meant rejecting the other (often derived from the other person's verbalizations in that regard), or as if to stop living enmeshed would lead to loneliness or distancing from others. If this happens, we need to introduce specific psychoeducation explaining how in healthy attachment, in which differentiation is clear, the person is able to have close and intimate relationships.

11. We install the idea of an autonomous self: "Notice Mary, Mary's feelings, Mary's opinions, while pushing away everything that is not yours... You let the other person decide what she wants to do with her own emotions and opinions. While looking at Rose, notice the boundary between who you are and who she is, feel who you are, try to tell yourself "I'm Mary," "I'm me," and see how you feel when you do (use BLS to process possible associated disturbance and then to strengthen the adaptive changes that might occur).

12. This exercise will probably need to be repeated several times and with different people (family members, partners, children...). Later during processing, it will be introduced as interweave, either pushing the wall as in this procedure, a cushion, or the therapist's hand.

## The Two Sides of the Story Procedure

As explained in previous chapters, borderline clients often have difficulty focusing on what depends on them. When analyzing their relationship problems, they often focus more on what others "do to them," rather than on their contribution to the problem.

In this procedure, we ask clients to tell us about a problematic interaction with others. Once they have told us about the situation, if we assess that there is a tendency to blame problems on others, we may propose an experiment.

We ask clients to visualize a screen on which to project the film of the situation, but they will only try to see what others did and did not do, what others said and what they did not say. When clients finish playing the movie, we ask them to identify what they say to themselves internally, the emotion and physical sensation, and we do a few sets of BLS.

Then we propose another experiment to clients. They will play the movie again, but this time they will be the only one on the screen - what they said and did not say, what they did and they did not do, just their part of the dialogue, only their own scenes. Once they finish, we ask again for the thought, emotion, and feeling generated by this second view, and we also process it.

We can assess doing a repetition of the second sequence, placing the phrases "it is important to see what part depends on me" or "this is the part I can manage, that is in my hand" next to it.

Therapists must not become frustrated when clients verbalize that they cannot do the second part of the exercise, as this is a big part of the issues they present. At first try, they will attempt to divert our attention to what others have done or not done, but after several tries, they will be able to complete it. It is recommended not to give up easily, because this is an exercise that can generate important insights.

For example, a client did the first exercise without any problems, verbalizing discomfort with how bad others had treated her. This was more of the same, in a client whose speech was often focused on how unfairly people usually treated her. However, the screening of the movie based on "her part" led to a powerful realization. She realized that she never looked at herself, and that the mere fact of doing so generated great discomfort. After processing this discomfort with several sets of BLS, she also became aware of how many of her attitudes fed problems that later tormented her. "I never realized I was living outwardly... I have always lived my life outside of myself."

Another client did this exercise by pure chance. She met with her ex-partner with the intention of recording the meeting and having proof of how badly he treated her. When she played the tape, she was scared of their own words, tone, and reactions: "I didn't recognize myself, I was scared of how I act."

## Processing the Positive Belief

As explained in Chapter 12 on beliefs, these need extra work in borderline clients, beginning in the initial psychoeducation and extending throughout all stages of therapy. Negative beliefs will be "eroded" with psychoeducational work and directed resource installation. As discussed in the previous chapter, the lack of positive affect tolerance can be addressed with the specific protocol proposed by Leeds (2006). Much of the work on beliefs will depend on the management performed during phases 3 to 7, in order to help the client identify realistic beliefs without extreme polarization. In this chapter, we will explain a specific procedure that can sometimes be useful for working with the positive belief.

The positive belief in itself is often associated with disturbance. The affirmation "I'm worth it" is of such intensity, it has always been so impossible and so unthinkable, that clients literally "can't get it into their heads." Thinking "I deserve to be happy" means feeling the hope that was abandoned many years ago because it was too painful. As we commented in prior chapters, this hope was changed to resignation, which would help survive a prolonged adverse situation. If this disturbance is not addressed before accessing and processing traumatic memories, as soon as the associative process activated by bilateral stimulation approaches positive networks, this negative resonance of the positive belief will become activated and will probably block the processing.

Sometimes, preparing this positive belief to be accessible may require the processing of the previously associated disturbance, taking the positive belief itself as a target. To do this, we ask clients to think about the positive belief "I'm worth it" and score from 1 to 7 how much they think they may feel like this at some point. In this scale, which we call VOC by analogy with phase 3 of the standard protocol, we will generally find scores on the low end of the scale. Emotional disturbance is measured on a SUD scale from 0 to 10, and we will ask for location of the sensation in the body. From these elements, several processing sets are done, returning to target every three or four sets of BLS, without waiting for positive or neutral associations, in order to maintain the processing focused.

Every time we go back to target, we will ask for the VOC, the SUD, and the sensation in the body again. If, when returning to target, the VOC increases some points and the SUD decreases to some extent, we will terminate the procedure, as it is not expected that the positive belief can be felt with a certainty of 7 before enough work with disturbing memories has been done. The goal is that clients be able to contemplate the possibility of change towards the positive belief. The therapist will help the client when necessary, introducing possibilities that are more modest but can feel more possible, such as "I can value myself more" or "I can learn to value myself."

## Emotional Integration Procedure

Borderline clients have significant difficulties with emotional regulation. Understanding their emotions, identifying primary and secondary emotions, mindfulness exercises with self-instructions, and identifying the most common triggers are various strategies that will help them expand their regulatory capacity. We will describe one of these exercises in this chapter.

Given that even BPD clients without marked dissociative symptoms have a certain degree of structural dissociation, clients are likely to present difficulty integrating different mental states, often associated with different emotions. To achieve an integrated perspective, we use a procedure inspired by the meeting place procedure.

If clients, when drawing a picture of how they see themselves, draw different emotions like "my angry self" or "my sad self," we will use this as a foundation. If not, we will specifically ask them to draw the various emotions and reactions they have inside the circle of the self. We will ask them to tell us about each one of them, what adaptive function they have (although the way in which clients manage them does not yet work adaptively), and how it feels to deal with that emotion (exploring their phobia of that state of mind, of that dissociative part that has little structure). Typically, clients will feel discomfort regarding their emotions, and probably this will be different with each one of them. One by one, we will process the discomfort clients feel about the emotion, focusing, as in working with dissociative phobias, on the sensation in the body. Even with the emotions that they apparently accept, we will ask for the somatic sensation that may hide an unconscious disturbance. When we have gone through each and every one of their emotions, we ask clients to look at the whole and feel how they all make sense, how they can balance and compensate each other, and to realize how they represent different resources for coping with life situations. This global and meta-conscious view stimulates the ability to distance themselves from their emotions, reduces blockages, and helps clients gain perspective. We will get back to this idea whenever we need to work a blocked processing in phase 4, using a secondary emotion: "What do you feel about that emotion that has appeared?" or "What do you notice when you see yourself feeling...?"

## Relational Bridge

This protocol can be used to address some of the difficulties that may arise in the therapeutic relationship and may interfere with therapy or processing. It can also be used to explore clients' relationships (past and present) and the dynamics that may be fueling some of the difficulties that clients experience and manifest in interactions with others (including therapists).

It is very important to be careful that clients do not feel criticized or judged during this intervention. We have to explain that understanding how they relate to others is very important to be able to move forward in treatment. Clients must understand that the therapeutic relationship can be conditioned by previous relationships and, because of this, it is important to pay attention to relational issues. This way, we will be able to identify possible interferences and find out where they come from or how they originated. It can be very useful to explain to clients that this is a team effort, something we will do together.

For starters, we can read the following to the client: Relationship problems can leave a deep imprint in people's lives. This can generate relational difficulties that can be replayed in therapy sessions. The therapeutic relationship can be an avenue for understanding how you learned to relate to others. It will be useful to identify and understand these connections.

**Prior considerations to the implementation of this protocol**

Prior to this intervention, therapists must have acquired some perspective regarding the relational situation and explored whether the relational pattern or their emotions are connected with THEIR own personal history. If therapists continue feeling intense anger, despair, etc. and are unable to get perspective, this intervention can be counterproductive. In such case, it is convenient to supervise the case previously. When events in therapists' biographies are emotionally charged and clearly connected with the dysfunctional interaction with clients, it would be advisable for therapists to do personal work processing the feeder memories.

**Possible options in using the relational bridge:**

1.　　Explore from the client's emotion in the relationship. I understand that you are feeling (I have the feeling) about me... Have you ever had this feeling before with other people?

2.　　Explore from our own emotion in the relationship. Sometimes in these situations, I have the feeling of...  Have you ever felt that way?

3.　　Explore from the relational pattern. I get the feeling that we are relating..., you function in this way..., and I function in this other way..., and I was wondering if you see the similarity of this with any previous relationship in your life. Notice your feelings about me and the relationship with me, close your eyes, and let your mind go back in time until you find the first time you were in a relationship that is somewhat similar or made you feel in a similar way.

# Limited Processing

To facilitate processing in BPD clients, we can do limited processing. We know that associations generated during reprocessing can be potentially destabilizing in clients with a lot of trauma. In BPD, it can be understood that emotional dysregulation is caused by multiple unprocessed memories that can "erupt," with no apparent evidence of the underlying disturbance.

The idea of limiting the processing derives from clinical experience with clients who connect with these multiple traumas continuously without any positive associations. With this variation of the standard processing, we may address the memories in a more contained way, while we encourage clients' emotional regulation and show them that this is a safe method.

The benefits of limited processing are higher containment and emotional regulation, potentially less destabilizing associations, and a sense of capacity and management that encourages the development of a sense of security, so we can then work on other traumatic targets.

One client got very nervous at the mere idea of working with traumatic memories. After an attempt at standard processing, where he was blocked by a cascade of disturbing memories, he explained to his therapist how his brain worked like a computer, where windows kept popping up until it collapsed and crashed. Going back to target often allowed the containment of the traumatic material and gave him greater sense of control. Over time, and after processing some of the most overwhelming memories, the client could understand and feel the benefits of working with EMDR, which resulted in increased confidence in the process, being able to move on to standard processing of memories.

The proposed changes are in line with the original EMD (Shapiro, 1989), where we go back to target after each set of bilateral stimulation. In our experience, it is useful to allow some room for associations in order for effective processing to take place; but instead of waiting for positive or neutral associations, we simply go back to target when we observe a change in sensation, in the memory, or some kind of insight or reflection. Even if there is no such change, we may go back to target after two or three positive associations, asking, "What is different now?" to avoid automatic responses such as "the same."

In this type of processing, sessions usually end as incomplete, since the goal is not just the processing of memories, but the reduction of traumatic burden while clients cope with their difficult experiences from a sense of regulation, containment, and control. In order to achieve this, the dynamic interweaves discussed below will be very useful.

Phase 3 is structured, as in the standard processing, based on an image, a negative and positive belief, emotion, and bodily sensation. For the selection of positive and negative beliefs, we must take into account what relates to beliefs in BPD, described in chapter 12. In relation to emotion and somatic sensation, it is necessary to assess aspects related to emotional regulation, as discussed in chapter 10. The specific characteristics of each client in this regard will lead to a greater or lesser need to adapt phase 3. For example, a client with a tendency to string together various negative beliefs may need help from the therapist to identify which one of them is more clearly associated with the memory being worked on, while enhancing the reflective capacity of the client. An individual whose negative belief acts as an activator of negative judgments about himself will need to remember the self-care interventions practiced in phase 2. A person who becomes "immersed" in the memory, will need orientation to present reality, and probably a shorter and somewhat "minimalist" version of phase 3, in order to introduce processing without the client delving too much into his negative emotions. A client who expresses a positive belief that it is rather the expression of an idealization defense must go back to the elements of the previous work with defenses.

All these difficulties should not lead, however, to ignoring phase 3 and starting the processing without a clear target. Each element of phase 3 is a different level of processing, and establishing these levels as a starting point is in itself a learning experience for clients with difficulties in emotion identification, differentiation of self, and reflective thinking. It is true that an extremely long phase 3 can lead to feelings of frustration, inadequacy, or incompetence in clients with a tendency to see themselves in that way, and it is important to facilitate that the experience of working with EMDR, especially the first targets, be positive. If we wait to establish a complete phase 3 before carrying out the processing, we may delay it more than would be beneficial. We can use the list of beliefs if clients feel unable to come up with a belief, or help them reduce the positive belief to a more realistic level, or accept a generic belief as "I can deal better with things" in clients with difficulties in this area. We may skip asking for different emotions, or the SUD, if clients are extremely activated. But at least, it is important for clients to understand that one thing is the memory and another thing is how it makes them feel; that they can distinguish a thought from an emotion and identify a current sensation in the body, since it is possible that the names used to describe emotions do not correspond with what clients are feeling or do not accurately describe it.

Phase 4 starts normally, making short associative chains as described above. In cases of high activation level, we can choose to focus the processing on one of the elements, for example, asking clients to put aside the thoughts and focus only on the physical sensation, or to focus on one of the many emotions or feelings that they are noticing, or just on one part of the memory. Therapists will need to dynamically introduce interweaves, not only cognitive ones, but also somatic, relational, or psychoeducational (Gonzalez & Mosquera, 2012). Therapeutic presence is the most important regulator, and often, memory processing needs more interventions than in PTSD, but only those which are necessary to channel the processing so it follows the usual route in simple trauma.

Even with an incomplete phase 4, which, as we mentioned, is common in BPD and may be more appropriate, especially in the early stages working with highly unstable clients, it is convenient to introduce a simplified version of phase 5. The memory, partially processed, will also become partially associated with a positive belief or insight. For example, a client who has managed to lower the disturbance associated with a memory of abuse, may end up with the image that he now has about the fact, associated with an insight about herself such as, "I was just a child, it was not my fault." There are still many emotions, physical sensations, and even negative beliefs associated with that moment in time, which will take time to process completely. But we are interested in reinforcing this change in perspective regarding the facts and connecting it to the memory using EBL, as a way to end the session.

Such limited processing is not mandatory in BPD and should not be used in cases in which standard processing works directly. Many clients with high levels of dysregulation have no problems identifying phase 3 elements, tolerate the standard processing of a memory perfectly well, and can complete it with a SUD of 0, a VOC of 7, and a negative body scan. Let us consider that many of these clients live habitually with intense emotions, and what comes up during processing, apparently very dramatic, is routine for them. Even those clients who need to start with limited processing may be able to work, as therapy progresses, in a way that resembles the standard protocol. We must also keep in mind that, for some people, BLS produces a relaxation effect that is rather straightforward and fast, so even when starting at high levels of disturbance, they can reach complete processing. A fully processed memory has a much greater impact on the improvement of symptoms. However, limited processing is better than delaying the processing, simply because all conditions are not met, in a client who could benefit from it. Phase 8, reassessment, will give us the most valuable information for deciding how to proceed with each individual client. When in doubt, starting cautiously and progressively is safer and allows us to introduce processing elements without the risk of decompensating clients or having them refuse to continue working with EMDR.

Up to this point, we were talking about an individual approach to therapy. But borderline clients are immersed in frequent and complex relational problems that should be well understood and managed. These issues will be discussed in the next section of the book.

# Part Four
# Borderline Personality Disorder in the Interpersonal Context

# Chapter 15
# The Family of the BPD Client

Carmen is a 54-year-old woman who brings her daughter Sara to therapy. With her attitude, Sara makes it clear that she would rather be anywhere else. In the first session, and in front of the therapist, they both show their ability to say offensive things to each other. Carmen makes ongoing negative comments about Sara, such as, "She doesn't take care of her daughter; she doesn't care about anyone but herself." When Sara becomes activated due to these comments, the mother looks at the therapist in a complicit way and says, "See what I have to put up with every day?" Sara anticipates that the therapist will ally with her mother to scold her, so she stands up pushing the chair and says she never asked to come here, and that the person who should to have her head fixed is her mother. Before the therapist can speak, she slams the door and leaves.

The therapist feels very uncomfortable with Carmen, who talks non-stop for the rest of the session and puts him in the impossible situation of finding an urgent solution to Sara's problem, while at the same time, affirming categorically that her daughter "is hopeless." She talks about the countless previous diagnoses that the client has received, including depression, eating disorder, substance abuse, and BPD, asking the therapist to tell her "what her daughter really has." The therapist, after experiencing different unpleasant feelings with this woman, ends up asking her to leave the office, telling her that Sara is the client, and that he needs to talk with her.

After her mother leaves, Sara walks in and, soon after being in the room with the therapist, her attitude becomes more cooperative, recognizing that she has serious problems and needs help fixing them. She talks about how hurtful her mother is and how badly she treats her, giving numerous examples, and asks the therapist to get her mother to stop treating her like a little girl. The therapist complies with the process of talking to the mother, but tries to avoid her presence in the following sessions. Carmen solves this with long, frequent, and highly charged emotional phone calls, in which she tells the therapist how little Sara is doing to change and how serious her behaviors are, while insisting on how unproductive and unaffordable the therapy is for her.

Can therapy work without trying to understand this relational problem? Can we do an effective EMDR treatment only with the client's information? Can expanding the focus help, both so the therapist can position himself regarding the case and so the client can change her position in her family?

Sara is the oldest of 4 siblings. As the origin of her problems, she mentions verbal abuse from her mother, which sometimes ends in physical abuse, and the feeling that her mother had always rejected her. Her father is quite an absent figure, the client saying that he is completely destroyed by the mother and does not intervene in family problems. Neither one of them understood her when she told them that a group of school children had harassed her and described an episode of sexual abuse by several of them. Both parents agreed that she had it coming because she was keeping bad company and she kept getting into trouble. Sara states generally not knowing who she is, where she is going, or what she wants or can do with her life. She has a daughter, with one of the many problematic partners she has had, who lives with her and her mother at home. She often feels that her mother "takes over" in caring for her child.

After the last phone conversation with Carmen, which lasted about an hour, the therapist understands that he has to reposition himself with this woman. He tries to listen and understand what is behind this mother's emotional and overwhelmed speech. He understands that many of her comments are justifications and disclaimers and formulates the hypothesis that a significant burden of underlying guilt is feeding her reaction. He speaks with Carmen from this perspective, reinforcing her interest in her daughter and how much she had fought for this girl. He understands all the helplessness that seeing her going from problem to problem without being able to do anything about it can bring. He is able to establish an alliance with this woman, enough to convince her to start therapy for herself with a coworker at the clinic.

Looking at the client's mother in terms of her own story made the global picture more understandable. The oldest of 5 siblings, Carmen spent all her childhood caring for her siblings and her home. She never wanted her eldest daughter to go through anything like that, so she tried to give her "everything she never had," devoting herself to her children. When Carmen was a child, she was not allowed to complain, be tired, or be sick. When this happened, she got screamed at and insulted, even beaten up, so she learned to ignore her needs, her fatigue, and her boundaries. This led to the accumulation of a lot of discomfort, which had no healthy channel for discharge and periodically turned into angry outbursts. She showed significant dissociative symptomatology, with extensive memory gaps in her early history and extreme changes in her behavior. At age 9, she was sexually abused by a close relative, situation that lasted until she was 13. Her family knew, but looked the other way. She had a very troubled adolescence. She identified with the daughter's diagnosis, "She is like me when I was young," which on the one hand generated extreme guilt for having "passed on" this inheritance and, on the other, made her react to her daughter's symptoms in the same way that her parents had reacted to her discomfort at home. She refers frequent suicidal ideation and believes it is "inherited" from her own mother, "She was always in bed, she never got up or paid attention to us. Since I was the oldest, I had to do everything." When she now feels "that she has to do everything," she experiences it as a punishment that the world imposes on her, which is reinforced by her husband's passivity toward the situation. Her parents talked to her about their problems, just as she does with her own children. She thinks good children should never bad-mouth their parents, and she understands her daughter's direct challenges as lack of affection, which triggers her background beliefs of "I must have done something wrong for my daughter not to love me" and "I´m a bad mother."

After having a few sessions with Carmen, she begins to offer very valuable information for her daughter´s therapy. This information is much more objective, now that the emotional burden has decreased. Sara sometimes severely neglects the care of her own daughter, who is a year and a half old. She may not change her diaper for an entire day or may forget to feed her a meal. The girl is very attached to her grandmother, something that bothers Sara very much. Carmen understands that her daughter is jealous, but focuses, healthily, on the interest of the child. Now she is able not to blame Sara for her attitude with her child and instead does things with the child and involves Sara, so arguments have improved. The mother acknowledges that when she loses her temper, she says very hurtful things, things that she does not really think (and that, in the worst moments, she sometimes does not even remember), but at the same time, she sees that her daughter functions like she does and that they upset each other.

This information helped the client´s therapist realize that Sara had a problem with responsibility, as part of a pathological relational dynamic in which the mother, with intense feelings of guilt, constantly reproached her daughter. On the one hand, Sara did not assume healthy responsibility, being overwhelmed by her mother´s constant blaming and, on the other hand, she participated in the same chain of reproaches as her mother. Guilt was a hot potato that no one wanted and both were throwing it at each other but, in this game, no one took responsibility for their own actions, which is the only position from which change can take place. If the therapist were to have continued to ally with the client and see that "Sara´s problem was her mother," he would have become part of the same pathological relational dynamic in which these two women were trapped. Later, they started analyzing the situation with the father and the story of both families, which gave the client a useful perspective, helping her locate her problem and reformulate her situation. Her parents became instrumental in Sara´s recovery.

EMDR allows us to see the client, but also her family, from a comprehensive model in which current behaviors make sense in light of the biographical history. It also gives us a tool to break these chains of beliefs and dysfunctional patterns that often are passed from generation to generation. It helps us not to stay in the apparent. Family histories that favor the development of pathologies such as BPD are complex and cannot be understood from a simplistic view or from a "search for the culprit." Once trauma is processed and the client can say "this is my story" and "this is me," the family history will be one of the elements that may be looked at with understanding and freedom to "start over," leaving behind shared dysfunctional inheritances.

## The Family of the BPD Client

As we saw in the first chapters, early attachment relationships play a key role in the development of borderline pathology. At other times, to a greater or lesser extent, there are genetically based biological features contributing to the genesis of borderline symptomatology. A history of trauma, especially intrafamilial trauma, is more common in clinical populations and, among them, more so in BPD.

But these are more than just statistics. When clients with BPD come to therapy, they do not usually come alone. Since the clinical picture usually acquires its greatest intensity in adolescence or early adulthood, at this stage in life, individuals are still closely attached to their families of origin. If they managed to establish a certain level of autonomy, their low functioning level makes this incomplete. For example, the person continues to depend partially on the family at a financial level, or has not done well at the work level due to impulsiveness or relational problems and had to move back home with the parents. Often, due to the interpersonal dependency characteristic of borderline pathology, attachment with the family of origin remains intense. It is also likely that, faced with repeated failures in relationships due to their pattern of relational instability, people who are unable to tolerate loneliness go back home or strengthen the relationship with their parents.

It is easy to imagine the complexity of this situation. Clients return to the breeding grounds in which their problem developed. But then again, family is often the only support that individuals have and due to their own pathology, they are still not able to operate without support.

Therapists used to working individually are often overwhelmed by family groups of high intensity and complexity. These families tend to hoard time from clients' sessions who, on their own, already consume lots of energy from the professional. When families are particularly critical or hostile toward clients, therapists may tend to ally with the clients, entering into a particularly pernicious dynamic. If, on the other hand, therapists try to understand the family's position, clients will probably react negatively, which can become an obstacle for the therapeutic relationship. Immersed in the dysfunctional triad, "the friend of my enemy can't be my friend," therapists become trapped in a complex situation. The only solution is that clients and families, who were enemies before, become allies. But transitioning between the more or less open conflict that the family system often has and a healthy and productive collaboration for the benefit of all is not something that can be achieved with a couple of guidelines to the family or some strategic prescription. Those who have had BPD clients and their families together in the same office for more than 10 minutes will understand the content of these paragraphs very well.

## Multigenerational Maps

In order to understand the complex picture of BPD in the family context, we must be aware of the transgenerational nature of all factors involved. Attachment patterns are transmitted in the relationship between caregivers and children, with more than a 70% correspondence between the parents' and their children's attachment style (Grossmann, Grossmann, & Waters, 2005; Van IJzendoorn, 1992), and it is often reproduced in previous generations (Benoit & Parker, 1994; Bowen, 1978; Van IJzendoorn, 1992). Trauma histories usually happen in this way as well. For example, if we trace intrafamilial sexual abuse or physical abuse in clients' family trees, we will probably see more cases in the family history. Genetic traits, of course, are passed on from generation to generation. Drawing this map is very helpful, not only to understand clients and their family dynamics, but also so therapists can gain perspective on the problem and can place themselves equidistant to the parts of the complex system before them.

Ruth comes to the clinic because she has several difficulties in her daily functioning. At intake, she says that there was a situation that had great impact in her life: sexual abuse at age 7. Working with EMDR, she realizes that what was worse for her was her mother's reaction, who minimized its importance when she told her about it. In family therapy, the client's mother said that she too was abused, and her mother had responded with minimization as well. We did not have access to the grandmother to understand the origin of her attitude. For the client, to take into account what had happened in the family history helped her gain perspective on what happened and to position herself differently in regards to her mother.

## Family Models and Attachment Styles

Descriptions that systemic authors do of family models are confluent with what attachment theorists have proposed (Marvin, 2003; Stevenson-Hinde, 1990). Minuchin (1974) classified family structures into adaptive, enmeshed, disconnected, and chaotic. The adaptive family sets appropriate boundaries, which allow for both connection and autonomy of its members. This is the context of secure attachment. The enmeshed family is "too close," and boundaries between individuals are fuzzy. The self does not develop fully or independently, as we discussed when talking about resistant-ambivalent attachment in children, which will lead to preoccupied attachment in adults. Disconnected families have rigid boundaries but lack connection, as in avoidant-dismissive attachment. There are no problems with the autonomy of the self, but there are with connection to the self and others. The chaotic family has erratic and inconsistent boundaries, sharing traits with disorganized attachment families.

In the BPD clients' families of origin, and given that, as mentioned, BPD is most frequently associated to preoccupied and disorganized attachment, we will find more of the families that Minuchin calls enmeshed and chaotic. The first are defined by concern, lack of boundaries, intrusion into the private psychological space of the other, and difficulties with autonomy. The latter are characterized by inconsistency in patterns, lack of predictability, and it is in this context where they often present situations of abuse.

In our experience, a frequent pattern in BPD is a client with an overprotective or overinvolved mother and an authoritarian or distant father. Relationship patterns are divergent but complementary. When one member appears authoritarian, inflexible, critical, and hostile, constantly invalidating the client's feelings, emotions, and achievements, the other member tries to compensate this first pattern, becoming emotionally overinvolved (usually the mother). In neither of these two models does the client find healthy understanding and validation.

These divergent patterns reflect and enhance problems in the family hierarchy. Minuchin (1974) observed that healthy families have a hierarchy in which parents have most of the power. Children respect the parents' power and feel they can go to them for comfort and advice. Families that lack a proper hierarchy experience more conflict.

Couples with BPD children often have problematic relationships that tend to deteriorate due to the client's problems. A pernicious dynamic is generated in these situations: The frequency and intensity of children's problems greatly activate the divergent parental reaction in response, thus accentuating the couple's relational conflict. For these couples, immersed in their dysfunctional relationship, authentic communication and connection become inaccessible, and the children's problem may turn into the only possible bond between them. When the family pattern is enmeshed and autonomy is not even a possibility, the clients' improvement may pose a threat, since the only "glue" that kept the system together is lost. Thus, paradoxically, these families that seem to show the greatest concern for their children, may end up boycotting the clients' improvement. This dynamic is far from being conscious for the participants and draws a complex relational landscape.

**How Do We See This in Clinical Practice?**

In our experience, a large group of family situations in BPD relate to enmeshed family structures and preoccupied attachment, often with several members presenting divergent but complementary patterns, as we mentioned in the previous example. When clients come to our clinic, often there has been a deterioration process in which these dysfunctional patterns become increasingly extreme and healthy forms of attachment decrease. Another group, less frequent in BPD, are chaotic families and disorganized attachment patterns, with more elements of emotional, physical, and sexual abuse. This group, as we already mentioned, will probably present more dissociative symptoms and share more elements regarding comprehension and treatment with dissociative disorders.

a)  **As part of the pattern of enmeshed family - preoccupied attachment - inconsistent patterns, situations observed in the families of our clients with BPD are described below:**

Emotional and behavioral variability and inconsistency in what is transmitted. The therapist may have a feeling of confusion and "not having heard correctly." When situations are discussed by the family in a state of emotional arousal, contents vary and people may not even recognize their own words, denying having said certain things. There is often a view of extremes, without proper integration between the good and bad aspects of people. This variability is reminiscent of the changes in mental state of borderline clients, and it probably points to some degree of structural dissociation in the parents.

Overprotection and overinvolvement with the child, with whom there may even be an emotional over-identification. This over-identification can often be framed in a marital conflict between parents, establishing a pathological alliance between the client and one of the parents against the other. Thus, children become parentalized and parents may end up involving them in family conflicts or trying to have them mediate in conflicts between the parents. Children may have too much information about the lives of the adults, who make them their confidant. The overinvolved parent who "gives everything" for the children, though supposedly does this by choice, often becomes overwhelmed and then blames the client, as if this was something that the child had asked for or required.

A characteristic feature of preoccupied attachment that the client usually shares with at least one parent is the difficulty of establishing differentiating and respecting boundaries. This style tends to highlight the relationship type in enmeshed families, and the result is a lack of psychological development of the self and of one's own identity, as described in chapter 7. The parent does not conceive that the child may have an opinion that is different from what the adult feels or thinks. When the parent is angry with a family member, the child automatically has to be angry too. If the child does not share an opinion or an emotion with the parent, it is often interpreted as "you don't love me," or "you're selfish," which pushes the child to fit the pattern: "If you don't eat, you don't love me," "if you really cared about me, you wouldn't move in with your girlfriend." Since concern is what constitutes the bond in this attachment style, not sharing the concern is experienced as equivalent to breaking the bond.

A common result of the lack of defined boundaries is that children are not treated as autonomous beings, but as extensions of the parents. One of the parents may have the tendency to live the lives of others, in this case the client's, or to try to live what they have not lived through their children, regardless of their feelings, thoughts, and preferences. Clients are burdened with too much responsibility, "As long as you keep living with me, I'll keep on fighting," or in a more extreme case, "I don't kill myself because I have you," and they will feel they are responsible for the welfare of others. Their own needs must remain in the background.

In enmeshed families, preoccupation is the usual background music in interactions. From the foundation of concern, any of the children's behaviors, thoughts, or feelings usually becomes magnified and dramatized, turning it into a serious problem. This catastrophic emotional resonance is transmitted to the children, so when they fail in school, they will feel like a failure, and when they are ill, they think they will die.

b) **In other cases, as we mentioned, the families of clients with BPD are closer to chaotic structures and disorganized attachment patterns. The threat is present in the attachments, and it takes the form of emotional, physical, or sexual abuse.**

In these cases, we can see angry outbursts in some of the parents, which at times may be violent. There may be alcohol abuse, but not always. Either parent may have significant psychiatric pathology or specifically borderline traits with self-destructive behaviors.

Interactions are more paranoid, the parent interprets the often harmless reactions of the client as hostile, "You're doing this to piss me off," "you've failed so you could embarrass me." There may be humiliations, mocking, invalidations, insults, and various types of aggressions. In milder cases, these verbal attacks come at times when the parent is upset and assumes that it means nothing because it was said while being angry or upset. In severe cases, emotional, physical, or sexual abuse is justified: "It's not him, it's the alcohol," "it's your father, you have to understand him."

But the family is not just the parents. The role of the siblings is also very significant. Comparisons with the "model child" are not uncommon and are very harmful for the client's self-esteem. Sometimes the BPD client's siblings are placed on the back burner regarding situations at home, which can generate different types of psychological problems that are more or less obvious, or they have to take too much responsibility for their age. This can end up feeding resentment in the siblings, which directly or indirectly, gets back to the client; or it may be that the BPD client finds a sense of control in the relationship with the sibling which is not easily obtained in other contexts. As in the rest of relational situations, scenarios can be very diverse.

## Problematic Relatives: Understanding the Origins

Families, who often bring in clients with weak or ambivalent motivation, will ask for guidance and solutions. The way in which each of the individuals in the household place themselves in regards to the client is different and unique, and it is important to establish an alliance with each one of them to transform a troubled family into a team of co-therapists.

Some families work well with just psychoeducational work (Mosquera, 2009). An interesting possibility are family groups, where aside from information about their problem, they can share situations with other families, feel accompanied in their troubles, and gain a different perspective on what is happening to the client.

But often, some family members present particular management difficulties. As we commented in previous sections, it is important to consider that some genetic traits and attachment patterns are transmitted transgenerationally. Parents and relatives of BPD clients carry their own difficulties, and this will influence how they attend therapy and how they bring up the client's problem. Some families have greater difficulty. As in borderline clients, these difficulties do not originate exclusively in the relative's behavior, but also in the emotional reaction it produces in the therapist. The burden of dealing with a problematic client's troubled relative and the difficulty of maintaining balance generate reactions of tiredness, frustration, and helplessness in the professionals. They may tend to ally with the client, who they feel have to protect from the authoritarian, critical, or manipulative attitude of the relative.

EMDR, aside from a therapeutic intervention, gives us a perspective for looking at people's problems. As we saw in the initial example, seeing these relatives with their own stories and their own weaknesses and trying to understand where they learned the patterns from which they are functioning helps the therapist gain insight. It allows us to expand the map to include the family history. From this perspective, we will try to understand some family prototypes that have management difficulties (based on Mosquera & Ageitos, 2007).

## The Authoritarian or Controlling Relative

Authority and control are one of the axes of interpersonal relationships. Keisler (1983) describes the interpersonal circle, defining interpersonal behaviors along two dimensions: the vertical of control (dominance-submission) and the horizontal of affiliation (warmth-coldness/distance). Lack of flexibility to move around this circle generates pathology. A rigid pattern of domination and emotional distance characterizes the authoritarian or controlling relative. The client's response may be rigid submission, settling into a pattern of learned helplessness, or adoption of the same pattern, entering into periodic escalations. Alternating between the two patterns of domination-submission is highly likely in borderline clients.

Control by this family member may be exercised by making unilateral decisions or interrogations that seek to know what the client is doing at all times, which often generates a cycle of lies-distrust. In some cases, the family member is extremely demanding and regardless of the many advances of the client, these are never enough. The relative usually solves all problems by stating, "What he has to do is..." Of course, even if he does it, it will not make the relative show any pride and satisfaction. In cases of higher family disorganization, there may be an extremely critical or openly abusive parent.

A family consisting of a couple and their three daughters has been in treatment at different times, with different therapists, except for the father. Two of the daughters meet criteria for BPD, the other one has gone to work in a different region of the country. The two daughters, still at home, have frequent conflicts. The mother is an extremely worried woman, although her traits have attenuated with therapy. The father is a rigid and authoritarian man, who solves situations by banging on the table. On occasion, he has become physically aggressive. After the latest of these explosions, he agrees to go to therapy.

This father is a man with an alexithymic profile. He presents almost no contact with his own emotions and does not understand the internal processes that lead him to explode. He talks about a childhood with a dictatorial and inconsiderate father, for whom he worked for years in the family business. When his father died, he left everything to his brothers, but nothing to him. Such inconsiderate attitudes were common in both parents, a fact he minimizes by saying, "It doesn't affect me." His younger brother committed suicide a few years ago, but he says, "I'm over it." The possibility of working with this man in individual therapy seemed complex, since there was much disconnection and motivation for personal work was scarce, but he agreed to do a few sessions, which at least helped to prevent aggressive explosions.

## The Pessimistic-Catastrophic Relative

The predominant insecure attachment subtype in BPD is preoccupied. Worry and anxiety dominate relational styles, at least with some of the family members. A frequent couple is an anxious and worried mother with a distant and authoritarian father. The mother's attachment style feeds the lack of differentiation and the client's dependency. The father's attachment style encourages the lack of emotional recognition and also impulsive responses. They are a family of "high emotional expression."

But aside from this prototype, pessimistic-catastrophic family members present another problem in therapy. Their speech will focus on what clients do "to them" and the little interest they show for others. But often, they will not welcome practical solutions, easily returning to the pessimistic discourse and listing all the times clients have previously failed. If clients try to do something independently, which is usually discouraged in enmeshed families, these relatives will discourage or disqualify them, and perhaps will take over the task so they can later show clients how indispensable they are and how unable clients are to do it themselves.

In Keisler's (1983) circle, some family members with this pessimistic profile will be in a role of victimization-submission regarding the other parent, with a dominant profile. But for others, excessive closeness combines with extreme dominance, usually with indirect forms of expression through emotional manipulation. Clients often feel confused, doubt their perceptions, or are easily convinced that things are not how they see and feel them. Relatives may present their actions with a halo of interest, concern, and affection, verbalizing with great conviction that "they would die for their child," making clients feel guilty or selfish for not following their instructions or criteria.

In both cases, these family members will have low expectations about clients' chances of recovery, and they will have difficulty recognizing achievements. The more that rigid control characterizes the relationship, the more likely its interference in therapy will be.

The mother of a 17-year-old client often speaks with the therapist about the girl, looking very distressed by her situation. She has always lived for her daughter, who presented behavior problems from a very young age. She asks repeatedly if her daughter's issues will be fixed someday, and her tone of voice seems to anticipate that this will not happen. Although there have been some improvements in the client's situation and severe episodes of self-harm are no longer present, the tone of the mother remains one of intense concern. She complains to her husband that she must always carry everything on her shoulders, and when she gives him any explicit indication, he follows it without a problem. She has recently called the client's therapist to ask him to take care of the girl because "I can't go on and I'm going to get out of the way." After this, she talks for an hour on the phone with the family therapist about how overwhelmed she is with the situation. Given this woman's difficulties having a minimally realistic point of view, the therapist does not confront her with it, taking her feeling of being overwhelmed as an argument to resume her personal therapy, which she left months ago. Given how focused her life is on her daughter's problem, this definition of herself as an essential caregiver is not initially dismantled. The therapist helps her understand that precisely because she is a "key player" in the family, she needs to be well in order to remain in place, but at the same time she also deserves to take care of herself.

This woman came from a family with an intrusive and hypercritical mother and an alcoholic father, not violent but very peripheral, who neither gave affection nor protected his children from his wife's abusive behavior. There were several siblings, and this woman assumed the role of the caregiver, but since she was almost the same age as her siblings, and there was a significant level of abandonment, she recalled feeling overwhelmed trying to take care of other children like her, distressed by her mother's criticism about how she did it, and burdened by a responsibility that was not appropriate for her age. She continued doing the same with her own daughter, and feeling the same feelings from her childhood, a mixture between the obligation to deal with her and the heavy load she wanted to drop but was not allowed to (even if she now was the one who did not allow herself to drop it). She wanted to be "the best mother" as to not replay what she had experienced, but interestingly enough, without realizing it, she reproduced many of the hypercritical and hostile behaviors that her mother had with her children.

## The Distant-Avoidant Relative

Sometimes, one of the parents is virtually absent, even when spending time at home. They delegate full responsibility on the other parent, who may take care of everything, apparently protesting, but reinforcing a sense of being indispensable. This distance may be due to lack of their own emotional resonance, little connection with their own emotions, or difficulties in managing the anxiety that conflict or problems generate. This difference is important, because in the latter case, the information, guidance on what to do in various situations, and recognition of his interest in the client can help this distant parent take a more active role in therapy. Sometimes this recovery of the absent parent can be made more difficult by a more or less explicit alliance between the client and the other parent.

In other cases, there is no avoidance from anxiety, just difficulty connecting. The bond is established based on material things: "I told him I was sick, and he gave me money to buy clothes." The parent does not understand the client's complaints of lack of attention, "We've given you everything, you have not lacked anything."

A client and his mother often speak of how difficult the father is. He says things that are inadequate and out of place, which make the client feel worse. He complains that his father is never there when there are difficulties, and that when he goes through a crisis, he always delegates to the mother, who is exhausted and overwhelmed. They think it would be good if he came to therapy, which he has not done in the year and a half that the client has been in treatment.

When the man arrives, he is visibly nervous. He minimizes his son's problem talking about other kids he meets in his business, "Kids today are like that, they don't take responsibility for anything, they don't care." When the therapist explains that his child has a serious problem, not comparable with those kids' behavior, and that he has been about to kill himself several times, the father's eyes fill up with tears and his voice trembles, nodding to what the therapist explains. However, a little later he returns to the example of "the teenagers nowadays," which appears to be a way to fend off some emotions he does not know how to manage.

The early history of this man took place in an emotional desert. His parents were extremely cold and hard working. He had to start working at a very young age. He grew up surrounded by loneliness and lack of attention. His wife - who had to take care of all her siblings, as well as an always-depressed mother, whom she protected from her alcoholic husband - was the caretaker that he never had. His lack of emotional learning made him unable to communicate at an emotional level with his wife or son, or care for them, since he had not had any model of caring in his early history.

In just one session with the therapist, this man greatly changed his attitude toward the client, showing signs of wanting to follow the guidelines that were given to him. The client and his mother, however, spoke of him in subsequent sessions in a derogatory tone, pointing out his lack of relational skills. The mother had found in the client someone that "resonated in the same emotional wavelength than her" and the client had formed an extreme alliance with the mother, because from the father's side he had not been able to establish a bond.

## The Narcissistic Relative

They demand constant appreciation from their environment, but do not respond reciprocally. They are unable to meet the needs of others and usually commit negligence by not supporting or collaborating in the family. Clients feel they cannot count on them, and for some kind of relationship to take place it must be centered in the relatives, their needs, and desires.

This egocentrism may be exercised from a victim position. For example, a husband or wife who is authoritarian and dominant; from this standpoint, the child's situation has never been central. When he becomes an adult, he still has to engage in caring for this emotionally weak or depressed relative. When the son finally falls ill, the relative becomes even more depressed.

These family members needs to be the center of attention, and regardless of how severe the client's distress is, they always end up taking it on themselves, "I spend the day working and you're lying there on the couch doing nothing," or they compete with the client for the attention of the other parent.

A man monopolized the therapy sessions of his only son, explaining how the therapist had to deal with the boy's problem. Both the client and the mother indicated the father's arrogance as highly traumatic, always speaking as if being in possession of the truth. The father also talked to the therapist about his wife, explaining what the psychological problems of his wife were and how to solve them.

For a while, the therapist listened attentively to the father's story, reinforcing those aspects that seemed reasonable and accurate, and simply accepting the rest of his opinions without confrontation. This man's narcissistic defense was intense and rigid, and working on dismantling it should be gradual. The goal was to initiate individual therapy with the father, whose functioning was an important trigger for family problems. After a long work of strengthening the relationship with the therapist, he agreed to some sessions.

In the history of this man, we could see an early abandonment at age 10. His father moved to another country where he began a new life with another woman and disappeared completely from their lives. His mother "chose" him from his 4 siblings and turned him into her pride and support. Everything he did or said was always good for her, but this generated a lot of pressure on him and numerous conflicts with his siblings. In his mother's mind, the father was greatly idealized, and he had always been trying to prove he was better than his father.

The past relationship with his mother, now deceased, also distorts his current relationship, because he feels that his wife does not love him enough, like his mother did. Working with EMDR on the memory of the father leaving, he is surprised at the painful feeling of vulnerability that is associated with that memory. When they worked on the relationship with his wife, using as target a time when both stared into each other's eyes, he interrupted the session by saying that such contact with another person was "too intense." The same happened with his son, reflecting that genuine connection with another human being, as well as contact with his vulnerable self, was intolerable and unmanageable. The client agreed to work for awhile, and had a good enough relationship with the therapist to change some attitudes, although they did not touch on all core wounds or completely repair contact with his child self. With his wife, apparently more collaborative, it was impossible to conduct individual therapy sessions in depth. The process of individuation of the child from the core of the family was complex, and several interventions with different family members were needed.

## Unstable or Variables Patterns

The more chaotic the family structure and the more disorganized the attachment patterns, the higher the degree of structural dissociation that we shall see, not only in clients but also among family members. We may observe extreme and changing behaviors, often unpredictable. Family members may say something in one emotional state and the opposite thing in another. They may appear solicitous, interested in, and dedicated to the clients, and later invalidate them when there are no witnesses or they lose their temper. They may appear to collaborate and then boycott clients' progress, in ways that are sometimes subtle and difficult to identify.

Unstable patterns can be of various types, from extreme and changing emotional reactions regarding children (urge to protect, anger, avoidance, imitation, etc.) to the most extreme degree of dissociation in which the family member has marked dissociative symptoms that prevent functioning coherently.

A client comes to the office demanding to "be able to feel something." In his day to day, he is totally disconnected from his emotions, but sometimes they overwhelm him and he has angry outbursts that put him and others at risk (fighting and assaulting authority figures, destroying local businesses, cornering his family and threatening them, etc.). The client does not remember what he does during the outbursts and feels he is dangerous, that he has to be away from his family to avoid harming them. During intake, the client states how his father, an alcoholic, had abused and assaulted him at an early age. As a child, he froze at the variable and unpredictable reactions of his father. As an adult, he starts defending himself by reacting aggressively and violently (exactly like his father).

## Continuity of Transgenerational Transmission: The Child of the Client with BPD

If we understand that attachment patterns are transmitted from generation to generation, it is expected that the children of the clients we serve also present different types of problems, which may be more or less evident during therapy. Clients' problematic situations and their handling of difficulties within the couple or the family of origin can monopolize the entire session, which will become insufficient to cover all difficult areas. A realistic treatment of borderline personality disorder requires a team of professionals that can focus on differential aspects in a specific way.

Clients with BPD can have serious difficulties dealing with their children, but sometimes show great concern for them. However, the disorder is a good example of how different issues that have nothing to do with affection and interest can interfere with bonding. People unable to differentiate who they are, what they feel, and what they think from what other people are, feel, and think will not be able to help their own children understand their feelings and develop their autonomy. People who do not identify their needs or do not satisfy them in a balanced way cannot help children to be aware of theirs, or will be so extremely focus on the needs of the children, denying their own, that they will enter into a different, but also dysfunctional, pattern.

The impact of borderline personality disorder symptoms and clients' histories of parenting can be very diverse. The impulsivity that BPD clients have will make them less patient with their children's lack of regulation, reinforcing it. What clients reject in themselves, they will find difficult to accept in their children. Their deep feelings of guilt will make them feel like "a bad mother" or "a bad father," overreacting in their parental functions or spoiling the child. Someone who has experienced traumatic situations with the father of her child, may be triggered in situations with the child, for example when he shows reactions that resemble those of the father. A thousand different situations are possible depending on the history of each client, but it is difficult for a child to live unharmed in the relationship with a caregiver with profound difficulties in emotional management and interpersonal relationships. Only when the other parent or another family figure in direct relationship with the child, like a grandfather, is very present in the child's upbringing, can the difficulties and needs of the client in the care of her child be compensated for, enough to provide the child with resilience.

## Frequent Reactions in Children of Parents Affected by Borderline Personality Disorder

In our clinical practice, we have observed different reactions in the children of affected clients, which can be clustered into five subgroups (based on Mosquera 2007b):

a) **Pleasing - submissive**: worried about fitting in, "doing everything right" to "make others happy." They will be the perfect child, they will do great in school and in all their activities. There are so many problems at home that they try to not add any. They may present obsessive symptoms and focus on control as a way to feel safe in the unpredictability of family context and attachment.

b) **Rebel - irritable**: presents episodes of behavioral lack of control, which a parent with little capacity for emotional regulation will not be able to help manage, or may even enhance. Also, when parents cannot provide their children with the attention they need, bad behavior may be the only way to reclaim it. They can also share genetic traits of impulsivity with the parent with BPD.

c) **Anxious - dependent**: they present major separation anxiety and behaviors seeking to monopolize constant attention from parents. Though saturated with the demands of the children, they feel extremely guilty if they separate from them and if they are not there 100%. For example, they will not bear to hear them cry and will try to calm them down, even when this may be counterproductive; they will give them anything to make them stop: hold them for hours or sleep with them. Children may also share traits of emotional dysregulation and anxiety with the borderline parent.

d) **Responsible - caregiver**: they assume responsibilities that do not correspond to their age, reversing roles and caring for their parents. Sometimes, one of the siblings will serve as parent to the others when the adults do not take care of the children. They are apparently very mature children and do not usually express, nor realize, their own discomfort.

e) **Avoidant - self-absorbed**: they try to avoid confrontation, in relationships both with the family and with other people. They do not talk about their problems and feelings, and they do anything to avoid conflict, which they do not know how to handle. They become isolated or blocked when their parent is not well, and they seem to be in their own little world and not realize what is happening.

These reactions may be more or less variable. Some children adapt to a role and have trouble getting out of it; others cannot tolerate acting in a certain way for a long time. The following example shows this variability:

"I've gone through several stages; in the first one I tried to help my mother, I was always checking on her, I tried to get the best grades, do everything right... I thought this way she would feel better, I wanted her to stop being sad, to stop suffering... I thought I could compensate her..., then I went into a stage of rebellion, I protested about everything, I argued all the time... I even fantasized with her hurting me... This stage was more bearable than the other one, in the other one I was in a void, I didn´t exist... In this one, I didn´t like what I did, but at least "I existed."

## How to Help Prevent Problems in the Children of Clients with BPD

With the right help, clients can understand their patterns and change them. When it comes to children, parents with BPD often have additional motivation to improve and change toward healthier patterns. Often, they have difficulty making changes to their advantage, but they do it for their children. While it is important for them to learn to consider and value themselves, the development of the relationship with their children will help them change many things in their reactions, while we prevent problems in these children and in the adults they will become.

Clients sometimes find it difficult to recognize these situations with their children, because they feel extremely embarrassed or guilty. At other times, their difficulties "looking inward" prevent them from seeing the child in front of them with real mindsight (Siegel, 2011). Maybe their own traumatic history can come between them and their children, interfering with the establishment of a healthy and genuine attachment:

"Now I deal better with my anger issue. Before, I hit him and became aggressive with him. Now, I don´t do it. But I have a hard time seeing him cry; I can´t tolerate it. When he expresses his emotions, it´s like a mirror in which I see my own repressed emotions. When he tells me that children treat him badly, my own abuse is activated. My reaction has nothing to do with him, it has to do with me."

It is especially important to pay attention to the very normative children, those who care for adults or siblings, who always behave well, and do not create any problems. These children may go unnoticed and give the impression of not having problems. Regardless of how children are, it is important to give them information about what is happening, in the most natural and clear way possible. Children, whether they clearly demonstrate it, and especially if they do not, catch on to all the difficulties at home and suffer different emotional reactions, with which they need help from someone. Giving this information in collaboration with the parents also helps them learn a healthy communication model.

Working with BPD clients and their children is a patient reconstruction of the attachment and a joint learning of emotional vocabulary and ability to understand one´s own mental states and those of others. Parents need help "realizing" what happens to the children, the concrete and real child in front of them, differentiated from themselves, without becoming infected with their emotional states. Some studies with mothers and children focusing on the development of the mentalizing ability (Sadler, Slade, & Mayers, 2006) have shown interesting possibilities for restructuring the mother-child relationship. From the field of EMDR, Wesselman (2007) has presented various methods for reestablishing bonds when there are disruptions in attachment between parents and children, which can be adapted to these cases. However, with a BPD parent, the personal therapy process has to be parallel to the work with their children. This is a privileged moment in which we can break the chain of intergenerational transmission of dysfunctional patterns.

234

The words of this client are a good description of the change process that clients are able to perform with their children and the difficulties they run into during the process:

> "I remember the first time that I had them as newborn in my arms, those conflicting emotions of joy, heavy responsibility, and thinking, 'Will we be prepared for this?' Every day I worry about whether I will be able to meet all the needs of my children and just like a body that needs food, whether we will be giving them all they need to have a life that does not lack affection. We try to plan family activities and make them see how valuable they are in our lives, but I also try to have them understand that I need my time to be alone with their father and that they have to respect that. I dedicate a lot of time and effort to them.
>
> The other day, I was upset with one of them. She wanted to negotiate and I said, 'No, no, there is not negotiation here, there is a structure, clear rules: yes is yes and no is no,' and I proposed a deal, 'We will make a list of 5 well-chosen family rules, along with each rule the punishment for disobeying it, including mom and dad, we will review them periodically to know what is expected of each one of us.' The fact that we were also included was funny for them and motivated them to comply with us. I'm also teaching them to distribute their schedule to study, work at home, and play, so they start organizing themselves, so they start learning.
>
> Another of the things we now have to be aware of is to listen. These last few days, I have been so very low that the last thing I wanted was to listen to anyone, much less talk. But, in fact, their problems and doubts are the most important and the biggest problem in the world for them, so even if they sometimes exaggerate, we have to consider their feelings, because if not, the communication channel is interrupted.
>
> The other day X told me: 'Mom, so and so said to me that his dad gets very nervous and I listened carefully and said: Don't worry, my mother also gets very nervous at times, she has an illness, BPD.' And I said, 'Baby, you don't talk about that (laughing).' 'But Mom, it's not the same! You don't hit me, and her father does. And the worst thing is that he doesn't want to get treatment, you're going to therapy, you're doing a lot for your life.'
>
> And she said it so naturally, I couldn't stop laughing. The truth is that we have addressed all the issues so naturally that the communication path is, for the moment, completely open."

In understanding and managing BPD clients, family dynamics are as crucial as couple relationship dynamics, as we will see in the next chapter.

# Chapter 16
# BPD and Couples: Complexity Squared

As part of their own disorder, clients with borderline pathology tend to be trapped in problematic relationships of different types, but some relational contexts present greater complexity. As we saw in the previous chapter, on the one hand, in the relationship with the family of origin, interaction patterns that were already present in early development often become apparent. We can see how different family members´ relational difficulties converge to generate situations that are sometimes difficult to manage and are closely linked to the maintenance of the client´s problem. On the other hand, the relationship, given the greater intimacy and intensity of the bond, easily triggers many of the symptoms and distortions that we see in BPD.

The issues we have been discussing throughout the chapters of this book will help us understand the interactions between BPD clients and their partners and their difficulties in establishing healthy intimate relationships.

In this chapter, we review previously mentioned issues in order to understand the origin of clients´ relational difficulties. We will think about different BPD subtypes and their possible connection with different personality profiles, referring to some of the conjunctions of pathological personalities that can often be seen in clinical practice (based on Mosquera & Gonzalez, 2013).

# Several Levels of Analysis

The attachment styles, cognitive processes, and specific symptomatic constellation of each individual with BPD can help us understand the borderline client in a couple relationship:

1. The attachment style helps us connect current problems in relationships with early history.

2. Altered cognitive and emotional processes in clients with BPD, such as mentalization deficits, emotional regulation, differentiation, or lack of integration can also help us understand some of their relational difficulties.

3. Relational difficulties may be different, depending on the type of BPD and its most important criteria.

# Attachment and Couple Relationships

Individuals with secure attachment are better at interpreting negative facial emotions and perceive positive emotions better than those with anxious attachment (Páez, Campos, Fernández, Zubieta, & Casullo, 2007). In individuals with BPD, in which insecure attachment is the norm, the reactions of people they live with are often inadequately interpreted. This is not only because many gestures or attitudes function as triggers of previous situations, but especially because of their difficulties in mentalization and identifying mental states and other people's motivations as different from their own.

Clients, unable to see others as individuals with different motivations and emotions, will interpret the others' emotions based on "their own state." For example, they can perceive another person as angry when they are the ones feeling anger. In addition, they will have trouble identifying and differentiating their own emotions, accepting that they feel "what they say they feel."

People with secure attachment are more responsive to the unexpected and are less reactive than those with insecure attachment. People with secure attachment usually deal with their problems, tend to focus on possible solutions, and see the positive in what is happening. On the contrary, people with insecure or disorganized attachment often have many difficulties coping effectively with problems and tend to resort to impulsive action, something very common in people with BPD. Given the inevitable frictions of cohabitation and the necessary adjustments of life as a couple, borderline clients will tend to "drown in a glass of water" and find themselves with the same problem over and over, being unable to think of any practical solution.

## Insecure - Ambivalent - Resistant – Preoccupied Attachment

Think of the early history of insecure-ambivalent attachment. The caregiver is scared, feels anxious, or becomes overwhelmed when the child cries or is upset. Continually, normal and adaptive emotions are associated in the child with a sense of alarm or rejection. As adults, BPD clients will not regulate certain emotions when they appear, showing overwhelmed and uncontrolled reactions, even in a calm couple. But if, as often happens, the partner is impulsive, anxious, rigid, or critical, the client's dysregulation will multiply. Lack of their own mechanisms of emotional regulation and autonomy leaves borderline individuals the only resource of using others to control their discomfort, even though other people not only may be ineffective at it, but even when their response is counterproductive.

On the other hand, and without these two situations overlapping, but instead alternating, children have times when the parents are emotionally accessible and close. At those times, children can develop a positive self-concept that is uncertain, as it may change at any given time or only be reached "under certain circumstances." Children can then learn to modify their emotional states to keep their caregiver in this receptive and accessible state, containing or disconnecting from the emotions that parents do not tolerate. When these moments are few and far between, children may overadapt, trying to do more and more, while internally generating the belief that "it is never enough." In other situations related to this insecure - ambivalent attachment subtype, very anxious parents establish symbiotic bonds with their children, in which their own insecurity is compensated through an extreme style of control that does not support individuation. In these cases, children become an extension of the parents, cutting off any possibility for autonomy through direct censorship or, more likely, through emotional coercion: "If you don't feel the same as me, if you don't see the world as I see it, it's that you don't love me , it's that you're a bad son."

In either of these cases related to preoccupied attachment in adults, we will see flaws in the basic differentiation of self, difficulties in "looking inside" (identity is obtained only through others), and sometimes rejected aspects of the self. In regards to a couple, this means that clients feel that, literally, they need others to exist. Separation is experienced as annihilation and, therefore, they will do anything to keep the relationship, no matter how many negative consequences it brings. The situations that arise in this type of attachment will have a lot to do with pathological emotional dependency, and conflict will be generated mainly from fear of abandonment or the real possibility of it occurring.

In these cases, we will work with EMDR on the memories associated to attachment situations with the necessary psychoeducation, since, as we mentioned, many of these situations probably will be experienced as "normal." In addition, we will work on events related to previous couple relationships, most likely with examples of problems arising from the same pattern. But it is essential to do specific work on the image of the self, as explained in Chapter 7, and to work with the self-care patterns discussed in Chapter 8, along with the necessary psychoeducation so that clients develop their own self-regulatory resources.

When individuals with BPD grow up with parents who combine this insecure ambivalent attachment style with a high level of criticism, rejection, or hostility, their self-image is often more negative and self-critical, while they see others as being more positive. Their beliefs usually refer to "there is something wrong with me that makes others not love me," while others are seen from an idealized perspective. The feeling that their partner is neither as close nor supports them as much as they would like (Hazan & Shaver, 1994) may be present regardless of the type of relationship they maintain, but they often end up with partners whose patterns have similarities with their experiences with their parents. Until early memories are processed, individuals will search for "everything they did not have" in their own childhood in each new relationship. From this dysfunctionally stored information, it is easy to imagine the never-fulfilled demand for attention that some of the people with this diagnosis may transfer to their partners, and how easy it can be to trigger the preverbal memory of the painful lack of a nutritional attachment.

A critical or even abusive partner telling them things about themselves that fit their nuclear negative beliefs fits well in their world. But on the other hand, their positive worldview makes them idealize this person, "omitting" the hostility or negative comments they receive. Intermittent reinforcement of the primary caregiver's inconsistency, overinvolved at times and rejecting at others, inconsistent and unpredictable, finds many echoes in a partner who seems to provide them with equally inconsistent affection. In session, a BPD client with this profile will focus on talking non-stop about their partner's insults, while being unable to leave the relationship or to explain why. This case has more similarities with insecure disorganized attachment, which we will discuss below. After the necessary work on early attachment experiences, it will be necessary to work with EMDR not only on the moments of aggression or criticism from the partner, but also on the best moments (real, idealized, or dreamt) and the view of the partner, including both the good and bad times.

## Insecure Disorganized - Disoriented or Unresolved Attachment

In disorganized (insecure) attachment, children's needs are not met by their parents, whose behavior is, on the contrary, a source of disorientation and/or fear. Instead of a safe haven, it generates alarm and confusion in children, placing them in a biological paradox. The biological attachment system is programmed to motivate children to seek proximity with the caregiver in times of distress, in order to be comforted and protected. But in this case, children are at a dead end because fleeing from what causes fear or alarm is also a biological mechanism. This is what Main and Hesse (1990) have called "fright without solution." Thus, as the only possible adaptation, the attachment system becomes disorganized and chaotic.

In BPD adults with disorganized attachment (with a more dissociative profile), responses will be more extreme and disconnected. Oscillation between the need for attachment and the defense-aggression-flight is much clearer, and both responses may occur simultaneously. The attachment object is experienced as a source of danger and ambivalent and contradictory responses are more pronounced.

From these early experiences, problems with responsibility and guilt are also often generated. Usually, children assume responsibility for the parents' behavior, who in turn often blame others for their own behavior or are excused by the other parent, "Your father is not bad, he has a temper, we must understand him." For the children, blaming themselves also meets an adaptive function: It preserves the idealization of the attachment figures, which is the only realistic way to bond in a dysfunctional family. This guilt is a common core belief in these clients, taking responsibility as adults for what happens around them. This is an emotional territory suitable for situations of domestic abuse. Clients will blame themselves for the insults or beatings, excusing their partners, "He loves me, he regrets it very much, he can´t control himself."

Others, after becoming tired of this role, go to the opposite extreme and blame others for everything that happens.

These attributions of responsibility and guilt can sometimes fluctuate from one moment to the next; clients enter into a discourse focused on "the story of the bad guy": talking about everything bad that their partners do to them. If interviewers innocently ask what the reason is for not leaving their partners, clients can go on to explain that they cannot live without them. Only when we understand that the first part of the speech is the expression of a defensive struggle and the second one is the activation of a primal cry of attachment, and we work on these alternating mental states with the perspective of where they learned them, can we find a framework from which to promote real change.

## Mentalization and Communication

In BPD, the development of a real image of the self, as an entity that manages mental actions and behavior, fails. They cannot see other people as autonomous beings with their own mental processes. Individuals do not understand what is inside, which they experience as an undifferentiated amalgam in which emotions, thoughts, and feelings are not differentiated or understood. In this context, even looking inside can be distressing. The reflective capacity is scarce, and impulsive responses predominate (Bateman & Fonagy, 2004).

At a cognitive level, validity of the primitive modes of mental functioning involves failures in many of the functions of mentalization. These manifest as concrete thinking, difficulty in forming a representation of one´s own and the other person´s mental world, predominance of rigid and stereotyped attribution schemas in interpersonal relationships, impulsivity, emotional dysregulation, a tendency to act out, etc. Individuals with BPD lack elements for interpreting others, their motivations, and their actions.

Problems in the couple that derive from a failure in mentalization ability go beyond the cognitive difficulty of understanding others as individuals. During childhood, they do not get to see their own emotional states reflected in the caregiver, so they have no choice but to internalize representations of the caregiver´s state as part of their representation of themselves. This creates a foreign experience inside: They have beliefs, an internal critic, and emotions that they do not feel as their own but which work inside as powerful slogans. Thus, ideas and feelings that do not seem to belong to the self are experienced as a part of it. Sometimes, this image colonizes the self and upsets its sense of identity and coherence, so it must be projected in an attempt to restore continuity of experience. In this projection, individuals with BPD accuse others of their own unacknowledged impulses. Attempting to process both current situations experienced as adverse (which are really projections) and early experiences with the caregiver (with whom they have not been able to develop an adequate differentiation) with EMDR will probably be fruitless without prior psychoeducational work and the development of a certain degree of autonomy of the self, which helps clients have a more realistic view of the their problems.

There are certain elements that must be developed throughout the therapeutic process, which are extremely necessary for managing relational and marital problems: reflective capacity; identification of basic mental states, such as thoughts, feelings, desires, intentions, and beliefs about oneself and others; and being able to think about and imagine such states. Affect-laden interactions complicate the possibility of influencing others by psychological means, leading to attempts to control the behavior of others. This is perceived as a hostile or coercive action, which, in turn, awakens strong feelings in them which foster less reflexive actions, thus starting a similar negative cycle. But this emotional and relational learning also lays the foundation for a more effective processing of the memories that feed clients´ problems, by improving the identification of elements to process and especially the required dual attention.

The processing of specific memories must not wait, however, for all this learning to take place, not even when clients are immersed in a troubled or even actively abusive relationship. Let us consider that prior trauma activates more primitive reactions and makes individuals stop having access to more adaptive later experiences. Reflective thinking, dependent on prefrontal areas, is disabled in situations of high emotional arousal and people start to run in "amygdala mode," or from a child mental state. Once the attachment relationship is activated, other people´s mental states are less clear. The end of the relationship is experienced as annihilation of the self. When this process takes place, dependence on the other person becomes total (Fonagy et al., 2007). Pure psychoeducational work in this case may be unproductive and frustrating. If clients´ capacity for tolerance makes the processing of the most activated memory possible, a standard EMDR session, or even an incomplete processing, can offer another emotional context from which to work on relational situations.

## Difficulties Depending on the Symptomatic Profile

For the understanding and conceptualization of cases, we have developed a classification of frequent partners for the BPD client (Mosquera & Gonzalez, 2013). This classification into subtypes is not aimed at multiplying diagnostic labels, but at helping us understand the different ways of presenting borderline pathology, beyond the prototypical clinical pictures. These subgroups also help us understand the many different situations that we see in BPD clients regarding couple relationships. We have called the first group relational BPD, in which we can see various kinds of difficulties with their partners, which obey the criterion related to problematic and unstable interpersonal relationships. The second group is called defensive BPD, and these are clients with a borderline structure, but whose defenses determine a more atypical appearance. A third group will be the seemingly self-centered, which may resemble personality disorders most associated to egocentrism, such as histrionic or antisocial, but in which there are prevalent underlying borderline traits.

# Group 1: Relational BPD

They tend to become immersed in problematic relationships, in which they appear to be trapped.

The predominant criteria for this group are: frantic efforts to avoid real or imagined abandonment, relational difficulties (relationships that, regardless of how problematic, they cannot do without), identity disturbance, emotional instability, and a feeling of emptiness.

We can divide the relational BPD in 2 subtypes: dependent borderline and ambivalent-unstable borderline.

## 1.1 Dependent Borderline

In these clients, efforts to avoid abandonment (be it real or imaginary) are really desperate, and the core criteria will be, along with this, an altered sense of self and chronic feelings of emptiness. The predominant attachment style is preoccupied and there is often less definition of the boundaries of the self and inner experiences.

Mood instability and suicide attempts often come from sometimes insignificant relational difficulties with the people they depend on. Any gesture of independence by the partner is experienced as abandonment, which can lead to intense jealousy. They present great difficulties in being autonomous, and tend to see the solution of their problems in what others would have to change. They only do things for themselves when they have no other choice, and they experience loneliness as something negative and unbearable.

The problem in therapy is often that their motivation is the disappearance of the discomfort that is generated by these situations, rather than the desire to change them, and that their position regarding the therapist will also tend to be dependent, hoping "to be healed." Depending on the type of partner they are with, the work of relational situations will vary.

## 1.2 The Ambivalent-Unstable Borderline

In this subgroup there is great ambivalence. When they feel they are getting too close to others, they experience great insecurity that drives them to hostile behaviors or avoidance of intimacy (whichever they feel is necessary to protect themselves). Their extreme need for attachment leads them to take the risk of intimacy despite their enormous difficulties with interpersonal bonds, reacting to any perceived danger in an extreme way (from an extreme hypersensitivity).

This subtype is characterized by instability, both in mood and behavior, and by responses that are often impulsive. The type of attachment may be ambivalent, but it is often disorganized, becoming more associated with dissociative features. There are more memories associated with criticism, hostility, or aggression with primary caregivers.

These clients may be "addicted to the intensity," understanding true love as a necessarily painful passion, which they seek to repeat from a pattern which is similar to addiction. From here, the partners they connect with will also be intense, but not particularly stable. Sometimes, the person is hung up on the few moments when the relationship brought them what they much needed or even on what they wanted to happen and that never took place. As mentioned, the treatment plan will include both early experiences and traumatic and idealized couple situations. In such cases, when working from a model of structural dissociation, with or without severe dissociative symptoms, it is essential to put the contradictory action tendencies in attachment relationships on the table.

# Group 2: Defensive BPD

Many borderline clients do not show a prototypical appearance, thus leading to confusion with other diagnostic labels. The borderline structure is present, but different types of defenses are established to protect themselves from intense emotions that are felt as intolerable.

We have divided defensive BPD into 5 subtypes: avoidant, rigid, paranoid, dissociative, and depressive-negativistic (Mosquera & Gonzalez, 2013).

### 2.1. The Avoidant Borderline

There is a predominant avoidant style and a tendency toward reactivity when exposed to situations that they do not know how to handle, especially in regard to relationships and possible situations of rejection, or when the fear of not fitting in, being judged, or being "attacked" by others comes up.

Feelings of inadequacy, which appear in avoidant personality disorder, are also present, but in this case they usually relate to previous experiences.

Sometimes, these are people who used to present previously flashy, impulsive, and histrionic behaviors that have caused constant problems, crises, and frequent hospitalizations, and they have learned to avoid any situation that could destabilize them. They tell themselves: "This way, I don´t have any problems or become disappointed," "I´m in a mini-world, so I have everything under control, any invasion of this space is too big a risk for me."

In extreme cases, clients may seem schizoid, reaching a degree of isolation from the world that, unlike the true schizoid, basically they do not want. Feeling of not fitting in, of being different, prevail, as well as thoughts like, "I´m better off alone," "others can hurt me," or "the world is dangerous, it´s better to avoid it." The diagnostic criteria of BPD may not be apparently present because the individual denies it, but they really feel loneliness as painful (associated with the feeling of emptiness) and their mood is unstable, as well as their identity.

The previous stage of open dysregulation that we mentioned earlier will not be evident in all cases. There may be individuals that are highly vulnerable to rejection and have strong feelings of shame, manifesting depressive episodes, isolation, anxiety, suicide attempts, or substance abuse as reactive decompensations to romantic disappointments. These reactions sometimes occur with platonic relationships they do not even dare to start or that they give up on at the first hurdle or sign of rejection or disinterest.

Working with EMDR in these individuals must be patient and progressive. It requires a much longer time for them to be able to feel any safety establishing bonds in the therapeutic relationship. Any attempt to force the pace can lead to an interruption in therapy or a relapse. For example, a client came to therapy once every three months. He recognized that working with EMDR gave him far more than his previous cognitive behavioral therapy, but he said the change was "too fast" for him. After working on a memory of physical abuse by his father, which for the first two years of therapy, he had failed to tell the therapist about, he interrupted the sessions for a year, falling into a state of deep depression. When resuming treatment, it was possible to negotiate more continuous work (one appointment per month) with a commitment to alternate working with EMDR with more psychoeducational interventions.

## 2.2 The Rigid Borderline

Their external appearance resembles obsessive personalities, but they are really people with high emotional instability, great fragility regarding the opinions and/or criteria of others, and many relational and cognitive difficulties. Rigidity is just a compensatory behavior that allows them to maintain a sense of control over the difficulties they present in many areas of their life.

This rigidity differs from obsessive personality disorder in that it is not structural: It is only a shell, a shaky defensive mechanism they hold on to desperately due to their difficulty tolerating uncertainty and chaos. Time and again, they tend to go back to what is familiar, even if it does not work, because leaving that familiarity generates insecurity and confronts them with their deep vulnerability. Due to this, they have trouble making changes in their lives, although they are willing and understand that it would necessary to do so in order to feel better. They may develop obsessive rituals and compulsions, and self-harm often serves a similar function.

BPD clients who use this rigid armor may come from either a very controlling, strict, or demanding environment (they internalize these features) or an extremely chaotic one (control being a way to survive absolute uncertainty). Control is the central feature in the relationships they establish, and since this control is a defense against uncertainty, there will be a tendency to take it to extremes when dealing with daily difficulties. When something unexpected and "beyond their control" comes up, they may become aggressive with themselves and others. The affective instability and the high reactivity of their mood are generally suppressed by compensatory behaviors and rituals.

Often, these clients do not get to establish significant couple relationships, since intimacy makes them feel too exposed.

Although in a different way than the previous subtype, EMDR work must be cautious because of the role that the defensive structure is playing. Although there are procedures to specifically target the defenses with EMDR, such as the procedures proposed by Knipe and Leeds, prematurely dismantling defenses before giving the individual sufficient resources, without a powerful therapeutic alliance and without a solid previous therapeutic process, can lead to a set-back rather than a positive development.

## 2.3. The Paranoid Borderline

A style of extreme distrust, in many cases related to previous experiences, predominates in these clients. When early attachment, at a time when we are developmentally most vulnerable, is a source of damage, it is easy to develop a belief such as "I can´t trust anyone." Later traumatic situations can feed this perspective on relationships, to the point of turning it into a core belief. Suspicion, distrust, and defensiveness can be understood as "neurological self-referentiality," but also as a reaction to triggers that remind the client of early experiences that are still stored in the nervous system. Many times certain genetic traits, consumption of certain drugs, and adverse experiences combine to exponentially generate the expression of this trait.

Clients´ discourse can be focused on the "list of grievances" that confirms their negative view of the human being, on an "intolerance of injustice or lies." In couple relationships, behaviors that are experienced by clients as betrayal or deceit are considered impossible to assume. A common expression of pathological distrust in the relationships of borderline clients is jealousy. Clients who present as most paranoid almost reach the dimension of pathological jealousy. When these behaviors are based on previous experiences, processing the specific memories with EMDR can be extremely helpful. The main difficulty of this work is that clients are greatly focused on what "other people" do, which at times makes it difficult to identify the underlying negative beliefs. Let us consider that in this case, the paranoid attitude is a defense against powerful feelings of inferiority, insecurity, and helplessness. Contact with these core issues should not be forced beyond the client´s tolerance, taking into account that the therapeutic relationship in a client with suspicion and distrust usually has specific complexities.

## 2.4. The Dissociative Borderline

As discussed in Chapter 2, although structural dissociation would be the basic mechanism from which borderline pathology develops, a subgroup of clients have more apparent dissociative symptoms. They meet criteria for the diagnosis of a dissociative disorder itself (Mosquera et al., 2011) and treatment with EMDR must be closer to the treatment of dissociation (Gonzalez & Mosquera 2012).

These clients frequently present amnesic gaps, depersonalization experiences (seeing themselves from outside their body, disconnection from the body, etc.), and fragmentation (different mental states that manifest as intrusive thoughts, auditory hallucinations, or very different behaviors at different times, some of which they may not remember). These behaviors are experienced as alien and ego-dystonic, as if "it were not me."

When in a couple relationship, they have dramatically different reactions, and sometimes they may not be able to remember what they do at other times. Partners usually have the feeling of "living with several different people," or that many times the other "does not seem like the same person."

The complexity of these cases can be addressed by working with the parts and with the internal system. For example, a client talks about her partner, describing numerous despotic and abusive behaviors. She says that she stays with him for financial reasons and because of her masochistic traits, which she describes elaborately after years of different psychotherapies. She hears a commanding voice that tells her to assault other people. In working with the meeting place, a technique for working with dissociative parts, she identifies a submissive child part that is attached to her partner, as she was to their parents, and an aggressive part connected with the voices. The submissive part is focused on the attachment to a violent father and a negligent and emotionally abusive mother, who she idealizes from this mental state. The aggressive part can see all the damage she received and, only from this state of mind, is she able to access memories of physical abuse and violent sexual assault by her father in adolescence. Working with EMDR to address dissociative phobias, as well as with the internal system, was helping with the progressive disappearance of the voices and the processing of traumatic content. This work was associated with changes in the relationship, improving not only the ability to set boundaries and develop autonomy, but also to recognize the attachment that kept her connected to that person and the reasons that led to this pattern of functioning.

## 2.5. The Depressive-Negative Borderline

Some clients with BPD present primarily depressive symptoms, and they are often initially diagnosed as major depression or dysthymia, but they respond poorly to antidepressants.

Negativity would be the most characteristic defense mechanism in this subtype, along with denial and despair, which, although they may be felt very intensely, eventually become their identity.

Affective instability with frequent depressive symptoms and mood fluctuations is characteristic of many borderline clinical pictures, but in these cases it ends up becoming a defense.

This can be due to the fact that:

a)  They cling to their depressive identity in the absence of a defined healthy identity.

b)  Due to early traumatic history, they operate from a state of learned helplessness.

c)  Although unpleasant, this depressive state is a familiar environment that they find more tolerable than the uncertainty of relating to others and making adaptive changes.

Thus, sadness becomes a safe place to which they return automatically when faced with the smallest difficulty. These clients may become victims of domestic violence, but this may end up becoming an identity, and they may tend to operate from the role of the victim.

In some cases, this is based on a traumatic history. As we commented in prior chapters, children that grew up in an abusive environment, with one violent parent and one victimized and submissive parent, may identify with the non-abusive parent because the alternative (being like the abuser) is unimaginable. Born in this world of opposites, only these two extreme roles will seem possible to the adult that has developed a borderline pathology.

People who fit this subtype may have difficulty empathizing with others because they are too focused on their own problems and, in some cases, come to share points in common with narcissistic personalities, although covered up with a mask of vulnerability and weakness.

As in any other case, the work with EMDR will depend on the context in which this pattern occurs. When what predominates is learned helplessness, working with patterns of self-care may be interesting. When suffering is a deeply rooted identity, psychoeducational work and the reformulation of the problem are equally essential and complex. Otherwise, processing the sources, presented by the client as the origin of that suffering, with EMDR will most likely be unproductive.

## Group 3: Apparently Egocentric BPD

Clients with little or no empathy, focused on meeting their needs, will be classified in the DSM-V as narcissistic or antisocial personalities. However, difficulties in mentalization have been considered core features of borderline pathology (Bateman & Fonagy, 2004), and they can be expressed as an absolute inability to understand the thought processes of others, their emotional reactions, and their motivations.

Unlike the authentic narcissistic and antisocial personality disorders, in BPD clients with this profile, we shall see that being self-centered compensates against core beliefs such as "I´m not important" or "I don´t exist" that hide underneath. Externally, these people seem to be led by their own needs and are often perceived as instrumentalists (using others to meet their own needs), but there is a significant underlying dependence based on the inability for autonomy and self-regulation.

We have divided the seemingly egocentric BPD into 2 subtypes: histrionic borderline and learned antisocial borderline (Mosquera & Gonzalez, 2013).

### 3.1. The Histrionic Borderline

There is a predominant dramatic, explosive, and intense style. Histrionic personality disorder seems destined to disappear in the DSM-V and perhaps a subgroup lacking empathy and emotional resonance may be included in the antisocial and narcissistic groups.

Many of these clients will share core BPD traits and behaviors and, under their dramatic behaviors, there will be a high emotional dependence on others, whose attention they reclaim by the only (dysfunctional) means to which they have access. They often behave as open and seductive, seeking acceptance and integration, but they can be very demanding in order to be able to feel good.

When they do not get to be the center of attention, they can act dramatically (make up stories, resort to self-harm, blackmail, and/or suicide attempts) to draw attention to themselves. Relational problems will be cumbersome and complex, presenting frequent manipulative behaviors, since they do not feel they can handle relationships or maintain the interest and attention of others by simply being who they are.

Sometimes, BPD clients are considered histrionic when they are assessed at the times when they operate from a more regressive and infantile mental state, from which they cling desperately to others, usually generating behaviors that imply more rejection than support.

### 3.2. The Learned Antisocial Borderline

People in this borderline subgroup may seem psychopathic and even meet the diagnostic criteria for antisocial personality disorder. But as we deepen the assessment, we will observe emotional responses and suffering, as well as inconsistencies and contradictions (Mosquera, 2007a).

Unlike antisocial and psychopathic individuals, borderline clients of the learned antisocial type can be disarmed when we mention the pain of others, and they are more aware of the damage they cause. Although there is considerable suffering in this subtype, they do everything they can to conceal it. Often, these traits have developed in traumatic histories that have taught them that it is better to be the strongest one (Mosquera, 2007a). Unlike dependent personalities, they opted for the abuser rather than the victim role, based on the idea that "it is better to be a demon in a world governed by God, than to be an angel in a world ruled by the Devil."

However, they are people who can (and often do) crumble when we mention the suffering of others. Since they are experts at blocking emotions and not expressing them, and given their excellent façade of invulnerability, toughness, and arrogance, this background structure may not be visible. However, sometimes they remain intensely bonded with their partners and children, reacting in an extreme way either to defend them or against any threat to the relationship. If they have aggressive or negative reactions toward their partner, they are usually generated by triggers that can be understood from early traumatic history. They lack premeditation or manipulative character, but these cases can be quite severe.

# When BPD Clients Have a Pathological Partner: Frequent Combinations

Although we cannot generalize, in many cases, the partner of a person with BPD is pathological but can have very different profiles. The most common in our clinics are the caregivers, the unstable and in need of affection, and the narcissists (Mosquera & Gonzalez, 2013).

### Profile 1: Caregivers

Borderline clients can fit with a caregiver personality who is attracted to their extreme vulnerability and dependence, but who ends up puzzled and hurt by the opposite reaction of hostile defense or extreme reactions that BPD clients present toward attachments.

Another more complex profile is the "passive-aggressive caregiver": seemingly kind people, but who are always expecting gratitude and recognition from others for what they give, using this to manipulate them to feel "in debt." These people always seem ready to care for others, without ever showing anger or disagreement. This disagreement can be expressed in an indirect and subtle way, generating reactions in the BPD client that they do not understand, given that there is nothing that motivates them.

These "passive-aggressive caregivers" come to sessions with their partners and they seem to appear collaborative, but end up boycotting therapy (for example, he continues using cocaine with the client even though much of her decompensation has been due to this).

In both cases, the identity of the person is pathologically based on the role of caregiver, which implies a relational trap. If the BPD client improves, it may represent a threat to the identity of the caregiver and to the unspoken rules on which the relationship is based. Some caregiver partners may benefit from exploring their own history and from personal learning about self-care, assertiveness, and boundaries. In other cases, the caregiver role is too rooted in their personal identity and change would require an individual therapeutic process, often complicated not only by the time it entails, but because of these individuals´ low awareness of the problem.

## Profile 2: The Unstable and in Need of Affection

BPD clients can also fit with people with similar traits of extreme need of attachment, prone to intense and unstable relationships and high impulsivity.

These relationships are based on intensity, and the oscillations of one of the partners trigger oscillations in the other, increasing the significant instability of borderline clients. However, in this case, partners, although feeding affect dysregulation, do not slow down clients´ improvement.

For example , a woman who was a victim of incest in her family home has many borderline features: attachment difficulties, oscillating between dependence and avoidance, high impulsivity, emotional instability, and a constant feeling of emptiness.

After many troubled relationships, she meets a man who suffered a history of severe abuse in his family of origin and spent quite some time in prison. The extreme need for attachment that both of them have bonds them in the strongest relationship either of them have ever had, which they interpret as real. After a while, this starts activating extreme reactions on both sides to triggers that can only make sense if understood as activators of the network of traumatic memories they each carry with them.

He reacts to her crying spells, shouts, and insults with hostility and alcohol consumption. Much of what happens in these episodes he does not remember later, even when he has not been drinking, just as had happened in the most violent situations with his father and several episodes of sexual abuse by a teacher at the school he was expelled from due to "problematic behavior."

These memories are not generally accessible to the individual´s ordinary consciousness, but are stored in a completely dissociated mental state, which manifests sometimes at a mental level as critical and hostile auditory hallucinations. When she criticizes his behavior, he is only half aware of his amnesic gaps, since he remembers most of the interactions, but not particularly those fragments in which he shows greater aggressiveness.

In this case, it is reasonable to become specifically disconnected from those emotions and behaviors that he so often endured from the adults who were supposed to take care of him during childhood. Therefore, he considers that his partner exaggerates and dramatizes something that "was not so bad."

When the situation ends up in an undeniable extreme (she has obvious injuries from his beatings), he feels extremely guilty ("How can I be doing what my father did?") and sincerely apologizes, distressed and crying.

At that moment, she does not see the aggressor, instead she sees the vulnerable and helpless child who, from his own pain, could recognize his partner through all his armors. This is why, despite the recommendations of the social worker, she is unable to abandon him.

Working with couples to help them see these interactions and their connection with their history can be tremendously helpful.

## Profile 3: Narcissistic Couples

Individuals with BPD lack identity and internal security, and can be hooked to the narcissist´s apparent sense of security, who initially may be perceived as a savior.

The narcissist tells her what to think, what to feel, how she should dress, etc., and the borderline client finds what she has been looking for.

But this security in the narcissist is merely a defense, and often does not reach a balance: it is never enough. His self-affirmation is based on superiority over others, and possibly others will never be low enough for the difference to place him in the highest place he needs to be.

Sooner than later, systematic suppression of the borderline partner also helps develop a depressive clinical picture that is refractory to any medication or psychotherapy. This person, voided and worn out, will be even more maligned and humiliated by the narcissistic partner, who believes that she is not "at his level."

Often, clinical BPD worsens dramatically, presenting suicide attempts or severe depressive symptoms. In many cases, paradoxically, we see how the children of such a couple end up under the custody of a narcissistic parent, who are perfectly able to show their best side and maintain exquisite control within the judicial system, while the parent with BPD is considered incapable of performing her function, due to the seriousness of her condition, which is interpreted not as a consequence but as the cause of the couple´s problems.

Managing these situations is complex, and in cases of severe narcissistic pathology, breaking the relationship is the only realistic option for the client with BPD to improve. In the following chapter, we will delve into particular aspects of the therapeutic relationship with the borderline client.

# Chapter 17
# The Therapeutic Relationship

*Few disorders could devote an entire volume to the emotional reactions that those who suffer generate in the professionals who treat them...*

Gabbard & Wilkinson, 2000.

As discussed in the introduction, clients with BPD have the ability to test us as therapists and as people. Often, this "test" is literal because, due to their history, many clients need to understand that "we are going to be different," that "in the moment of truth, we will not fail them." In order to check this, they take things to such extremes that they often end up generating what they fear so much: rejection. This not only happens to them with us, but also with their partners, friends, and family. What happens in therapy is the story of their lives.

Problems in the therapeutic relationship are an excellent opportunity to understand issues about clients' functioning that otherwise they cannot explain, either because they are not aware of them or because they have too many defenses. It is also a privileged time to analyze issues as they are taking place and to be able to redirect tendencies and change dysfunctional patterns that show up. Numerous reflections and proposals on this topic have been written in psychoanalytic theory. Taking the concept of reciprocal roles from Cognitive Analytical Therapy (Ryle & Kerr, 2002, 2006), we can read a more elaborate development relative to complex trauma in Gonzalez & Mosquera (2012), which may also be applicable in borderline disorder.

This chapter describes some common reactions that therapists have to clients with BPD and the relational situations that often occur. The most obvious are the relatively "intense" thoughts, feelings, or responses to the client or the therapy session itself, which can be positive or negative. At other times, we do not understand very well what is happening in the session, and we have a sense of confusion, blocking, or perplexity. But it is also important to note that many seemingly positive feelings are not really productive for the psychotherapeutic process, as we will point out below.

Often, in therapy with borderline clients, therapists go through emotional roller coasters. Borderline individuals living through this emotional rollercoaster and their extreme and changing reactions often generate the activation of complementary roles and their mirror neurons in therapists. We may feel provoked, despised, attacked, blamed, overwhelmed, saturated, pressured, manipulated, coerced, and even responsible for the life of a client. In the same session or in the following sessions, we may also feel idealized, cared for, admired, obeyed, pleased, exceedingly well treated, etc. All these reactions are common among professionals working with these cases and provide a valuable diagnostic and therapeutic tool. The only problem with these reactions is that we keep them to ourselves, considering them shameful, or we let ourselves be carried away by them, losing our perspective on what is happening.

We will now outline some examples of reactions in the therapist and how they can be related to the experiences the client has lived and sometimes is still living (based on Mosquera, 2004a, 2013a).

## Anxiety, Fear, Insecurity

Regardless of what happens in the course of therapy, these clients make therapists feel anxious very easily. This makes perfect sense if we think of the anxiety, fear, insecurity, and terror that clients may have experienced during the situation that caused the trauma which brings them in to see us, sometimes repeated abuse over the years. Therapists' fear of harming or even retraumatizing clients who appears so fragile can make them neglect important issues during the session. Therapists try to protect clients by avoiding sensitive issues. It is very important to take into consideration clients' limitations, for example, realizing that they need time and resources before delving into trauma territory. But it becomes a problem when it is the clinicians' defensive response, "It's better not to get into this issue because she may get worse and kill herself," which is the result of therapists' insecurity or difficulty connecting with their own unresolved biographical experiences. If, during a session, we fear that the client may commit suicide, we must take into account our intuition, which can help us read the warning signs and help us take protective measures for the client. But we must have enough perspective on the client's problem, our own issues, and the therapeutic relationship in order to assess other possible factors involved, and not react in a direct and non-reflexive manner.

## Feeling Attacked and Challenged

Challenges to the therapist may be present, especially in the early sessions. While some clients have a hard time making eye contact, expressing their concerns, and talking openly about their difficulties, others are accustomed to using attack as a defense (sometimes as a strategy to ensure that the environment is safe and that the therapist is able to hear horrible things). The attack will not always be obvious; sometimes they can be very subtle behaviors with very passive-aggressive undertones.

Therapists must avoid an impulsive and personal response. Even when professionals do not respond aggressively or defensively at an explicit level, at an implicit level a word, a certain tone of voice, or a look that transpires hostility, rejection, or insecurity can emotionally activate clients and make them react negatively. In the best-case scenario, they might drop therapy, because they do not consider it useful, and look for another alternative. They might also react aggressively, breaking things, throwing things, yelling, threatening, or slamming the door when they leave. In the worst-case scenario, they can relive the trauma or present self or hetero-aggressive behavior.

The solution to this relational trap is to always count on it, especially if there is a first stage of idealization or a tendency to please. It can be useful to put it on the table before it occurs, and get perspective when it shows up, trying to analyze this problem with the same neutrality as any other that presents in therapy. It is also important that therapists be willing to admit their own mistakes, without implying the acceptance of whatever clients say because they are angry.

## Feeling Blackmailed or Manipulated

Sometimes clients function with a manipulative relational style, which logically will also manifest in therapy. The risk of this situation is not that it come up, since it is just one of the issues to work on with clients. The problem is that the therapists may experience it as something directed at them personally, as a lie, or as being used. Therapists can also fall into interpreting everything as manipulation, due to the fact that the clients have a personality disorder. For example, sometimes clients´ desire to die and the fact that they verbalize it are interpreted as personal attacks on the therapist or attempts to get more attention. But sometimes, all that clients are doing is informing us of a real risk, which is high in BPD, as we saw in Chapter 9 on self-harm. If clients are dramatic individuals, who often behave childishly and are constantly demanding attention, or have made manipulative threats of autolysis in the past, therapists are more likely to assume that this time it is "more of the same." Unfortunately, sometimes after many low lethality attempts, clients end up committing suicide due to the deterioration of their personal circumstances or relationships, or because this time they go "a little bit further" or it gets out of hand.

It is also common for therapists to feel blackmailed if clients establish conditions for coming to therapy and seem demanding, or to perceive that such threats are a criticism or a questioning of the therapy. Therapists with little tolerance for criticism will easily interpret clients' intentions as personal attacks, whether or not they are calls for attention.

## Feeling Guilty or Responsible of the Therapy or the Client

Therapists may feel guilty about the deterioration of the psychotherapy, because clients do not progress, are not constant, do not bring homework, self-harm, etc. Client many times actively contribute to making therapists feel guilty: "I took the pills because I called you at 3:00 a.m. and your cell was off," "I self-harmed because I felt really bad after our last session." If therapists take these sentences from clients directly as realities, they can become responsible for their feelings and reactions. Therapists with a tendency to care a lot for other people, sometimes exceeding healthy boundaries in their relationship with clients, will focus on themselves the entire responsibility of the therapeutic process. This experience prevents therapists from seeing the situation with enough perspective, and the main problem for the therapy process is that it does not enhance clients assuming responsibility for themselves and regaining control over their lives.

A common example of this situation is in relation to the management of suicidal behavior. Some professionals may easily fall into relational traps, assuming the responsibility of keeping clients alive. When clients say, "I'm still alive because of you," therapists may feel significant pressure and run out of room for maneuver. Clients will experience every frustration as the therapist's responsibility, "I told you I don't want to live, it's not worth it, and here I am with another shitty situation because I made a promise to you."

Sometimes, therapists may feel guilty, even without clients manifesting anything. When a session ends up with clients not coming in to the next appointment or decompensating, and therapists attribute this to their own failure, they may, moved by a sense of guilt, make desperate attempts to "fix it," losing the opportunity to learn from what has happened. Unproductive or counterproductive sessions can provide more useful information for therapy than dramatically positive ones. For example, the phobia of trauma in clients, which becomes activated while trying to process a memory, teaches us that it is too early for them to do this and helps us calculate their pace. Recognizing this and repairing it is an important learning for clients, like what happens in healthy attachment where attachments disruptions are repaired and have their adaptive function.

As therapists, the only realistic option is to "make better mistakes tomorrow." In order to do this, we have to learn from previous mistakes.

## Sense of Unworthiness or "Feeling like a Fraud"

Clients with BPD may question the therapists' competence, as a result of the pattern of idealization/devaluation that characterizes them. Sometimes they do it directly and vehemently: "This case has gotten too big for you. Admit that you don't know how to treat me and let's get this farce over with." An insecure professional, with an internal conviction of being a fraud, will resonate powerfully with these sentences. Such situations sometimes make us aware of the areas we have to work on at a personal level and other times help us control our own narcissism.

In other situations, clients are simply transmitting through the therapeutic relationship all the frustration, distrust, and feeling of worthlessness that they have felt throughout their lives, which has resulted in persistent hopelessness and lack of motivation. Therapists who tend to become easily emotionally infected also end up feeling that "we´re not going anywhere" and "this case has no solution." If this is identified, we can do important psychoeducational work with clients, helping them understand how their reactions and feelings in the here-and-now are conditioned by the experiences of the there-and-then. At the same time, the safety of the therapist will help the client move forward. If someone feels that they will not be able to do something, and are accompanied by an influential figure who trusts their capabilities, they learn to trust themselves. But it is important for this not to become "pulling the client" and also not to let the interaction become polarized, with therapists encouraging "come on, you can do it" and clients getting increasingly stuck at the other extreme. The cushion that clients need from therapists is a realistic, not patronizing, sense of security.

## Feeling "Invaded"

People with complex trauma have many difficulties with interpersonal boundaries and differentiation. If we do a good intake, we can understand why they have no concept of personal space and boundaries. Clients, drawn by their intense need to attach, start searching for a figure of reference to hold on to and rely on. Most likely, they do not measure how far they can go, trying to figure out things about their therapists and even trying to "be part of their life," sometimes reaching extremes that can intimidate therapists and interfere in therapy. Not agreeing with these demands will generate strong reactions to what they experience as rejection. Agreeing to them eventually leads to the therapists´ exhaustion, because whatever they give, it will never be enough. The way out of this dynamic is to get some distance with clients and talk about it with perspective, also understanding the contexts of childhood in which it was generated.

Sometimes, extreme need for affection is followed by a defensive reaction. Clients demand involvement and closeness from therapists, which when achieved, trigger all the warning signs. Early attachment experiences were not only of preoccupation and lack of individuation, but damage was inflicted by the attachment figure. Closeness is sought and feared in extreme ways. Therapists´ feeling of being invaded is followed by bewilderment at clients´ apparently contradictory reaction, reflecting the ambivalence, and sometimes the disorganization, of the attachment pattern.

## The Client´s Idealization

Ooohhh...! My therapist is the most wonderful woman in the world!!

Individuals with early traumatization often have been voided as people. Some fear showing themselves as they are, because they are not able to see themselves or because they are convinced that they are horrible, at times internalizing things they were told. They fear that others will be frightened or reject them if they discover their true self. With therapists, clients may be complacent, trying to please. Their difficulty trusting others and showing themselves does not come out in therapy, let alone what they can feel towards the therapist. Clients can do the homework, state that a memory is being processed without a full decrease of the disturbance, say, very convincingly, how wonderful this therapy is, and praise the therapist´s ability. When the attitude is very exaggerated, it can raise suspicion, but if not, therapists may believe that the case is going well and that sessions are very rich and productive, feeling gratified by the results they are getting. However, the external life of the client can stay exactly the same as in the beginning; there is no real change, or only change that is not solid. Sometimes, the seemingly problematic cases advance more than the apparently easier ones. The important thing is not to lose objectivity and try periodically to see how things are going on the client´s day to day.

## Emotional Contagion

As we commented in prior chapters, some therapists tend to become infected with the emotions of others. They take home clients´ sadness or their stories, and turn them around in their head for days. Clients´ desperation may also become the therapist´s. When clients experience problems intensely, therapists may feel that it is a priority to focus on them, only to find themselves in the same situation in the next session, with a different problem. It can also happen in reverse, clients´

phobia of traumatic memories can lead to therapists feeling insecure about exploring these issues, thinking that the person will not tolerate it.

This contagion of clients' emotional reactions makes therapists lose objectivity and analyze the problems and the therapeutic process 100% from the client's perspective. Although it is important to respect clients' decisions, it is equally important to help them make those decisions. Emotional decisions are part of our clients' problems and for therapists to share these problems does not help clients find a different way of analyzing and dealing with things.

While emotional contagion is more common in the early stages of therapists' professional lives, some professionals have a higher tendency due to their own structure and their own history. Sometimes, therapists who have worked for many years with therapeutic approaches focused on symptoms or the here-and-now may find themselves without resources to handle painful and often terrible stories.

## Aggressiveness

Although aggressiveness is a universal reaction, clinicians may not recognize it in themselves because they may not consider it appropriate for a therapist. Some professionals feel bad about having this type of reaction: "How can I be a good therapist if I'm feeling that I want to attack this client?" This is even more disturbing when clinicians empathize with one part of the client and at the same time experience rejection or aggression towards other parts.

As with any relational situation, different therapists may have different reactions to the same scenario. For example, with a client who shows great distress and asks for help, one professional can feel like helping, while in another one this may generate helplessness, and in another one, rejection.

Interestingly, in some cases, the therapists' reactions have a lot to do with clients' traumatic history. A woman with a piercing cry that leaves her breathless generates in her therapist the feeling of wanting to shake her, as well as great empathy when connecting with her pain and helplessness. While supervising the case, the therapist learns that this woman was brutally abused and tortured and that one of the usual attacks she received was being shaken when she cried desperately.

## Rescuing Fantasies

Therapists feel compelled to "save" clients, to the point of believing that they are the only ones who can help them. This is sometimes verbalized directly by clients: "You're the only person who can help me and understand me, if it wasn't for you I wouldn't be alive." This is not just a consequence of the tendency to idealize, but also a part of the externalization of solutions that is common in BPD. Clients believe that their problems will be solved magically, and the idea of an omnipotent rescuer is one of those solutions devoid of realism. If individuals have grown up in an adverse family environment, rescue fantasies might have been common mechanisms to mentally escape their situation.

This childish position of dependence and magical thinking will be further enhanced if therapists assume the role of the rescuer, doing things for clients. They will not develop their autonomy, assume adult responsibility, or regain control over their lives. Therapists with a hypertrophied role of caregiver or a narcissistic profile may fit in a pathological way into this relationship pattern presented by clients.

## Excitement or Sexual Fantasies

Some clients are used to relating through sex and reproduce this in therapy. The clearest example is the client who was sexually abused in her family and presents hyper-sexualized or seductive behaviors with the therapist. It makes sense to think that if early attachments were associated with sexual contact or ambiguity, the therapeutic relationship will end up presenting these nuances. Other times, clients talk in detail about their sexual encounters seeking the therapist's attention or thereby building a smokescreen to avoid contact with more delicate or difficult aspects. Clients who have suffered sexual traumatization may need to test and see if they can address that part of their story by checking their reactions.

In other cases, clients, as a result of the lack of interpersonal boundaries, end up seeing the therapist as the "love of their life," someone who can give them all the love that was missing in their childhood. Clients may verbalize these feelings to the therapist, interpreting the attention given to them as signs of romantic or sexual interest.

Therapists may feel uncomfortable and interrupt therapy or refer the case to another therapist, which is often experienced by clients as a repetition of the abandonment and neglect they suffered in childhood. Unfortunately, in many cases, therapists end up responding to clients' demands, having romantic or sexual relationships with clients. This is a serious problem, not only ethically, but of course, for clients' recovery.

Sexual or sexualized behaviors, from the perspective of EMDR, are not only aspects of the therapeutic relationship that must be managed, but also entry points for the identification of material that needs to be processed. For example, a client with BPD was constantly trying to call the therapist´s attention to her breasts or legs. If he looked at her, she suddenly changed and started seeing him as a disgusting pig, sometimes to the point of losing control or insulting him. If he did not look at her, she became annoyed, felt she was not important, and complained that "he didn´t care for her" or that he was not paying enough attention. This client was referred to a woman therapist. Through a careful examination of her history, we found that this client was not normally "seen" by her father, except when he sexually abused her. The client´s complex emotional response to her father made the relational situation with the therapist understandable: "I felt disgusting after sleeping with him, but being invisible was much worse."

## Avoidance of Traumatic Content

To survive in a traumatic environment, children have to think that this never happened or that it has never happened to me. Being fully aware of all the traumatic past is emotionally intolerable. Adults who have grown up without having fully assimilated this information may want to talk about the past, without being aware that in doing so, they become destabilized. If therapists interrupt, they feel misunderstood. If therapist lets them talk as much as they "need," the client decompensates.

Another possibility is that they present some level of amnesia, minimization, or denial of the traumatic history. Clients want to understand with the same emphasis with which they avoid the contents of those experiences. Therapists can also share these opposite reactions. On the one hand, they may not explore a possible history of trauma, may distrust the story that the client is telling, or may consider that past traumatic events are not relevant to the client's current problems. On the other hand, therapists may experience vicarious traumatization with the terrible stories they have to listen to. In this case, they may stop or directly avoid EMDR reprocessing because they themselves (but not the client) cannot tolerate the intense emotions of the desensitization phase.

## Boredom, Tiredness

The benefits of limited processing are higher containment and emotional regulation, potentially less destabilizing associations, and a sense of capacity and management that fosters the development of a sense of security that will facilitate working on other traumatic targets.

BPD therapy is a marathon. There may be times when the sessions are intense and, at times, spectacular. But there are many times when sessions are the umpteenth repetition of previous sessions. Therapists may find themselves repeating the same story, or they can see how clients, after months or years of hard work, get back into the exact same problem. After huge advances, clients get involved again in pathological relationships, and it seems that nothing has been achieved. Many sessions are bland, boring, confusing, tiring, and exhausting. If therapists do not review the history and periodically assess progress, the clients' negativism and the dramatic current crisis may give the impression that there is no progress.

It is difficult for BPD therapy to have linear progression and not suffer frequent dropouts and resumptions of the therapeutic process, punctuated by more or less dramatic crises and decompensation. Often, the therapeutic relationship, being difficult to manage, enters into a standstill situation in which the functioning patterns of both members of the relational dyad become chronic and blocked.

The best way for preventing this type of situation is to periodically review the goals, share cases, discuss them with colleagues, supervise, and conduct research. They can be hugely rewarding clients, but our ability to accept delayed gratification has to be great. Our backpack for a marathon cannot be the same one as for a sprint.

# Confusion

Clients with BPD live in chaos and it may be difficult for them to work with structure. Often, with the best of intentions, therapists "follow the client", fearing that they are not being sufficiently empathetic if they interrupt when clients are highly activated talking about something that affects them. At the end of the session, both client and therapist are confused, and the client may even blame the therapist for not taking over. At other times, confusion responds to the rapid successive or simultaneous activation of different emotional parts that generate changeable and contradictory or ambivalent reactions. In some clients, the mixture of messages is very powerful and ongoing, although some of them are sent at a much more subliminal level. Therapists may see an apparent behavior and not understand their apparently contradictory reaction toward clients.

EMDR therapists accustomed to precise and clear sessions with some clients who are willing to work, who can process a memory in an hour, and who experience sometimes spectacularly fast changes, may struggle to handle these cases. In them, situations are more closely related to attachment than to concrete events, develop slower, and present numerous defenses that make approaching traumatic content and full, effective processing very complex. After a first phase of fascination with EMDR as a therapeutic tool and with its therapeutic potential, when entering into the territory of complex trauma, therapists start to work from very different conditions. While EMDR therapy gives us the opportunity to completely restructure a personality with severe shortcomings and dysfunctions, working directly with the profound experiences that underlie these cases can be a challenge. In this case, we cannot expect to find a protocol, or a set of protocols, to be applied in a linear fashion. Therapists will have to introduce numerous modifications (see Chapter 13), which will be different from client to client and from session to session. This can also be a source of confusion for clinicians, who are left without the clear references they had for EMDR work with simple trauma.

In summary, relational problems are not really problems, but excellent entry points to deepen the understanding of the individual's difficulties. For clients to present the problems they have in their relationship with us in therapy gives us the opportunity to see those problems live, put them on the table, understand them, and identify options for intervention.

Treatment of borderline personality disorder can generate many different emotions in therapists. These reactions not only give us information about the client, but also about ourselves. It is important to reflect on how the elements of our own memory networks are activated in our clients. Knowing ourselves and being well rooted in our ability to regulate and contain our emotional reactions, discriminating about when they are related to our own problems and when with those of clients, gives us the possibility of using them as indicators of clients´ internal organization and early history. Getting perspective is the key element in this process and, for this reason, sharing and supervising cases is essential, especially with this type of problem.

# Chapter 18
# Maintaining Improvement

To close this book, we are going to tell you a story based on a very well known children's tale, *The Three Little Pigs*. This tale has been used in numerous occasions as a metaphor for clients (based on Mosquera 2004a, 2013b) and we are now adapting it to our work with EMDR.

Let us remember the story. The first pig, as we know, built his house in one day, with a bunch of straw. The second one had to work a little more, looking for reeds and pieces of wood in the forest, and finished it in three days. And finally, the third one dedicated many months and effort to build a solid brick and cement house with a door, windows, and a fireplace. When the wolf came, just a strong puff knocked down the first house. The second only fell after a strong attack, but eventually ended up collapsing. The third house resisted the wolf, the harsh winter, the torrential rains, and the summer sun. The third pig was then truly aware of how worthwhile his effort had been.

The client's history and therapy may have a lot to do with this children's story. If the person resorts to alcohol, binge eating, cuts, etc., discomfort seems to be covered up (like the straw house), but in reality, it is not. With EMDR therapy, something similar could happen. If we target the symptoms or discomfort that clients bring to the office on any specific day, it is possible for them to improve, but if we do not work on the root of the problem, we may not have anything more than a straw house.

In the second case, clients take medication or are in therapy while feeling bad, but stop as soon as they recover or find "love." Improvement is clear, but when there is a downturn or when any small setback takes place, they seem to "go downhill." EMDR therapists can also go "half way," but not because clients drop out, but because, given the improvement clients are experiencing, they "don't want to stir them up more, in order not to destabilize them" and avoid entering the processing of harder or more nuclear memories.

The third pig represents clients who, sometimes after several attempts, the most common scenario, or, at other times, from the very beginning, want to solve their problems and do anything it takes. EMDR therapists working in this way are putting up brick after brick, building on a solid foundation from a good case conceptualization and a comprehensive work plan that does not really set aside any nuclear area.

What they do not tell us in the story of the three little pigs is about all the maintenance, repairs, and work that a home needs so the wood does not rot, the metal does not rust, the walls do not deteriorate, and the roof does not leak. The most solid and well-built home in the world needs attention and care. This happens to all of us human beings, we all have unexpected events and problems, but if addressed on time, we learn from them and enable the maintenance of the improvement; the house continues being solid and even gets strengthened with each new setback.

It is important to remember that people with this diagnosis often have relapses when this is least expected, after they have been stable for a while, and when it seems that everything is under control. Contrary to what it may seem, increased functionality gained as therapy progresses can complicate things, because people will face new challenges that once seemed far from their possibilities. All this, mixed with low self-esteem, which can come back even if it has been corrected, and overly high expectations of oneself and others, can trigger unexpected reactions in clients at moments of frustration or when something unexpected happens.

Sometimes, pressure from the environment and fear of not being able to maintain the acquired and unfamiliar "stability" can be a burden that ends up destabilizing clients. During periods of instability, "bad moments" are nearly normal and clients are well used to them. However, when they think everything "has gone away" and their life is finally under control, seeing themselves with similar feelings as those they had when they were at their worst may be intolerable. Feeling anxious, upset, or sad may trigger the fear that everything is starting over again and make them feel unable to go through it again. One of the biggest changes clients have to face is "learning to feel bad without the world falling apart." They must learn to feel sad without being depressed, worry about their problems without becoming overwhelmed or anxious, deal with conflict without becoming upset or trying to avoid it, and feel responsible without tormenting themselves with guilt. Emotions, worries, and everyday life must be experienced without additional resonance, without arousing fears. Preparing clients to be able to look back without disturbance and fear, to simply feel bad on some days like everyone else does, and to see themselves functioning in the midst of the problems, disappointments, and frustrations of normal life is important in order to maintain the improvement.

When we advance in therapy, usually people have acquired a new set of resources, and they have made changes that greatly improve their quality of life and their way of adapting to unexpected or unforeseen situations, as well as the way they deal with the discomfort characteristic of this disorder. They often feel much safer, less confused, less lost, more hopeful for their near future, and especially more "deserving." Guilt, usually present in the early stages of therapy, and destructive behaviors decrease significantly, to the point of remission. But this is a delicate stage in the change process, which is important to anticipate. The new life clients reach after their progress is a stage with new and unknown complexities. The devil we know is good because it is known, and therefore, it is predictable. The good that we do not know is tinged with uncertainty, and this can make clients freak out and feel fear and lack of control. Interestingly, this seemingly good stage can be a much greater challenge in therapy than the first phase of treatment.

The key to this stage is that it should not be experienced by either clients or therapists as a failure, but rather as the result of a breakthrough. In order for this to be obvious when the moment arrives, it is important to have anticipated it repeatedly in previous stages. If we have explained that it is normal for the completion of therapy to activate many fears, that normal life can be intimidating, that making decisions is complex and we do not always succeed, and we have discussed the various challenges that the client will have to face, this period can be easily channeled. Unpredictability becomes predictable and the feeling of control and safety increases.

The completion of the therapeutic process must be natural and gradual. In this stage we must adopt an almost contemplative attitude and stop doing. Clients should be the ones who make decisions, who propose the intersession intervals, and who realize, in a natural way and attending to their own needs, that their current lifestyle does not allow them to come see us as often as they would like. Over time, they will realize that they no longer need the therapy. In a way, it is similar to when children learn to ride a bike with training wheels. While they have the wheels on, they get on the bike without fear and feel that "everything is under control." Seeing that their friends take off the training wheels and keep on riding their bikes, they will also want to have them removed. While many children outgrow this first fear and realize that they can continue without training wheels, others simply end up falling and feeling like a failure, due to the fear of not doing well or falling. Adults calculate children's pace, neither letting go suddenly on a ramp nor always taking them by the hand. There is always a moment, in which little by little, children realize that they really know how to do it alone. In therapy, the same thing happens. There is a moment when therapists realize that clients have acquired autonomy, security, and resources to live and solve issues. There comes a day when clients become aware of it.

It is important not to make closure definitive, to make it clear that the door will always be open, and to insist that if there is any problem, the client should not wait until things get complicated, trying to fix it themselves at all costs. Some clients occasionally come to "pay a visit," or bring up issues on which they feel they can use the therapist's point of view. They are no longer in therapy. They just know we are still there.

# References

Ainsworth, M.D., Blehar, M.C., Waters, E., & Wall, S. (1978). *Patterns of attachment: assessed in the strange situation and at home.* Hillsdale: Lawrence Erlbaum.

Akiskal, H.S., Chen, S.E., & Davis, G.C. (1985). Borderline: an adjective in search of a noun. *Journal of Clinical Psychiatry*, 46: 41-48.

Allen, D.M. (2003). *Psychotherapy with borderline patients. An integrated approach.* Mahwah, NJ: Lawrence Erlbaum and Associates.

Allport, G.W. (1981). Personality and social encounter. Chicago: University of Chicago Press.

American Psychiatric Association. (2013). *Diagnostic and statistical manual of mental disorders* (5th ed.) Arlington, VA: American Psychiatric Publishing.

Bakermans-Kranenburg M.J. & Van IJzendoorn M.H. (2009). The first 10,000 Adult Attachment Interviews: distributions of adult attachment representations in clinical and non-clinical groups. *Attachment and Human Development*, 11(3): 223-63.

Ball, J.S. & Links, P.S. (2009). Borderline personality disorder and childhood trauma: evidence for a causal relationship. *Current Psychiatry Reports*, 11: 63-8.

Barone, L. (2003). Developmental protective and risk factors in borderline personality disorder: a study using the Adult Attachment Interview. *Attachment and Human Development*, 5(1): 64-77.

Bartholomew, K. & Horowitz, L.M. (1991). Attachment styles among young adults: a test of a four-category model. *Journal of Personality and Social Psychology*, 61: 226-44.

Bateman, A. & Fonagy, P. (2004). *Psychotherapy for borderline personality disorder: mentalization based treatment.* Oxford: Oxford University Press.

Bateson, G. (1972). *Steps to an Ecology of Mind: Collected Essays in Anthropology, Psychiatry, Evolution, and Epistemology.* Chicago: University Of Chicago Press.

Batson, C.D. (2009). These things called empathy: Eight related but distinct phenomena. In J. Decety and W. Ickes (Eds.), *The Social Neuroscience of Empathy* (pp. 3–15). Cambridge: MIT Press

Battle, C.L., Shea, M.T., Johnson, D.M., Yen, S., Zlotnick, C., Zanarini, M.C.,… & Morey, L.C. (2004). Childhood maltreatment associated with adult personality disorders: findings from the Collaborative Longitudinal Personality Disorders Study. *Journal of Personality Disorders*, 18: 193-211.

Benjamin, L.S. (1993). *Interpersonal diagnosis and treatment of personality disorder.* New York: Guilford.

Benoit, D. & Parker, K. (1994) Stability and transmission of attachment across three generations. *Child Development*, 65: 1444-56.

Bisson, J., Roberts, N.P., Andrew, M., Cooper, R. & Lewis, C. (2013). Psychological therapies for chronic post-traumatic stress disorder (PTSD) in adults (Review). Cochrane Database of Systematic Reviews 2013, DOI: 10.1002/14651858.CD003388.pub4

Bleuler E. (1911). *Dementia Praecox oder Gruppe der Schizophrenien*. Leipzig, Germany. English version: Zinkin, J (Ed.) (1950). *Dementia praecox or the group of schizophrenias*. New York: International Universities Press.

Blizard, R.A. (2003). Disorganized attachment, development of dissociated self states and a relational approach to treatment. *Journal of Trauma and Dissociation*, 4(3): 27-50.

Bowen, M. (1978) *Family therapy in clinical practice*. Nueva York: Aronson.

Bowlby, J. (1969). *Attachment and loss: Vol. 1. Attachment*. New York: Basic Books

Bradley, R., Greene, J., Russ, E., Dutra, L., & Westen, D. (2005). A multidimensional meta-analysis of psychotherapy for PTSD. American Journal of Psychiatry, 162: 214-227.

Brazier, J., Tumur, I., Holmes, M., Ferriter, M., Parry, G., Dent-Brown, K., & Paisley, S. (2006). Psychological therapies including dialectical behaviour therapy for borderline personality disorder: A systematic review and preliminary economic evaluation. *Health Technology Assessment* (Winchester, England), 10(35): iii, ix-xii, 1-117.

Brennan, K.A., Clark, C.L., & Shaver, P.R. (1998). Self-report measurement of adult romantic attachment: An integrative overview. In Simpson, J.A. & Rholes, W.S. (Eds.) *Attachment theory and close relationships (*pp. 46-76). New York: Guilford Press.

Briere, J. & Conte, J. (1993). Self-reported amnesia in adults molested as children. *Journal of Traumatic Stress*, 6: 21-31.

Brodsky, B.S., Cloitre, M., & Dulit, R.A. (1995). Relationship of dissociation to self-mutilation and childhood abuse in borderline personality disorder. *American Journal of Psychiatry*, 152: 1788-92.

Bromberg, P.M. (1998). *Standing in the spaces: Essays on clinical process, trauma & dissociation*. Hillsdale, NJ: Analytic Press.

Brown, S. & Shapiro, F. (2006). EMDR in the treatment of borderline personality disorder. *Clinical Case Studies*, 5(5): 403-20.

Brussoni, M.J., Jang, K.L., Livesley, W.J., & MacBeth, T.M. (2000). Genetic and environmental influences on adult attachment styles. *Personal Relationships*, 7: 283-9.

Buchheim, A., George, C., Liebl, V., Moser, A., & Benecke, C. (2007). Affective facial behavior of borderline patients during the Adult Attachment Projective. *Psychosomatic Medicine and Psychotherapy*, 53(4): 339-54.

Bychowski, G. (1953). The problem of latent psychosis. *Journal of American Psychoanalytic Association*, 1: 484-503.

Charcot, J. M. (1887/1991). *Clinical lectures on diseases of the nervous system, Volume, III*. London: Tavistock/Routledge.

Chu, J. (1998). *Rebuilding shattered lives: The responsible treatment of complex post-traumatic and dissociative disorders*. New York: Wiley and Sons.

Chu, J., Matthews, J., Frey, L., & Ganzel, B. (1996). The nature of traumatic memories of sexual abuse. *Dissociation*, 10:2-17.

Chu, J.A. & Dill, DL. (1991). Dissociation, borderline personality disorder, and childhood trauma. *American Journal of Psychiatry*, 148: 812-3.

Classen, C., Pain, C., Field, N., & Woods, P. (2006). Posttraumatic personality disorder: A reformulation of the complex posttraumatic stress disorder and borderline personality disorder. *Psychiatric Clinics of North America*, 29: 87-112.

Cohen, P; Crawford, TN; Johnson, JG; & Kasen, S. (2005). The children in the community study of developmental course of personality disorder. *Journal of Personality Disorders*, 19:466-86.

Connell-Jones, G. (2011). *Drug modulated EMDR treatment for borderline personality disorder*. 12th European Conference on Traumatic Stress (ECOTS). Vienna, Austria.

Coons, P. M. (1994). Confirmation of childhood abuse in child and adolescent cases of multiple personality disorder and dissociative disorder not otherwise specified. *Journal of Nervous and Mental Disease*, 182, 461-464.

Cox, C.L., Uddin, L.Q., Di Martino, A., Castellanos, F.X., Milham, M.P., & Kelly, C. (2012). The balance between feeling and knowing: affective and cognitive empathy are reflected in the brain's intrinsic functional dynamics. *Social Cognitive and Affective Neuroscience*, 7 (6): 727–37.

Crawford, T.N., Livesley, W.J., Jang, K.L., Shaver, P.R., Cohen, P., & Ganiban, J. (2007). Insecure attachment and personality disorder: A twin study of adults. *European Journal of Personality*, 21: 191-208.

Crittenden, P.M. (1997). Toward and integrative theory of trauma: a dynamic maturation approach. In Cicchetti, D. & Toth, S.L. (Eds.) *Rochester Symposium on Developmental Psychopathology. Vol 8: Developmental Perspectives on Trauma*. Rochester, NY: University of Rochester Press. pp. 33-84.

Dammann, G. (2003). Borderline Personality Disorder and Theory of Mind: An Evolutionary Perspective. In Brüne, Ribbert, & Schiefenhövel (Eds.) *The Social Brain: Evolution and Pathology*. John Wiley & Sons, Ltd.

Damasio, A. (2010). *The self comes to mind: constructing the conscious brain*. Pantheon.

Davidson, P.R., & Parker, K.C.H. (2001). Eye movement desensitization and reprocessing (EMDR): A meta-analysis. *Journal of Consulting and Clinical Psychology, 69,* 305-316.

Decety J. & Meyer M. (2008). From emotion resonance to empathic understanding: A social developmental neuroscience account. *Development and Psychopathology, 20* (4): 1053–1080.

Dell, P. F. (2006). A New Model of Dissociative Identity Disorder. *Psychiatric Clinics of North America*, 29: 1–26.

Driessen, M., Beblo, T., Reddemann, L., Rau, H., Lange, W., Silva, A.,... & Ratzka, S. (2002). Is the borderline personality disorder a complex post-traumatic stress disorder? - The state of research. *Nervenarzt.* 73(9): 820-9.

Dubovsky, S.L. & Weissberg, M.P. (1981). *Clinical Psychiatry in Primary Care.* Williams & Wilkins Baltimore.

Einolf, C. (2012). Is Cognitive Empathy More Important than Affective Empathy? A Response to "Who Helps Natural-Disaster Victims?" *Analyses of Social Issues and Public Policy,* 12 (1): 268–271.

Eisenberg, N.J. (1987). *Empathy and its development.* Cambridge University Press.

Elliot, C.H. & Lassen, M.K. (1997). A schema polarity model for case conceptualisation, intervention and research. *Clinical Psychology Science and Practice,* 4, 12–28.

Erickson, M. & Rossi, E.L. (1975). Varieties of Double Bind. *The American Journal of Clinical Hypnosis.* 17: 143-157.

Erikson, E.H. (1980). *Identity and the life cycle.* New York: Norton.

Ey, H. (1959). Unity and diversity of schizophrenia: clinical and logical analysis of the concept of schizophrenia. *American Journal of Psychiatry,* 115:706-14.

Fanselow, M.S. & Lester, L.S. (1988). A functional behavioristic approach to aversively motivated behavior: Predatory imminence as a determinant of the topography of defensive behavior. In Bolles, R.C. & Beecher, M.D. (Eds.) *Evolution and learning* (pp. 185-212). Hillsdale, NJ: Erlbaum.

Federn P. (1947). Principles of psychotherapy in latent schizophrenia. *American Journal of Psychotherapy,* I, 2: 129-44.

Fenichel O. (1945). *The psychoanalytic theory of neurosis.* New York: Norton.

Fitzpatrick, C.J. (1985). Children's development of event-bound conceptions of their emotions. In: Fast, I. (Ed.) *Event theory: A Piaget-Freud integration.* Hillsdale. NJ: Erlbaum. pp. 79-109.

Fonagy, P. & Bateman, A. (2007). Attachment theory and mentalization-oriented model of borderline personality disorder. In Oldham, J.M., Skodol, A.E., & Bender, D.S. *Textbook of personality disorders.* Chapter 12. Elsevier Masson. pp. 189-203.

Fonagy, P. (2000). Attachment and borderline personality disorder. *Journal of the American Psychoanalytic Association,* 48: 1129-1146; discussion 1175-1187.

Fonagy, P., Gegerly, G., Jurist, E.L., & Target, M. (2002). *Affect regulation, mentalization and the development of the self.* New York: Other Press.

Fonagy, P., Target, M., & Gerfely, G. (2000). Attachment and borderline personality disorder: a theory and some evidence. *Psychiatric Clinics of North America,* 23:103-22.

Fossati, A., Madeddu, F., & Maffei, C. (1999). Borderline personality disorder and childhood sexual abuse: A meta-analytical study. *Journal of Personality Disorders,* 13: 268-80

Freud, S. (1923). *The ego and the id.* Standard Edition. pp. 13-59.

Frolov, Y.P. (1938). *Pavlov and His School*. Trans. by C.P. Dutt. Kegan Paul, Trench, Trubner, London.

Frosch JP. (1960). Psychotic character. *Journal of the American Psychoanalytic Association*, 8: 544-51.

Gabbard, O. & Wilkinson, S.M. (2000). *Management of countertransference with borderline patients.* Jason Aronson. New edition.

Gallese, V. (2003). The Roots of Empathy: The Shared Manifold Hypothesis and the Neural Basis of Intersubjectivity. *Psychopathology,* 36 (4): 171–180.

Galletly C. (1997). Borderline-dissociation comorbidity. *American Journal of Psychiatry*, 154: 1629.

García, G., Junquero, A., Jiménez, R., Villegas, C., & Sánchez, P. (2009). *Experiencia piloto en terapia grupal con pacientes con patología dual adaptando el programa psicoeducativo Diamantes en bruto*. Póster presentado en las XII Jornadas Nacionales de Patología Dual. Madrid.

George, C., Kaplan, N., & Main, N. (1985). *Adult Attachment Interview: Unpublished Manuscript*. Berkeley: University of California.

Giesen-Bloo, J., van Dyck, R., Spinhoven, P., van Tilburg, W., Dirksen, C., van Asselt, T., … Arntz, A. (2006). Outpatient Psychotherapy for Borderline Personality Disorder: Randomized Trial of Schema-Focused Therapy vs Transference-Focused Psychotherapy. *Archives of General Psychiatry*, 63: 649-658.

Gnepp, J., McKee, E., & Domanic, J. (1987). Children′s use of situational information to infer emotion: understanding emotionally equivocal situations. *Developmental Psychology*, 23: 114-23.

Goldberg, J.F. & Garno, J.L. (2009). Age at onset of bipolar disorder and risk for comorbid borderline personality disorder. *Bipolar Disorder*, 11: 205-8.

Goldsmith, H.H. & Harman, C. (1994). Temperament and attachment: Individuals and relationships. *Current Directions in Psychological Science*, 3: 53-7.

Golier, J., Yehuda, R., Bierer, L., Mitropoulou, V., New, A., Schmeidler, J., … & Siever, L.I. (2003). The relationship of borderline personality disorder to posttraumatic stress disorder and traumatic events. *American Journal of Psychiatry*, 160: 2018-24.

Golynkina, K. & Ryle, A. (1999). The identification and characteristics of the partially dissociated states of patients with borderline personality disorder. *British Journal of Medical Psychology*, 72: 429-45.

Gonzalez, A. (2010). *Trastornos disociativos*. Madrid: Ed. Pléyades.

Gonzalez, A. & Mosquera, D. (2011). Working with self-care patterns: a structured procedure for EMDR therapy. *Revista Iberoamericana de Psicotraumatología y Disociación*, 4, 3.

Gonzalez, A. & Mosquera, D. (2012). *EMDR and Dissociation: The Progressive Approach*. Ed Createspace. Spanish Edition: *EMDR y Disociación: El Abordaje Progresivo*. Madrid: Ed. Pléyades.

Gonzalez, A., Seijo, N., & Mosquera, D. (2009). *EMDR in complex trauma and dissociative disorders*. Annual meeting of the EMDR International Association. Atlanta, GA.

Goodman, M. & Yehuda, R. (2002). The relationship between psychological trauma and borderline personality disorder. *Psychiatric Annals*, 33: 337-45.

Gratz, K.L. & Roemer, L. (2004). Multidimensional assessment of emotion regulation and dysregulation: Development, factor structure, and initial validation of the Difficulties in Emotion Regulation Scale. *Journal of Psychopathology and Behavioral Assessment*, 26: 41-54.

Graybar, S. & Boutilier, L.R. (2002). Nontraumatic pathways to borderline personality disorder. *Psychotherapy: Theory, Research, Practice, Training*, 39:152-62.

Greenson, R.R. (1954). The struggle against identification. *Journal of the American Psychoanalytic Association*, 2: 200-17.

Grossmann, K.E., Grossmann, K., & Waters, E. (2005). *Attachment from Infancy to Adulthood: The Major Longitudinal Studies.* New York: The Guilford Press.

Grover K.E., Carpenter L.L., Price L.H., Gagne G.G., Mello A.F., Mello M.F., and Tyrka, A.R. (2007). The relationship between childhood abuse and adult personality disorder symptoms. *Journal of Personality Disorders*, 21(4): 442-7.

Guimón, J., Maruottolo, C., Mascaró, A., & Boyra, A. (2007). Results of a brief crisis program for people with borderline personality disorders. *European Psychiatry*, 22(1) (supplement).

Gunderson, J.G. (1984). *Borderline personality disorder.* Washington, DC: American Psychiatric Association.

Gunderson, J.G. (1996). The borderline patient´s intolerance of aloneness: Insecure attachments and therapist availability. *American Journal of Psychiatry*, 153: 752-8.

Gunderson, J.G. & Kolb, J.E. (1979). Discriminating features of borderline patients. *American Journal of Psychiatry*, 135: 792-6.

Gunderson, J.G. & Sabo, A. (1993). The phenomenological and conceptual interface be- tween borderline personality disorder and post-traumatic stress disorder. *American Journal of Psychiatry*, 150:19-27.

Gunderson, J.G., Berkowitz, C., & Ruiz-Sancho, A. (1997). Families of borderline patients: A psychoeducational approach. *Bulletin of the Menninger Clinic*, 61(4): 446-58.

Gunderson, J.G., Daversa, M.T., Grilo, C.M., McGlashan, T.H., Zanarini, M.C., Shea, M.T., ... & Stout, R.L. (2006). Predictors of 2-year outcome for patients with borderline personality disorder. *American Journal of Psychiatry*, 163:822-6.

Harned, M.S., Rizvi, S.L., & Linehan, M.M. (2010). Impact of co-occurring posttraumatic stress disorder on suicidal women with borderline personality disorder. *American Journal of Psychiatry*, 167(10): 1210-7.

Harris, P. (1985). *What children know about the situations that provoke emotion, in the socialization of emotions.* Lewis, M. & Saarni, C. (Ed). New York: Plenum. pp. 161-85.

Harter, S. (1999). *The construction of the self: a developmental perspective.* New York: Guilford Press.

Harter, S.E. & Buddin, B. (1987). Children´s understanding of the simultaneity of two emotions: a five-stage developmental acquisition sequence. *Developmental Psychology*, 23:390-9.

Hatfield E., Cacioppo J. L., & Rapson R. L. (1993). Emotional contagion. *Current Directions in Psychological Sciences,* 2 (3): 96–99.

Hayes, S.C., Strosahl, K.D., & Wilson, K.G. (2003). *Acceptance and Commitment Therapy: An Experiential Approach to Behavior Change.* The Guilford Press. NY.

Hazan, C. & Shaver, P. (1987). Romantic love conceptualized as an attachment process. *Journal of Personality and Social Psychology*, 52:511-24.

Herbst ,G., Jaeger, U., Leichsenring, F., & Streeck-Fischer, A. (2009). Effects of traumatic stress. *Praxis der Kinderpsychologie und Kinderpsychiatrie*, 58(8): 610-34.

Herman, J.L. (1992). Complex PTSD: A syndrome in survivors of prolonged and repeated trauma. *Journal of Traumatic Stress*, 5(3): 377-91.

Herman, J.L. & Schatzow, E. (1987). Recovery and verification of memories of childhood sexual trauma. *Psychoanalytic Psychology*, 4: 1-4.

Hesse, E. (1999). *The Adult Attachment Interview: Historical and Current Perspectives.* En: Cassidy J, Shaver PR (Eds.) Attachment theory, research and clinical applications. NY: Guilford Press.

Hesse, E. & Main, M. (2001). Disorganized infant, child, and adult attachment: Collapse in behavioral and attentional strategies. *Journal of the American Psychoanalytic Association*, 48: 1097-127.

Higgitt, A. & Fonagy, P. (1992). Two psychotherapeutic treatment of borderline and narcissistic personality disorder. *British Journal of Psychiatry*, 161: 23-43.

Hill, A.B. (1965). The environment and disease: association or causation? *Proceeding of the Royal Society of Medicine*, 58: 295-300.

Hoch P. & Polatin, P. (1949). Pseudoneurotic forms of schizophrenia. *Psychiatric Quarterly*, 23(2): 248-76.

Hoffman, M.L. (1982). Affect and moral development. *New Directions for Child Development*, 16: 83-103.

Horesh, N., Ratner, S., Laor, N., & Toren, P. (2008). A comparison of life events in adolescents with major depression, borderline personality disorder and matched controls: a pilot study. *Psychopathology*, 41(5): 300-6.

Horevitz, R. & Loewenstein, R.J. (1994). *The rational treatment of multiple personality disorder. In Kynn, S.J. & Rhue, S.W. (Eds.) Dissociation: Clinical and theoretical perspectives.* New York: Guilford. pp. 289-316.

Howell, E.F. (2002). Back to the "states": victim and abuser states in borderline personality disorder. *Psychoanalytic Dialogues*, 12: 921-57.

Howell, E.F. (2005). *The dissociative mind.* London: The Analytic Press.

Hunt, M. (2007). Borderline personality disorder across the lifespan. *Journal of Women and Aging*, 19(1-2): 173-91.

Janet, P. (1907). *The major symptoms of hysteria*. London & New York: Macmillan.

Janet, P. (1919). *Les médications psychologiques*. Paris: Félix Alcan. English edition (1925): Psychological healing. New York: Macmillan.

Johnson, J.G., Cohen, P., Brown, J., Smailes, E.M., & Bernstein, D.P. (1999). Childhood maltreatment increases risk for personality disorders during early adulthood. *Archives of General Psychiatry*, 56: 600-6.

Kamphausen, S., Schröder, P., Maier, S., Bader, K., Feige, B., Kaller, C.P., … Tüscher, O. (2013). Medial prefrontal dysfunction and prolonged amygdala response during instructed fear processing in borderline personality disorder, *World Journal of Biological Psychiatry* 14 (4): 307-318 (doi:10.3109/15622975.2012.665174)

Keisler, D.J. (1983). The 1982 interpersonal circle: a taxonomy for complementarity in human transactions. *Psychological Review*, 90: 185–214

Kelly, G. A. (1961). *Suicide: The personal construct point on view*. In Faberow, N. & Schneidman, E. (Eds). The Cry for Help. New York. McGraw-Hill.

Kernberg O.F. (1965). Notes on countertransference. *Journal of the American Psychoanalytic Association*, 13: 38-56.

Kernberg O.F. (1967). Borderline personality organization. *Journal of the American Psychoanalytic Association*, 15: 641-85.

Kernberg, O.F. (1979). Two reviews of literature on borderlines: An assessment. *Schizophrenia Bulletin*, 5:53-8.

Kernberg, O.F. (1993). *Severe personality disorders: psychotherapeutic strategies*. Yale University Press.

Kingdon, D.G., Ashcroft, K., Bhandari, B., Gleeson, S., Warikoo, N., Symons, M., … & Mehta, R. (2010). Schizophrenia and borderline personality disorder: similarities and differences in the experience of auditory hallucinations, paranoia, and childhood trauma. *Journal of Nervous and Mental Disease*, 198(6): 399-403.

Knipe, J. (1998). It was a golden time… Treating narcissistic vulnerability. In Manfield, P. (Ed.) *Extending EMDR: A casebook of innovative applications* (1st ed.) (pp. 232-255). New York: W.W. Norton & Co.

Knipe, J. (2005). Targeting positive affect to clear the pain of unrequited love, codependence, avoidance, and procrastination. In Shapiro, R. (Ed.) EMDR Solutions: Pathways to healing (pp.189-212). New York, NY: W.W. Norton & Co.

Knipe, J. (2008). Loving eyes: Procedures to therapeutically reverse dissociative processes while preserving emotional safety. In Forgash, C. & Copeley, M. (Eds). *Healing the heart of trauma and dissociation with EMDR and ego state therapy*. New York: Springer Pub. C. pp. 181-225.

Kohut, H. & Wolf, E.S. (1978). The disorders of the self and their treatment. *International Journal of Psychoanalysis*, 59: 413-25.

Korzekwa, M. (2010). *Strategic developmental model for EMDR in borderline personality disorder post-dialectical behavior therapy.* Annual meeting of EMDR International Association. Minneapolis.

Korzekwa, M.I., Dell, P.F., & Pain, C. (2009). Dissociation and borderline personality disorder: an update for clinicians. *Current Psychiatry Reports*, 11(1): 82-8.

Kremers, I.P., Van Giezen, A.E., Van der Does, A.J., Van Dyck, R., & Spinhoven, P. (2007). Memory of childhood trauma before and after long-term psychological treatment of borderline personality disorder. *Journal of Behavior Therapy and Experimental Psychiatry*, 38(1): 1-10.

Kröger, C., Harbeck, S., Armbrust, M., & Kliem, S. (2013). Effectiveness, response, and dropout of dialectical behavior therapy for borderline personality disorder in an inpatient setting. *Behaviour Research and Therapy*, 51(8): 411-416. doi:10.1016/j.brat.2013.04.008

Lamm C., Batson C.D., & Decety J. (2007). The neural basis of human empathy: Effects of perspective-taking and cognitive appraisal. *Journal of Cognitive Neuroscience,* 19 (1): 42–58.

Lang, P.J. (1995). The emotion probe: Studies of motivation and attention. *American Psychology*, 50: 372-85.

Laporte, L. & Guttman, H. (1996). Traumatic childhood experiences as risk factors for borderline and other personality disorders. *Journal of Personality Disorders*, 10:247-59.

Lawson, C.A. (2004). Treating the borderline mother: Integrating EMDR with a family systems perspective. In McFarlane, M.M. (Ed.) *Family treatment of personality disorders: Advances in clinical practice.* New York: Haworth Clinical Practice Press. pp. 305-34.

Lee, C., Taylor, G., & Drummond, P. (2006). The active ingredient in EMDR: Is it traditional exposure or dual focus of attention? *Clinical Psychology and Psychotherapy*, 13: 97-107.

Leeds, A.M. (2006). *Learning to feel good about positive emotions with the Positive Affect Tolerance and Integration Protocol.* EMDRIA Conference. Philadelphia.

Leeds, A.M. & Mosquera, D. (2012). *Borderline personality disorder and EMDR. Annual meeting of the EMDR International Association.* Arlington, VA.

Levine, P. & Frederick, A. (1997). *Waking the Tiger: Healing Trauma: The Innate Capacity to Transform Overwhelming Experiences.* North Atlantic Book.

Lieb, K., Zanarini, M.C., Schmahl, C., Linehan, M., & Bohus, M. (2004). Borderline personality disorder. *The Lancet*, 364: 453-60.

Liebowitz, M.R. (1979). Is borderline a distinct entity? *Schizophrenia Bulletin*, 5: 23-38.

Linehan, M. (1993). *Cognitive-behavioral treatment of borderline personality disorder.* New York: Guilford Press.

Linehan, M. (2006). *Treating borderline personality disorder: The dialectical approach.* New York: Guilford Press.

Liotti, G. (1999). Disorganization of attachment as a model for understanding dissociative psychopathology. In Solomon, J. & George, C. (Eds.) *Attachment disorganization*. New York: Guilford Press. pp. 297-317.

Liotti, G. (2004). Trauma, dissociation and disorganized attachment: three strands of a single braid. *Psychotherapy: Theory, Research and Practice Training*, 41: 472-86.

Litt, B. (2012). The child as identified patient: integrating Contextual Therapy and EMDR. In Shapiro, F., Kaslow, F.W., & Maxfield, L. *Handbook of EMDR and family therapy processes*. Wiley and Sons, Inc. Hoboken, NJ. pp. 306-324.

Little, M. (1966). Transference in borderline states. *International Journal of Psycho-Analysis*, 47:476-85.

Lobo, I. & Shaw, K. (2008). Phenotypic range of gene expression: Environmental influence. *Nature Education*, 1(1).

Luber, M. & Shapiro, F. (2009). Interview with Francine Shapiro: historical overview, present issues, and future directions of EMDR. *Journal of EMDR Practice and Research*, 3(4): 217-31.

Luborsky, L. & Crits-Christoph, P. (1990). *Understanding transference: The Core Conflictual Relationship Theme Method.* New York: Basic Books.

Lyons-Ruth, K. & Jacobovitz, D. (1999). Attachment disorganization: unresolved loss, relational violence and lapses in behavioral and attentional strategies. In Cassidy, J. & Shaver, P.R. (Eds.) *Handbook of attachment: Theory, research and clinical applications*. New York: Guilford. pp. 520-54.

Lyons-Ruth, K., Yellin, D., Melnick, S., & Atwood, G. (2005). Expanding the concept of unresolved mental states: hostile/helpless states of mind on the Adult Attachment Interview are associated with disrupted mother-infant communication and infant disorganization. *Developmental Psychopathology*, 17: 1-23.

Main, M. & Hesse, E. (1990). Parent's unresolved traumatic experiences are related to infant disorganized attachment status: Is frightened and/or frightening parental behavior the linking mechanism? In Greenberg, M.T., Chichetti, D., & Cummings, E.M. (Eds.) *Attachment in the preschool years: Theory, research and intervention* (pp 161-182). Chicago: University of Chicago Press.

Main, M. & Solomon, J. (1986). Discovery of a new, insecure-disorganized/disoriented attachment pattern. In Brazelton & Yogman (Eds.) *Affective development in infancy*. Ablex. pp. 95-124.

Main, M., Kaplan, M., & Cassidy, J. (1985). Security in infancy, childhood, and adulthood: A move to the level of representation. *Monographs of the Society for Research on Child Development*, 50: 66-104

Marvin, R. S. (2003) Implications of attachment research for the field of family therapy. In Erdman, P. & Caffery, T. (Eds.). *Attachment and family systems: Conceptual, empirical, and therapeutic relatedness.* New York: Brunner-Routledge. Pp. 3-27.

Masterson, J.F. (1976). *Psychotherapy of the borderline adult.* New York: Brunner-Mazel.

Mathiesen, B.B. & Weinryb, R.M. (2004). Unstable identity and prefrontal injury. *Cognitive Neuropsychiatry*, 9(4): 249-66.

McLean, L.M. & Gallop, R. (2003). Implications of childhood sexual abuse for adult borderline personality disorder and complex posttraumatic stress disorder. *American Journal of Psychiatry*, 160: 369-71.

McLean, P.D. (1990). *The triune brain in evolution: role in paleocerebral functions*. New York: Plenum Press.

Meijer, S. (2006). Who *does not dare not win: If you do nothing you lose for sure! Applications of EMDR in patients with borderline personality disorder*. National EMDR Conference. The Netherlands.

Mikulincer, M. (1995). Attachment style and mental representation of the self. *Journal of Personality and Social Psychology,* 69, 1203–1215.

Minuchin, S. (1974) *Families and family therapy*. Cambridge, MA: Harvard University Press.

Modell, A.H. (1963). Primitive object relationships and the predisposition to schizophrenia. *International Journal of Psycho-Analysis*, 44: 282-92.

Mosquera, D. (2004a). *Diamantes en bruto I. Un acercamiento al trastorno límite de la personalidad. Manual informativo para profesionales, pacientes y familiares*. Madrid: Ediciones Pléyades.

Mosquera, D. (2004b). *Diamantes en bruto (II). Manual psicoeducativo y de tratamiento del trastorno límite de la personalidad: programa estructurado para profesionales*. Madrid: Ediciones Pléyades.

Mosquera, D. (2007a). *Desmontando corazas. El trastorno social aprendido: Un mecanismo de defensa extremo.* Madrid. Ediciones Pléyades.

Mosquera D (2007b). *¿Cómo afecta el trastorno límite a los hijos? Asociación Cántabra de Rehabilitación Psicosocial* (A.C.A.R.P.). I Encuentro Nacional de Asociaciones.

Mosquera, D. (2007c). *Trastorno Límite de la Personalidad. Profundizando en el caos.* Madrid. Ediciones

Mosquera, D. (2008). *La autolesión: el lenguaje del dolor*. Madrid: Ediciones Pléyades.

Mosquera, D. (2010). *Trastorno límite de la personalidad. Una aproximación conceptual a los criterios del DSM-V.* Revista Persona, 10(2).

Mosquera, D. (2011). *Trastorno Límite de la Personalidad. Una aproximación conceptual a los criterios del DSM-IV-TR.* Revista digital de medicina psicosomática y psicoterapia, SEMPPM, Vol. 1, no 1.

Mosquera, D. (2013a). *Diamantes en bruto I. Un acercamiento al trastorno límite de la personalidad. Manual informativo para profesionales, pacientes y familiares.* Madrid: Ediciones Pléyades.

Mosquera, D. (2013b). *Diamantes en bruto II: manual psicoeducativo y de tratamiento del trastorno límite de la personalidad.* (2ª Ed.) Madrid: Ediciones Pléyades.

Mosquera, D. & Ageitos, L. (2007). *Patrones de relación frecuentes en los familiares de personas con trastorno límite de la personalidad.* Revista Persona.

Mosquera, D., Ageitos, L., Pitarch, S., & Bello, M.J. (2009). *Llenando el vacío: un espacio para la familia.* Madrid: Ediciones Pléyades.

Mosquera, D. & Gonzalez, A. (2009). *Disociación estructural y trastorno límite de la personalidad.* I Jornadas gallegas sobre trastornos de personalidad. TP-Galicia. A Coruña.

Mosquera, D. & Gonzalez, A. (2011). Del apego temprano al TLP. *Revista Mente y Cerebro.* January-February: 18-27.

Mosquera, D. & Gonzalez, A. (2012). Disturbo borderline di personalità, trauma e EMDR [Borderline personality disorder, trauma and EMDR]. *Rivista di Psichiatria.* 47(2 Suppl 1): 26S-32.

Mosquera, D. & Gonzalez, A. (2013). El trastorno límite de la personalidad y sus subtipos: relaciones interpersonales patológicas y violentas y su rol en la violencia intrafamiliar y de pareja. In *Trastorno mental, desviación social y delito: Manual de Psicología Jurídica, Psiquiatría Forense y Psicopatología Criminal.* Ed. EOS.

Mosquera, D., Gonzalez, A., & Van der Hart, O. (2011). Borderline personality disorder, childhood trauma and structural dissociation of the personality. *Revista Persona,* 11: 44-73.

Mosquera, D., Gonzalez, A., & Vazquez, I. (2012). Terapia EMDR en el trastorno límite de personalidad: Reflexiones en torno a un caso de patología dual. *Revista Española de Drogodependencias.* 37(1): 82-95.

Mosquera, D., Gonzalez, A., Baldomir, P., Vázquez, I., Bello M.J., Eiriz A.C., ... & Soto, A. (2013). *Trastornos de personalidad y trauma temprano intrafamiliar.* Poster. V Simposio sobre Trastorno Límite de la Personalidad. Sant Cugat, Barcelona.

Mosquera, D., Leeds, A. & Gonzalez, A. (2014) Application of EMDR therapy to Borderline Personality Disorder. *Journal of EMDR, Practice and Research,* 8(2): 74-89. doi:10.1891/1933-3196.8.2.1

Myers, C.S. (1940). *Shell shock in France 1914-1918.* Cambridge: Cambridge University Press.

Neuringer, C. (1964). Rigid thinking in suicidal individuals. *Journal of Consulting Psychology,* 28(1): 54-58.

Newman, L.K., Harris, M., & Allen, J. (2010). Neurobiological basis of parenting disturbance. *Australian and New Zealand Journal of Psychiatry,* 45: 109-22.

Nijenhuis, E. R. S., Spinhoven, P., Van Dyck, R., Van der Hart, O., & Vanderlinden, J. (1998). Degree of somatoform and psychological dissociation is correlated with reported trauma. *Journal of Traumatic Stress,* 11, 711-728.

Novella, E.J. & Plumed, J. (2005). Difusión de identidad y posmodernidad: una aproximación sociocultural al trastorno límite de la personalidad. In Cervera, G; Haro, G; & Martinez-Raga, J (Eds.) *Trastorno límite de la personalidad, paradigma de la comorbilidad psiquiátrica* (58-71). Madrid: Ed. Médica Panamericana.

O'Connell, S.M. (1995). Empathy in chimpanzees: Evidence for theory of mind? *Primates.* 36: 397-410.

O'Connor, T.G. & Croft, C.M. (2001). A twin study of attachment in preschool children. *Child Development,* 72: 1501-11.

Ofshe, R.J. & Singer, M.T. (1994). Recovered-memory therapy and robust repression: Influence and pseudomemories. *International Journal for Clinical and Experimental Hypnosis,* 42:391-410.

Ogden, P. & Minton, K. (2000). Sensorimotor psychotherapy: a method for processing traumatic memories. *Traumatology.* VI (3): Article 3.

Ogden, P., Minton, K., & Pain, C. (2006). *Trauma and the Body: a sensorimotor approach to psychotherapy.* W. W. Norton & co.

Ostacoli, L. (2010). *Il trattamento intensivo con EMDR nel disturbo borderline de personalita [Intensive treatment of BPD with EMDR].* In Ostacoli L. (proponent). L´EMDR: un approccio psicoterápico. XII Congresso Nazionale della Sezione di Psicologia Clinica e Dinamica. Torino, Italia.

Páez, D., Fernández, I., Campos, M., Zubieta, E. y Casullo, M. M. (2006). Apego seguro, vínculos parentasles, clima familiar e Inteligencia Emocional: socialización, regulación y bienestar. *Ansiedad y Estrés,* 12 (2-3): 319-341.

Pagura, J., Stein, M.B., Bolton, J.M., Cox, B.J., Grant, B., & Sareen, J. (2010). Comorbidity of borderline personality disorder and posttraumatic stress disorder in the U.S. population. *Journal of Psychiatric Research,* 44(16): 1190-8.

Panksepp J. (1998). *Affective neuroscience: The foundations of human and animal emotions.* New York/Oxford: Oxford University Press.

Paris, J. & Zweig-Frank, H. (1997). Dissociation in patients with borderline personality disorder. *American Journal of Psychiatry,* 154: 137-8.

Paris, J. (1994). *Borderline personality disorder: A multidimensional approach.* Washington, DC: American Psychiatric Publishing.

Paz, C., Palento, M., & Olmos, T. (1977). *Estructuras y estados fronterizos en niños, adolescentes y adultos.* Buenos Aires: Nueva Visión.

Perez, S. & Mosquera, D. (2006). *El suicidio. Prevención y Manejo.* Ediciones Pléyades, S.A.

Personality Disorders Guideline. (2011). *Grupo de trabajo de la guía de la práctica clínica sobre trastorno límite de la personalidad. Forum de salud mental y AIAQS, coordinadores. Guia de practia clínica sobre trastorno límite de la personalidad.* Barcelona. Agència d'Informació, Avaluació i Qualitat en Salut. Servei Catalá de la Salut. Pla Director de Salut Mental i Addiccions. Departament salut. Generalitat de Catalunya.

Pietrzak, R.H., Goldstein, R.B., Southwick, S.M., & Grant, B.F. (2011). Personality disorders associated with full and partial posttraumatic stress disorder in the U.S. population: results from Wave 2 of the National Epidemiologic Survey on Alcohol and Related Conditions. *Journal of Psychiatric Research,* 45: 678-86.

Plomin, R., DeFries, J.C., McClearn, G.E., & McGuffin, P. (2001). *Behavioral genetics.* 4th ed. New York: W.H. Freeman.

Pope, H.G. & Hudson, J.I. (1995). Can memories of child sexual abuse be repressed? *Psychological Medicine,* 25: 121-6.

Porges, S.W. (2003). The polyvagal theory: Phylogenetic contributions to social behavior. *Physiology and Behavior*, 79: 503-13.

Putnam F. (1997). *Dissociation in children and adolescents: a developmental perspective*. The Guilford Press.

Reinders, A., Nijenhuis, E., Paans, A.M., Korf, J., Willemsen, A.T., & Den Boer, J.A. (2003). One brain, two selves. *Neuroimage*, 20: 2119–2125.

Rizzolatti, G. & Craighero, L. (2004). The mirror-neuron system. *Annual Review of Neuroscience,* 27: 169–192.

Rogosch, F.A. & Cicchetti, D. (2005). Child maltreatment, attention networks and potential precursors to borderline personality disorder. *Developmental Psychopathology*, 17: 1071- 89.

Ross CA. (2007). Borderline personality disorder and dissociation. *Journal of Trauma and Dissociation*, 8(1): 71-80.

Roth, S., Newman, E., Pelcovitz, D., Van der Kolk, B.A., & Mandel, F.S. (1997). Complex PTSD in victims exposed to sexual and physical abuse: Results from the DSM-IV-R field trial for posttraumatic stress disorder. *Journal of Traumatic Stress*, 10: 539-55.

Ryle, A. (1997). The structure and development of borderline personality disorder: a proposed model. *British Journal of Psychiatry*, 170: 82-7.

Ryle, A. & Kerr, I. (2002). *Psicoterapia cognitivo analítica*. Ed. Desclee De Brouwer.

Ryle, A. & Kerr, I. (2006). *Introducción a la psicoterapia cognitivo analítica*. Ed. Desclee de Brouwer.

Sabo, A.N. (1997). Etiological significance of associations between childhood trauma and borderline personality disorder: Conceptual and clinical implications. *Journal of Personality Disorders*, 11: 50-70.

Sachsse, U. & Tumani, V. (1999). Be *borderline! A successful inpatients´ treatment program for (type II) traumatized female patients with PTSD/DES/BPD and the symptom of self-mutilation.* Annual meeting of the International Society for Traumatic Stress Studies. Miami, FL.

Salter, A. (2003). *Predators, pedophiles, rapists and other sex offenders. Who they are, how they operate and how we can protect ourselves and our children.* New York: Basic Books.

Sansone R.A., Sansone L.A., & Wiederman M.W. (1995). Trauma, borderline personality, and self-harm behaviors. *Archives of Family Medicine*, 4(12): 1000-2.

Sansone, R.A., Gaither, G.A., & Songer, D.A. (2002).The relationships among childhood abuse, borderline personality, and self-harm behavior in psychiatric inpatients. *Violence and Victims*, 17(1): 49-55.

Sar, V., Akyüz, G., & Doğan, O. (2007). Prevalence of dissociative disorders among women in the general population. *Psychiatry Research*, 149(1-3): 169-76.

Sar, V., Akyuz, G., Kugu, N., Ozturk, E., & Ertem-Vehid, H. (2006). Axis I dissociative disorder comorbidity in borderline personality disorder and reports of childhood trauma. *Journal of Clinical Psychiatry* 67(10): 1583-90.

Schmideberg, M. (1959). The borderline patient. In Arieti S., (Ed.) *American Handbook of Psychiatry*, Vol 1. New York: Basic Books.

Schneidman, E. (1985). *Definition of suicide.* New York: John Wiley & Sons.

Schneidman, E. (1987). A psychological approach to suicide. In Vandenbos, G.R. & Bryant, B.K. (Eds.) *Cataclysms, Crises and Catastrophes: Psychology in action.* Washington: American Psychological Association.

Schore, A. (2001). The effects of early relational trauma on right brain development, affect regulation and infant mental health. *Infant Mental Health*, 22:201-69.

Schore, A (2003a). *Affect dysregulation and disorders of the self.* New York: Norton.

Schore, A (2003b). *Affect regulation and the repair of the self.* New York: Norton.

Schuder, M. & Lyons-Ruth, K. (2004). "Hidden trauma" in infancy: attachment, fearful arousal and early dysfunction on the stress response system. In Osofsky, J. (Ed.) *Trauma in infancy and early childhood.* New York: Guilford Press. pp. 69-104.

Seijo, N. (2012). *Eating Disorders and EMDR.* Workshop. EMDR Spanish Association. Madrid.

Seligman, M.E.P. & Maier, S.F. (1967). Failure to escape traumatic shock. *Journal of Experimental Psychology*, 74: 1-9.

Selman, R.L. (1980). The growth of an interpersonal understanding of others. *Developmental Psychology*, 22: 649-54.

Semerari, A., Carcione, A., Dimaggio, G., Nicolò, G., Pedone, R., & Procacci, M. (2005). Metarepresentative functions in borderline personality disorder. *Journal of Personality Disorders*, 19: 690-710.

Shamay-Tsoory, S.G., Aharon-Peretz, J., & Perry, D. (2009). Two systems for empathy: a double dissociation between emotional and cognitive empathy in inferior frontal gyrus versus ventromedial prefrontal lesions. *Brain* 132 (3): 617–627

Shapiro, F. (2001). *Eye Movement Desensitization and Reprocessing. Basic Principles, Protocols and Procedures.* Second edition. New York: Guilford Press.

Shin, L.M., Wright, C.I., Cannistraro, P.A., Wedig, M.M., McMullin, K., Martis, B., ... Rauch, S.L. (2005). A functional magnetic resonance imaging study of amygdala and medial prefrontal cortex responses to overtly presented fearful faces in posttraumatic stress disorder. *Archives of General Psychiatry*, 62 (3): 273-81.

Siegel, D.J. (2011). *Mindsight: The New Science of Personal Transformation.* Bantam Books. New York.

Siegel, D.J. & Hartzell, M. (2004). *Parenting from the inside out.* Jeremy P. Tarcher/Penguin.

Siever L.J., Torgersen, S., Gunderson, J.G., Livesley, W.J., & Kendler, K.S. (2002). The borderline diagnosis III: identifying endophenotypes for genetic studies. *Biological Psychiatry*, 51(12): 964-8.

Silbersweig, D., Clarkin, J.F., Goldstein, M., Kernberg, O.F., Tuescher, O., Levy, K.N., ... Stern, E. (2007). Failure of Frontolimbic Inhibitory Function in the Context of Negative Emotion in Borderline Personality Disorder. *American Journal of Psychiatry; 164:1832-1841.* doi:10.1176/appi.ajp.2007.06010126

Silk, K.R., Lee, S., Hill, E.M.D., & Lohr, N.E. (1995). Borderline personality disorder symptoms and severity of sexual abuse. *American Journal of Psychiatry*, 152: 1059-64.

Skodol, A.E., Siever, L.J., Livesley, W.J., Gunderson, J.G., Pfohl, B., & Widiger, T.A. (2002). The borderline diagnosis II: biology, genetics, and clinical course. *Biological Psychiatry*, 51(12): 951-63.

Slade, A., Sadler, L.S., & Mayers, L. (2005). Minding the baby: Enhancing parental reflective functioning in a nursing/mental health home visiting program. In Berlin, L., Ziv, Y., Amaya-Jackson, L., & Greenberg, M. (Eds.). *Enhancing Early Attachment: theory, Research, Intervention and Policy* (pp 152-177). New York: Guilford Press.

Spinella, M. (2004). Neurobehavioral correlates of impulsivity: Evidence of prefrontal involvement. *International Journal of Neuroscience* 114: 95-104.

Spitzer, C., Effler, K., & Freyberger, H.J. (2000). Posttraumatic stress disorder, dissociation and self-destructive behavior in borderline patients. *Psychosomatic Medicine and Psychotherapy*, 46(3): 273-85.

Spitzer, R.L. & Endicott, J. (1979). Justification for separating schizotypal and borderline personality disorders. *Schizophrenia Bulletin*, 5: 95-100.

Steele, K., Van der Hart, O., Nijenhuis, E. (2005). Phase-oriented treatment of structural dissociation in complex traumatization: overcoming trauma-related phobias. *Journal of Trauma and Dissociation*, 6(3): 11-53.

Steele, H. & Siever, L. (2010). An attachment perspective on borderline personality disorder: advances in gene-environment considerations. *Current Psychiatry Reports*, 12(1): 61-7.

Stevenson-Hinde, J. (1990). Attachment within family systems: An overview. *Infant Mental Health Journal*, 11: 218-27.

Stoffers, J. M., Völlm, B. A., Rücker, G., Timmer, A., Huband, N., & Lieb, K. (2012). Psychological therapies for people with borderline personality disorder. *Cochrane Database of Systematic Reviews (Online)*, 8, CD005652. doi:10.1002/14651858.CD005652.pub2

Szerman, N. (2012). *Patología dual en los trastornos de personalidad.* II Jornadas Gallegas sobre Trastornos de Personalidad. TP-Galicia. Santiago de Compostela.

Tanielian, T. & Jaycox, L.H. (Eds.) (2008). *Invisible Wounds of War: Psychological and Cognitive Injuries, Their Consequences, and Services to Assist Recovery.* Santa Monica, CA: RAND Corporation, MG-720-CCF.

Taylor, K.E. (2004). *Brainwashing: The Science of Thought Control*. Oxford University Press.

Terr, L.C. (1988). What happens to memories of early childhood trauma? *Journal of the American Academy of Child and Adolescent Psychiatry*, 27: 96-104.

Terr, L.C. (1991). Childhood traumas: An outline and overview. *American Journal of Psychiatry*, 148: 10-20.

Tyrka, A.R., Wyche, M.C., Kelly, M.M., Price, L.H., & Carpenter, L.L. (2009). Childhood maltreatment and adult personality disorder symptoms: influence of maltreatment type. *Psychiatry Research*, 165(3): 281-7.

Van der Hart, O., Nijenhuis, E., & Steele, K. (2005). Dissociation: An insufficiently recognized major feature of complex PTSD. *Journal of Traumatic Stress*, 18(5): 413- 24.

Van der Hart, O., Nijenhuis, E., & Steele, K. (2006). *The haunted self: structural dissociation and the treatment of chronic traumatization.* New York: Norton.

Van der Hart, O., Nijenhuis, E., & Solomon, R.M. (2010). Dissociation of the personality in complex trauma-related disorders and EMDR: Theoretical consideration. *Journal of EMDR Practice and Research*, 4: 76–92.

Van der Kolk, B.A., Weisaeth, L., Van der Hart, O. (1996). History of trauma in psychiatry. In van der Kolk, B.A., McFarlane, A.C., Weisaeth, L. (Eds.). *Traumatic Stress*. New York: Guilford Press.

Van der Kolk, B., Roth, S., Pelcovitz, D., Sunday, S., & Spinazzola, J. (2005). Disorders of extreme stress: The empirical foundation of a complex adaptation to trauma. *Journal of Traumatic Stress*, 18(5): 389-99.

Van Derbur, M. (2004). *Miss America by day: Lessons learned from ultimate betrayals and unconditional love*. Denver: Oak Hill Ridge Press.

Van IJzendoorn, M.H. (1992) Intergenerational transmission of parenting: A review of studies in nonclinical populations. *Developmental Review,* 12: 76-99.

Watson, S., Chilton, R., Fairchild, H., & Whewell, P. (2006). Association between childhood trauma and dissociation among patients with borderline personality disorder. *Australian and New Zealand Journal of Psychiatry*, 40(5): 478-81.

Wesselmann D. (2007). Treating attachment issues through EMDR and a family systems approach. In Shapiro, F., Kaslow, F.W., & Maxfield, L. (Eds.) *Handbook of EMDR and family therapy processes*. Wiley and Sons, Inc. Hoboken, NJ. pp. 113-130.

Williams, L.M. (1994). Recall of childhood trauma: A prospective study of women´s memories of child sexual abuse. *Journal of Consulting and Clinical Psychology*, 62: 1167-76.

Winnicott, DW. (1967). *Mirror-role of the mother and family in child development*. In the Predicament of the family: A Psycho-Analytical Symposium. London: Hogarth Press and the Institute of Psycho-Analysis.

Winnicott, D. W. (1969). The Use of an Object. *International Journal of Psychoanalysis*, 50: 711-716

Wisper, L. (1986). The distinction between sympathy and empathy: to call for a concept, a word is needed. *Journal of Personality & Social Psychology*, 50:314-21.

Wolberg, A. (1952). The borderline patient. *American Journal of Psychotherapy*, 6: 694-701.

Woller, W. (2003). EMDR in der psychotherapie von persönlichkeitsstörungen [EMDR in the treatment of personality disorders]. *Zeitschrift für Psychotraumatologie und Psychologische Medizin*, 3: 3-8.

Yen, S., Shea, M.T., Battle, C.L., Johnson, D.M., Zlotnick, C., Dolan-Sewell, R., ... & Mcglashan, T.H. (2002). Traumatic exposure and posttraumatic stress disorder in borderline, schizotypal, avoidant, and obsessive-compulsive personality disorders: findings from the collaborative longitudinal personality disorders study. *Journal of Nervous and Mental Disease*, 190: 510-8.

Yeomans, F.E., Clarkin, J.F., & Kernberg, O.F. (2002). *A Primer of Transference Focused Psychotherapy for the Borderline Patient*. Jason Aronson.

Young, J., Klosko, J., & Weishaar, M. (2003). *Schema Therapy: A Practitioner's Guide*. New York: Guilford Publications.

Zanarini, M.C. (2000). Childhood experiences associated with the development of borderline personality disorder. *Psychiatric Clinics of North America*, 23: 89-101.

Zanarini, M.C., Frankenburg, F.R., Dubo, E.D., Sickel, A.E., Trikha, A., Levin, A., & Reynolds, V. (1998). Axis I comorbidity of borderline personality disorder. *American Journal of Psychiatry*, 155(12): 1733-9.

Zanarini, M.C., Ruser, T.F., Frankenburg, F.R., Hennen, J., & Gunderson, J.G. (2000). Risk factors associated with the dissociative experiences of borderline patients. *Journal of Nervous and Mental Disease*, 188(1): 26-30.

Zanarini, M.C., Frankenburg, F.R., Reich, D.B., Marino, M.F., Lewis, R.E., Williams, A.A., & Khera, G.S. (2000a). Biparental failure in the childhood experiences of borderline patients. *Journal of Personality Disorders*, 149:264-73.

Zanarini, M.C., Yong, L., Frankenburg, F.R., Hennen, J., Reich, D.B., Marino, M.F., & Vujanovic, A.A. (2002). Severity or reported childhood sexual abuse and its relationship to severity of borderline psychopathology and psychosocial impairment among borderline inpatients. *Journal of Nervous and Mental Disease,* 190: 381-7.

Zetzel, E.R. (1971). A developmental approach to the borderline patient. *American Journal of Psychiatry*, 127: 867-71.

Zweig-Frank, H. & Paris, J. (1991). Parents' emotional neglect and overprotection according to the recollections of patients with borderline personality disorder. *American Journal of Psychiatry*, 148: 648-51.

# About the authors

**Dolores Mosquera, MD.**         **Anabel Gonzalez, MD., PhD.**

Dolores Mosquera is psychologist and psychotherapist. She is the director of the Institute for the Study of Tauma and Personality Disorders (INTRA-TP), a private institution where she has worked with EMDR for many years on cases related to severe traumatization. She works in a program for the treatment of abused women as well as in a male offenders program. Dolores also collaborates in the treatment programs of adolescents in youth correctional facilities.

Dolores Mosquera is an EMDR Europe Consultant and Facilitator. She has extensive teaching experience, leading seminars, workshops and lectures internationally. She has published many books and many articles on personality disorders, complex trauma and dissociation and is a recognized expert in this field. Dolores Mosquera is a member of the ESTSS Board and a member of the Editorial Board for the ESTD Newsletter.

Anabel Gonzalez works as psychiatrist and psychotherapist in Public Mental Health System and Private Practice. She coordinates a Trauma and Dissociation Program into the Severe Mental Disorders Services of the Universitary Hospital of A Coruña and has a broad clinical experience with Dissociative Disorders and Complex Trauma. Trained in different psychotherapeutic approaches she works with EMDR from 1999 and is EMDR Therapist, Consultant and Facilitator.

Anabel Gonzalez is Vice-President of the Spanish EMDR Association and ESTD Board Member. She is head of the ISST-D online training on complex trauma and dissociation, and has presented several workshops and courses about EMDR interventions in dissociative disorders, personality disorders and psychosis. She is author of several articles, presentations, and books.